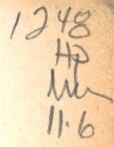

Acrobat 2.1: Your Personal Consultant

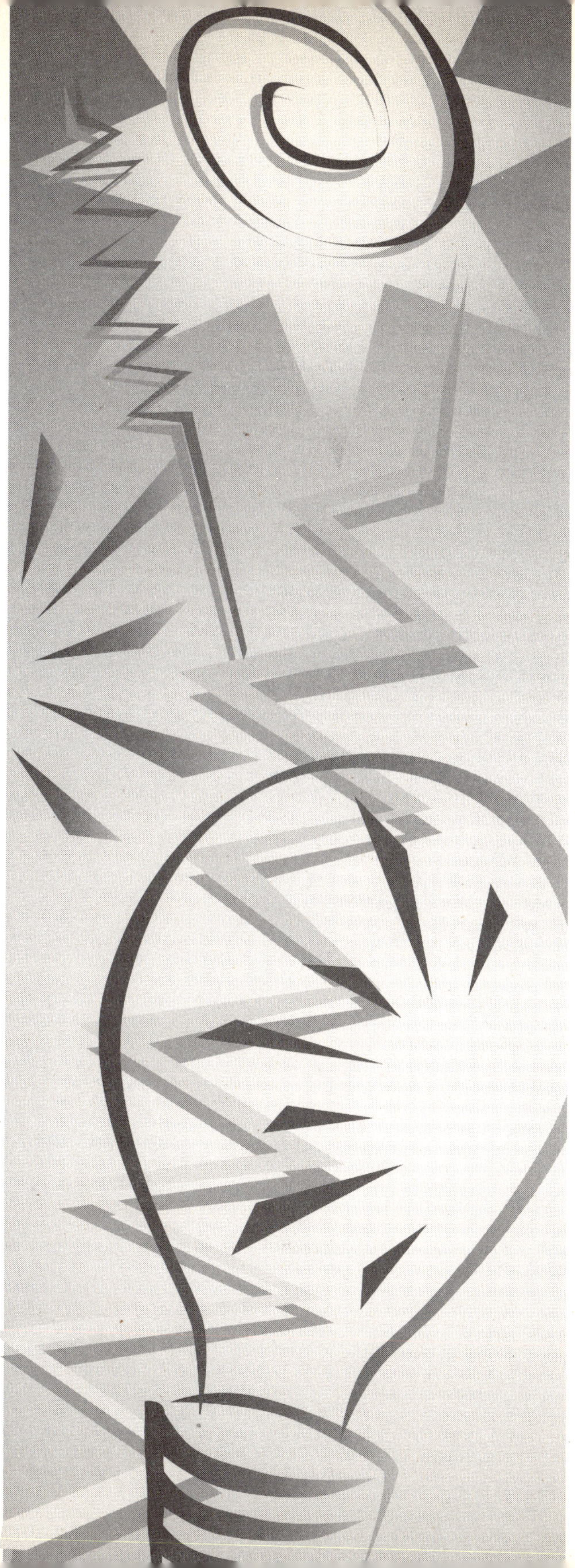

Acrobat 2.1: Your Personal Consultant

Roy Christmann

Ziff-Davis Press
Emeryville, California

Copy Editor	Stephanie Raney
Technical Reviewer	Mark Donohoe
Project Coordinator	Ami Knox
Proofreaders	Carol Burbo and Jeff Barrish
Cover Illustration and Design	Regan Honda
Book Design	Regan Honda
Word Processing	Howard Blechman
Page Layout	Bruce Lundquist
Indexer	Valerie Robbins

Ziff-Davis Press books are produced on a Macintosh computer system with the following applications: FrameMaker®, Microsoft® Word, QuarkXPress®, Adobe Illustrator®, Adobe Photoshop®, Adobe Streamline™, MacLink®*Plus*, Aldus® FreeHand™, Collage Plus™.

If you have comments or questions or would like to receive a free catalog, call or write:
Ziff-Davis Press
5903 Christie Avenue
Emeryville, CA 94608
800-688-0448

Copyright © 1995 by Ziff-Davis Press, a division of Macmillan Computer Publishing USA. All rights reserved.
PART OF A CONTINUING SERIES

Ziff-Davis Press and ZD Press are trademarks of Macmillan Computer Publishing USA.

All other product names and services identified throughout this book are trademarks or registered trademarks of their respective companies. They are used throughout this book in editorial fashion only and for the benefit of such companies. No such uses, or the use of any trade name, is intended to convey endorsement or other affiliation with the book.

No part of this publication may be reproduced in any form, or stored in a database or retrieval system, or transmitted or distributed in any form by any means, electronic, mechanical photocopying, recording, or otherwise, without the prior written permission of Ziff-Davis Press, except as permitted by the Copyright Act of 1976, and except that program listings may be entered, stored, and executed in a computer system.

THE INFORMATION AND MATERIAL CONTAINED IN THIS BOOK ARE PROVIDED "AS IS," WITHOUT WARRANTY OF ANY KIND, EXPRESS OR IMPLIED, INCLUDING WITHOUT LIMITATION ANY WARRANTY CONCERNING THE ACCURACY, ADEQUACY, OR COMPLETENESS OF SUCH INFORMATION OR MATERIAL OR THE RESULTS TO BE OBTAINED FROM USING SUCH INFORMATION OR MATERIAL. NEITHER ZIFF-DAVIS PRESS NOR THE AUTHOR SHALL BE RESPONSIBLE FOR ANY CLAIMS ATTRIBUTABLE TO ERRORS, OMISSIONS, OR OTHER INACCURACIES IN THE INFORMATION OR MATERIAL CONTAINED IN THIS BOOK, AND IN NO EVENT SHALL ZIFF-DAVIS PRESS OR THE AUTHOR BE LIABLE FOR DIRECT, INDIRECT, SPECIAL, INCIDENTAL, OR CONSEQUENTIAL DAMAGES ARISING OUT OF THE USE OF SUCH INFORMATION OR MATERIAL.

ISBN 1-56276-336-9

Manufactured in the United States of America

10 9 8 7 6 5 4 3 2 1

This book is dedicated to my grandmother, Catherine Conreaux.

TABLE OF CONTENTS

Introduction

xi

CHAPTER 1:

Introduction to Acrobat

1

CHAPTER 2

The Acrobat Reader

12

CHAPTER 3

Acrobat Exchange and PDF Writer

36

CHAPTER 4

Acrobat Distiller

90

CHAPTER 5

Indexing and Searching PDF Documents

132

CHAPTER 6

Acrobat Capture

174

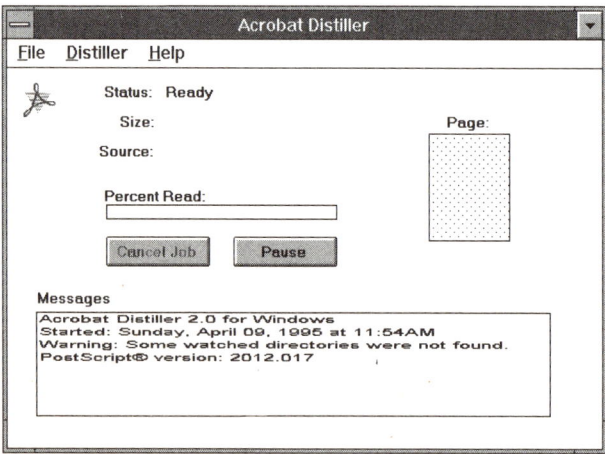

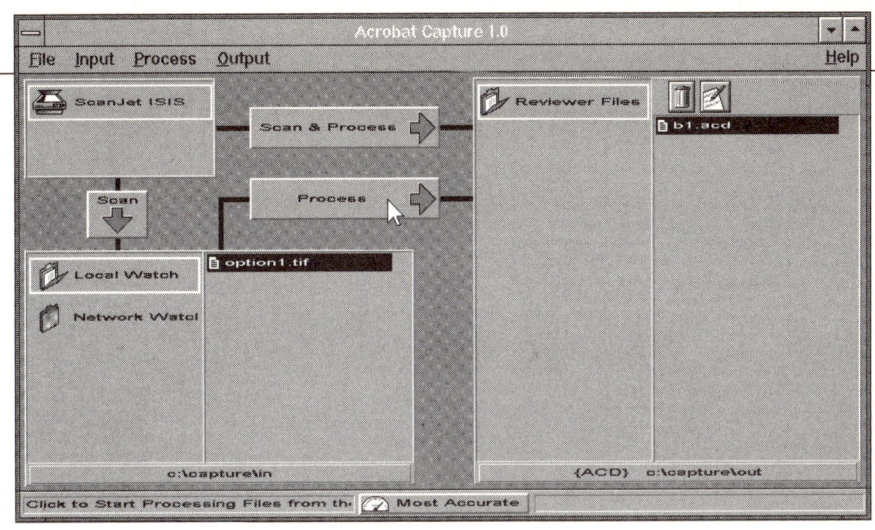

CHAPTER 7

Plug-ins

230

CHAPTER 8

Integrating Applications with Acrobat

258

CHAPTER 9

Publishing with Acrobat

320

CHAPTER 10

Writing PDF Source Code

346

APPENDIX

Windows INI File Settings

376

References for Further Reading

382

Index

386

ACKNOWLEDGMENTS

The author would like to thank the following people for their assistance with this book: Carol and Belinda at Waterside Productions, the able crew at Adobe Systems (including Rob Babcock, Rick Brown, John Ciccarelli, Mark Donohoe, Mark Gutkowski, and Jena Yankovich), and the calm, cool, and collected people at Ziff-Davis Press (including Cynthia Hudson, Suzanne Anthony, Lysa Lewellan, Stephanie Raney, and Ami Knox). Katherine Catmull, Dave Fisher, and Neil Milsted provided invaluable assistance with Macintosh versions of Acrobat software, and John Warrilow's help was crucial in producing the chapter on Capture. Additionally I'd like to thank Dave Fisher for getting me started with Acrobat and this project, and Margaret Robbins for introducing me to writing as a profession.

INTRODUCTION

What Is This Book About?

This book is essentially a tutorial on using the Acrobat tools to produce electronic documents. The focus is primarily on the tools themselves: How to use them and how to solve problems with them. This book is not a style guide for electronic publishing, but we do advocate a few basic principles in the form of guidelines where appropriate.

Who Should Use This Book?

Designers, writers, programmers, and publishers looking for a leg up with the Acrobat tools. This book is intended to supplement the on-line help provided by Adobe with additional real-world information gleaned from using Acrobat.

Acrobat: Your Personal Consultant Online

This book has a World Wide Web page on the Ziff-Davis home page; the URL of the Ziff-Davis Press home page is

```
http://www.zdnet.com/~zdpress/
```

From here, you can get to the page for this book, where you will find several utility programs the author has developed in the course of his work with Acrobat. The first is a progam that takes DDE commands from a file and "plays" them to Acrobat Exchange. The second is a program that embeds a PDF file into a Lotus Notes database. These programs are available as executables for Microsoft Windows and as source code in C. Check this book's page for more details.

You can contact the author online through the CompuServe network at user ID 71141,132 or via Internet mail at:

```
1141.132@compuserve.com.
```

CHAPTER

Introduction to Acrobat

Acrobat Components

Uses for Acrobat

The Portable Document Format

PDF Document Basics

Integrating Acrobat with Other Applications

Acrobat Components

Authors and publishers have been struggling for years to come up with a way to deliver their documents electronically. Today, documents are almost exclusively produced using electronic technology rather than paper and the typewriter. The enormous advantages of keeping documents in an electronic form, though, haven't been widely realized due to a small but crucial obstacle: Not everyone uses the same computer software to produce and view their documents. The result is that today's successful electronic communications (such as plain text electronic mail and now the World Wide Web) don't allow the author very much control of the look and feel of the document the reader sees.

Adobe Systems is well on the way to changing this situation with their Acrobat family of tools for creating and maintaining electronic documents. Leveraging off of the success of Adobe's PostScript page description language, Acrobat software creates electronic documents in a file format that is portable, device independent, and extensible. Acrobat preserves the fonts, graphics, and layout used to create the original document, in a format that can be viewed on many different computers. Prior to Acrobat, only paper was as portable, but Acrobat also delivers the advantages that only an electronic document provides: It can be stored conveniently, searched quickly, and transmitted across the continent in a few seconds.

Acrobat Components

Acrobat software works with the publishing tools you use today to create documents in Adobe's *Portable Document Format* (PDF). Files in this format can be viewed on any computer that can run Acrobat viewer software; currently, for Acrobat version 2.1 this includes

 Chapter 1: Introduction to Acrobat

Apple Macintosh, Microsoft Windows, Windows NT, and Sun and Hewlett Packard workstations. The entry-level viewer software, called Acrobat Reader, is free and can be licensed for redistribution with your documents, or downloaded from a number of online sources. Adobe sells the other components in the Acrobat family:

- Acrobat Exchange lets you view and modify PDF files. You use Exchange to add PDF features like bookmarks, links, and notes to your PDF files, and you use it to add, move, and delete pages in the document.

- Acrobat PDF Writer lets you create PDF files directly from any Macintosh or Windows application by using the application's own print function. You select and use PDF Writer just like it was another printer attached to your system.

- Acrobat Distiller lets you create PDF files from existing PostScript files. This is useful for several reasons. In some cases, you can get higher quality output by printing your documents to a PostScript file and then converting them to PDF. Also, Distiller lets you work with documents created on platforms not supported by PDF Writer.

- Acrobat Capture lets you scan a document and convert it to PDF. Capture can use optical character recognition (OCR) technology to convert text in the scanned image to a form that can be indexed and searched.

- Acrobat Catalog creates a database you can use to perform a full-text search of a collection of PDF files. Publishers use Catalog to index the document collections they distribute. The searches themselves are performed with Acrobat Search software that is supplied with Exchange.

Uses for Acrobat

Adobe sells the Acrobat programs named above in several configurations designed to meet different user's needs. At the time of this writing, Adobe offered three packages:

- Acrobat. Includes a single-user license for Exchange and PDF Writer, and copies of the Reader software for all supported platforms.
- Acrobat Pro. All the above plus a license for Distiller.
- Acrobat for Workgroups. A 10-user license for Acrobat Exchange and PDF Writer, plus a single-user license for Distiller and Catalog.

Acrobat Capture is sold separately.

Uses for Acrobat

Publishers are using Acrobat in all the new technologies for information delivery, wherever they want to control the look and feel of a document. For example, PDF documents are being incorporated into World Wide Web sites as a complement to the basic Hypertext Markup Language (HTML) documents already in use there. While HTML provides a format that lets anyone quickly view a document, HTML does not offer the publisher any control over what the user ultimately sees through his Web browser. HTML graphics may or may not be displayed, and the layout of the text in the document, and the fonts used to display it, are all subject to the whim of the user's software. In contrast, Acrobat delivers to the end user a document with the same format—and the same impact—that the author originally intended it to have. Acrobat tools support Web browsing and links to and from PDF documents on the Web.

CD-ROM publishing is another area where Acrobat use is spreading. A CD-ROM disc offers enough room to store a large document

 Chapter 1: Introduction to Acrobat

collection plus the database used to support full-text searches of the collection. Publishers can incorporate Acrobat viewers onto their disc as well, allowing the disc to be used on any system that can support the Acrobat software.

A third area where Acrobat is proving itself is within the organizational workgroup. Acrobat is providing a long-sought bridge between personal computers based on Microsoft's Windows and those based on Apple's Macintosh. Thanks to their incompatibilities, the widespread use of the Macintosh within certain key applications like desktop publishing has long been a sticking point for companies where the average desktop computer is an IBM-compatible. Using Acrobat (and following the advice we give you) you can eliminate those problems by sharing PDF documents.

Acrobat also excels where timely communication is important. Acrobat files can be transferred as easily as a fax, but with color and resolution intact. As an example of what you can do with this capability, AlphaGraphics Printshops offers a service where you can drop off a disk of your Acrobat files as you leave for the airport and pick up the printed results at your destination, saving you the trouble and expense of carrying the printed documents with you.

The Portable Document Format

Acrobat creates files in the Portable Document Format, which is based on Adobe's second generation PostScript Level 2 printing language. Both PostScript and PDF are open, published specifications, so there's no reason you need Acrobat software to create PDF documents. However, you can't just send a PDF document to your printer, even if it is a PostScript printer—for that, you need a viewer (either Acrobat Reader or Exchange) to translate the PDF file to PostScript. For the PostScript literate, we discuss some basics of writing PDF files in Chapter 10.

PDF Document Basics

The "page" is the atomic building block of the PDF document. For each page in the original document, PDF incorporates a page description written in PostScript. Acrobat itself does not allow users to change the contents of an individual page. Acrobat Exchange users can move pages from one document to another, or attach hypertext links and annotations to the page, but the original page itself remains intact, just as it was created. In general, this is what you want in a published document; you don't want the user to have unlimited power to modify it. However, Adobe's Illustrator 5.5 for the Macintosh does allow users to edit a single page of a PDF file and then put the modified page back into the document, with bookmarks and links intact (as long as the file is not protected by a password).

Text and Fonts

One of the goals of the PDF standard is to allow you to distribute documents using fonts that you like, but that aren't universally available. This is a big job, considering that there are several different kinds of fonts Acrobat might have to deal with (TrueType, PostScript Type 1, and PostScript Type 3 are commonly used on personal computers, and there are still other types). Acrobat provides three ways to create portable documents using a variety of fonts:

- Using the "standard" fonts (like Times Roman or Helvetica). These fonts are built into every PostScript printer and into every copy of Acrobat.

- Substituting synthetic fonts. Synthetic fonts are created using Adobe's multiple-master font technology. Multiple-master fonts are fonts that have many more parameters in their descriptions than a normal font. As a result, a single multiple-master font can be programmed to look like other fonts that aren't present on the

 Chapter 1: Introduction to Acrobat

system. Acrobat provides both serif and sans serif multiple-master fonts that can accurately emulate the look of a wide variety of commonly used fonts. Font substitution using multiple-master fonts does not work for every font, but when it does, it can result in substantial savings in the size of the PDF file produced.

- Font embedding. Font embedding allows the original font to be stored in the PDF file along with the document. This allows the viewer software to display the font exactly as originally intended. Acrobat software can embed both PostScript Type 1 and TrueType fonts in the PDF file—not as fixed bitmaps, but as fonts that can be rendered at any size or resolution.

Pictures

Acrobat supports many options for displaying bitmapped graphics images within a PDF document. Pictures can be monochrome, gray-scaled, or up to 24-bit color. Acrobat also addresses another problem with color images: their large storage requirements. Acrobat provides picture compression options that let you select a good tradeoff between the size of the compressed image and the quality of the resulting image in your document.

Links

Links (as in hypertext links) are one of the chief ways that electronic publishers can add value to a document. Links take you from one view of a document to another (that is, to a different page and perhaps a different magnification level). Links give your readers a way to break the linear presentation of information in your document, to get more specific data about topics of greater interest to them.

Links can also take you to a different document or start a completely different application to present related information. Acrobat supports links that can play sound files or display video clips, and in version 2.1, this data can even become a part of the PDF file. Adobe also provides tools that allow you to link your PDF files to the Internet using the World Wide Web. When used with a Web browser, a link created in your document can take the user to any other address on the Web.

Bookmarks

Bookmarks are to a PDF file what the table of contents is to this book, only better. Bookmarks are displayed in a separate pane of the viewer window, allowing the user to see the bookmarks alongside the current page. Selecting a bookmark displays the page the bookmark refers to. The creator of the bookmark can even control the magnification of the page when the bookmark is displayed. Bookmarks are really just another kind of link, and they have all the features that links have, including the ability to open other documents or even run other applications.

Thumbnails

Thumbnails are little postage-stamp-size sketches that represent the full page of a PDF document. Acrobat can display thumbnails of the pages of the document in a pane of the viewer window, next to the text of the current page. Thumbnails are handy for several purposes. When you are viewing a page at high levels of magnification, thumbnails let you see where you are on the page. Thumbnails are also very useful for composing a PDF document: adding, inserting, and deleting pages. They can also provide a quick way to find pictures, tables, and other items in the document that vary the page layout significantly.

Notes

One of the most useful things about a real paper document is that you can annotate it. Most key documents are at least reviewed (if not produced) by a committee, and scribbling in the margins of the document is the preferred way to add a needed comment to a page. Acrobat lets Exchange users annotate PDF documents using notes. Acrobat's notes look like little sticky notes attached to the page. These notes come in different colors (you choose) and can be labeled with the writer's name or any other line of text. Exchange also provides functions to take you directly to the notes in your document, so you can see what others have written, and you can also print a listing of all the notes in the document.

Actually, third-party add-on software written for Acrobat allows you to write in the margins or anywhere else on the pages of your PDF document. You can use regular ink or colored markers (even transparent highlighters). Other users with the add-on software will see your annotations, while those without the software will not notice the difference. This is a great example of the robust extensibility mechanisms built into the PDF file format.

Integrating Acrobat with Other Applications

Acrobat tools come with *interapplication communication* (IAC) interfaces that let you use them from other applications. These interfaces vary by platform. On the Macintosh, Acrobat tools support Apple Events; on Windows, they support Dynamic Data Exchange (DDE) and Object Linking and Embedding (OLE). Adobe sells an IAC Software Development Kit (SDK) and provides training classes in using it; they also provide most of the contents of the SDK for free on the Internet. We discuss these capabilities and how to use them in Chapter 8.

 **Integrating Acrobat with Other Applications** 9

Acrobat PDF files can be embedded into Lotus Notes databases, and Acrobat supports Lotus Notes/FX field exchange technology. Document information fields within a PDF file can be exchanged with Notes database fields, allowing you to display the document's title and author (among other things) within a Notes database view. We discuss these capabilities in Chapter 9.

Plug-ins

Acrobat Exchange provides an Application Programming Interface (API) that developers can use to extend the capabilities of PDF files and Acrobat Exchange itself. This API is called the Plug-in interface and products developed for it are called plug-ins. You can use the Plug-in interface to add menu items and toolbar buttons to the Exchange user interface to support proprietary functions. You can also use the interface to add proprietary data to a PDF file. These documents are still portable, even to those who do not have the software to support your extensions (though they won't be able to use the proprietary data without the plug-in).

Adobe sells the Plug-in Software Development Kit and training courses to get you started developing plug-ins. Because of the power of the Plug-in SDK, Adobe requires developers to sign a non-disclosure agreement before purchasing it. For more information contact the Adobe Developers Association at (415) 961-4111 or fax them at (415) 967-9231.

Support

Adobe provides extensive support for Acrobat products. The following services are provided free of charge:

- Adobe FaxYI. Call (206) 628-5737 from your fax machine to receive faxes covering various technical support topics for Adobe products. Documents cover bugs and work-arounds for them as

 **Chapter 1: Introduction to Acrobat**

well as how-to articles. First call and get the current catalog. Macintosh users should ask for document #220099; Windows users want #330099. This is an excellent source of information for troubleshooting Acrobat products.

- Adobe Automated Technical Support. A computer asks you questions to help you diagnose common problems with installation and use of Adobe products; however, when we called they only discussed problems with Distiller. Try it yourself at (206) 628-2757 with a touch-tone phone.

- Adobe forums on CompuServe. Adobe sponsors two forums on CompuServe: GO ADOBEAPP for questions about how to install and use Acrobat and other Adobe products, and GO ADOBESYS for developer questions (developer questions are those that relate to using IAC and developing plug-ins). These forums are staffed by volunteers who can refer problems to Adobe technical support and engineering. Be patient with them.

- Adobe's BBS at (206) 623-6984.

Adobe also provides paid support in several forms. Prices quoted below were accurate as of May 1995.

- Call (900) 555-ADOBE and talk your problem over with a helpful Adobe Technical Support representative. Charge is $2.00 per minute.

- Call (800) 872-3623 for the same telephone support service but charged at a flat $25 for up to 15 minutes of support time. Purchase telephone support calls in advance and receive a discount. You can purchase 10 support calls for $175 and receive a technical support CD-ROM as well.

- Adobe Acrobat Corporate Help Desk. This package provides 100 telephone service calls, a free technical support CD-ROM, and

 **Summary**

three days of classroom training for two people, among other things, for $3,000.00.

- Acrobat training classes. Adobe provides training classes for developers using the IAC and Plug-in SDKs.

Summary

Adobe has set its sights on the goal of making electronic publishing feasible without compromising either quality or accessibility. This book is about how to use Acrobat to realize those goals in your own work. In this chapter we've described the products that make up the Acrobat family and introduced the basic terms that describe Acrobat's features. We've also mentioned the mechanisms available to you to integrate Acrobat programs into your working environment and products. In Chapters 2 through 7, we describe how to use each of the Acrobat products in detail. In Chapter 8, we discuss Acrobat on a more technical level, describing in some detail how to integrate Acrobat with other programs and make use of its built-in automation features. Chapter 9 discusses publishing with Acrobat on the Internet, on CD-ROM, and using Lotus Notes. In Chapter 10, we introduce the basics of enhancing PostScript files for PDF and of writing PDF files directly from your application.

CHAPTER 2

The Acrobat Reader

Versions of the Reader
Viewing Documents
Browsing a Document
Controlling Document View Scaling
Full Screen Display Mode
Searching for Text
Using Notes
Reading Articles
Copying to the Clipboard
Windows OLE and the Reader
Preferences

 **Versions of the Reader**

The Reader is your basic, royalty-free tool for delivering PDF documents to your clientele. The Reader allows you to display the pages of a PDF document, including any bookmarks, notes, hypertext links, or thumbnails in the document. The Reader will also print the PDF document to the system printer. However, true to its name, the Reader only allows you to look at the PDF document. If you want to make changes or add annotations to the document, you must use the Exchange product described in Chapter 3. The Reader also provides only a very limited set of interapplication communication (IAC) capabilities. For more advanced IAC without the full cost of Exchange, Adobe provides Exchange LE to developers only; this program is also discussed in Chapter 3.

This chapter gives a synopsis of how to use the version 2.*x* Reader to view PDF documents. Exchange has all the same functions, so everything in this chapter applies to Exchange as well.

Versions of the Reader

As this book is being written, Adobe is preparing a new version of the Reader (version 2.1 will probably be available by the time you read this). This version not only runs on the usual Windows and Macintosh platforms (including PowerMac), but also on OS/2, Windows NT, Sun Solaris and SunOS, and Hewlett-Packard HP-UX. Another new feature of version 2.1 is that the Reader now includes a restricted version of Adobe's plug-in interface. The plug-in interface allows new code modules to be developed and added to the reader without having to replace the whole installation. We discuss plug-ins in Chapter 7.

In this book we cover the Macintosh and Windows versions of the Reader, which are so similar in appearance and operation that we

**Chapter 2: The Acrobat Reader**

can largely ignore their differences. The only important difference you should be aware of between the two versions has to do with differences between Macintosh and Windows keyboard support. The Windows version uses the Ctrl key combined with other keys to issue commands, while the Macintosh usually uses the Command (⌘) key instead. In the command summary tables in this chapter, under the heading Keyboard Accelerators, we show the keyboard combination that issues the command we are describing. To indicate a Ctrl or Command key combination, we use the format Ctrl/⌘ + X, where the X is replaced by the key you should press to activate this command. So Ctrl/⌘ + A means you would hold down the Ctrl key on a Windows machine, or the ⌘ key on a Macintosh, and press the letter A.

Viewing Documents

Figure 2.1 shows the main Reader window. At the top of the window is a standard menu bar and toolbar—these provide access to all of the Reader's functions (you can also use keyboard equivalents for many of these functions). The main portion of the window presents a view of the document (or it is blank if no document is open for viewing). The version 2.1 Reader for Windows and Macintosh will likely have additional toolbar buttons because of the plug-ins expected to ship with it.

The Reader gives you a view of your document in one of three different screen layouts. All three feature a view of the current page of the document, but two of them provide an additional window pane where you can view either the bookmarks or the thumbnails contained in your document. You select among these views in one of two ways—either from the View menu or the toolbar push buttons.

Viewing Documents 15

Figure 2.1
Acrobat Reader in Page Only view

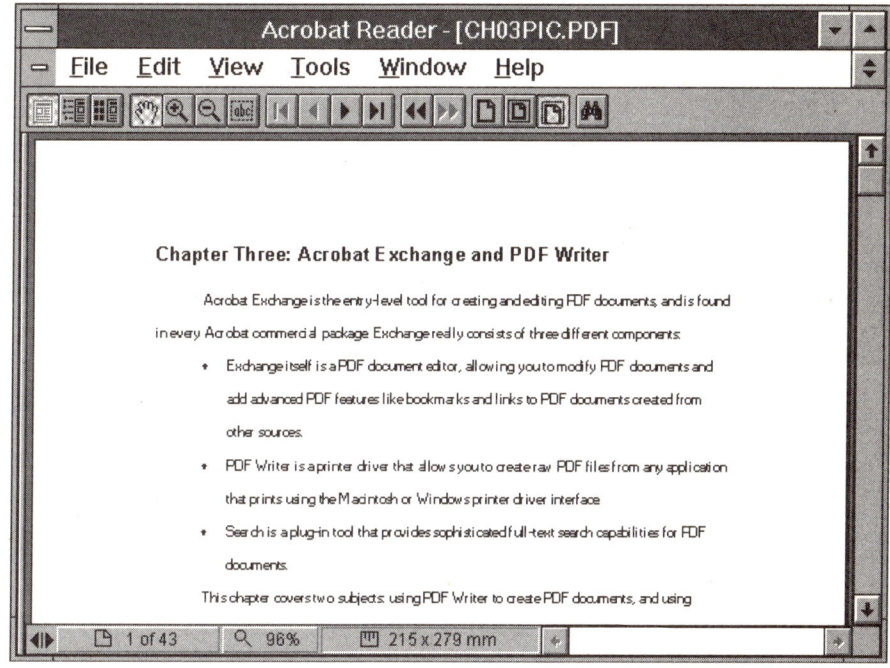

- Page Only view displays the document page by itself in the main window.

- Bookmarks and Page view displays the page alongside a list of the bookmarks found in the document. Clicking on a bookmark displays the page associated with that bookmark (see Figure 2.2 for an example).

- Thumbnails and Page view displays the page along with any thumbnails in the document. Clicking on a thumbnail displays the page associated with that thumbnail (see Figure 2.3 for an example).

When you first open a PDF document, the Reader will display the document with the screen layout established for that file (if it has

 **Chapter 2: The Acrobat Reader**

Figure 2.2
Bookmarks and Page view

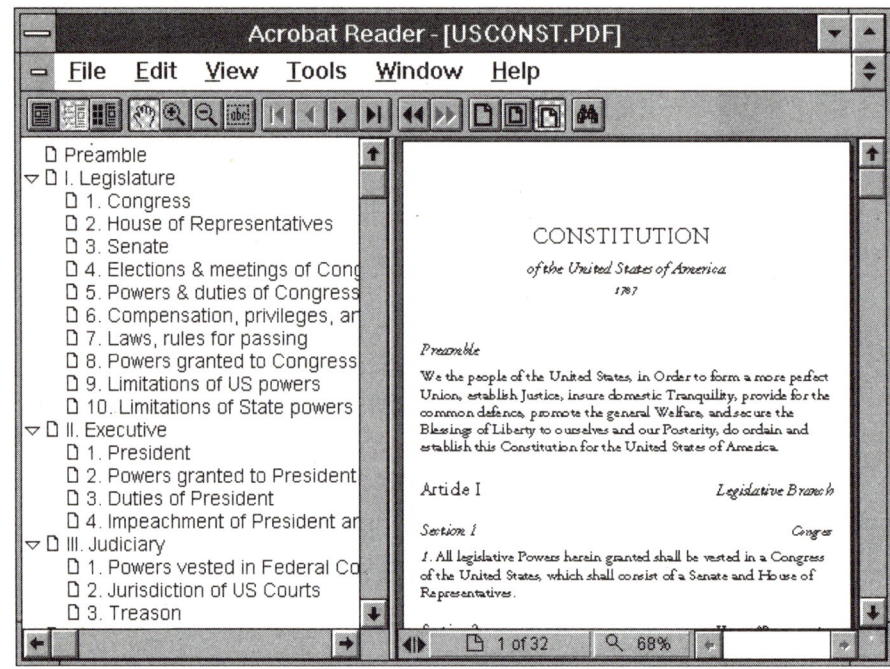

one) or it will use the current default. You can change the current view using any of the following methods:

Viewing Mode	Menu Bar Command	Keyboard Accelerator	Button
Page only	View | Page Only	Ctrl/⌘+6	
Bookmarks alongside the page	View | Bookmarks and Page	Ctrl/⌘+7	
Thumbnails alongside the page	View | Thumbnails and Page	Ctrl/⌘+8	

 **Viewing Documents** 17

Figure 2.3
Thumbnails
and Page view

When you are using one of the combination views, you can change the size of the bookmark or thumbnail pane of the window by dragging the double-arrow control in the bottom-right corner of the page view pane to the right or left. With Windows, you can also click and drag anywhere on the dividing bar. In fact, Page Only view is created by sliding the dividing bar all the way to the left, shrinking the bookmark/thumbnail pane to nothing (you can verify this by setting Page Only view and then dragging the dividing bar back into the document from the left border of the window). While the Reader doesn't provide Bookmark Only or Thumbnail Only commands, you can create these views by sliding the window pane dividing bar all the way to the right side of the window.

 Chapter 2: The Acrobat Reader

Browsing a Document

The Reader provides digital equivalents to most of the ways we already use to browse through a document. The most elementary page-turning commands are listed in the table below; they include commands to turn to the next or previous page, go directly to the first or last page, or go directly to any other page in the document by specifying a page number. You can also use the scroll bar on the right-hand side of the window to scroll through the document. One minor annoyance is that the Reader will not scroll smoothly between the pages of the document—instead it "jump scrolls" to the next page. In other words, you cannot view the bottom of one page and the top of the next page simultaneously.

Browsing Command	Menu Selection	Keyboard Accelerator	Button
Next page	View | Next Page	Ctrl/⌘+3 or Down Arrow	▶
Previous page	View | Previous Page	Ctrl/⌘+2 or Up Arrow	◀
Next full screen	None	Page Down	None
Previous full screen	None	Page Up	None
First page	View | First Page	Ctrl/⌘+1 or Home	◀◀
Last page	View | Last Page	Ctrl/⌘+4 or End	▶▶
Go to a specific page	View | Go To Page	Ctrl/⌘+5	1 of 5

Bookmarks are probably the single most important way to randomly browse through a document. A properly constructed set of bookmarks acts as a table of contents, enabling you to quickly scan the document's subject matter and head directly for the areas that interest you. We'll discuss creating bookmarks for your documents in the next chapter. Using bookmarks is easy: Select the Bookmarks

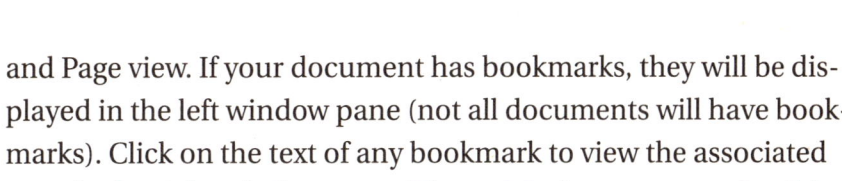

Browsing a Document

and Page view. If your document has bookmarks, they will be displayed in the left window pane (not all documents will have bookmarks). Click on the text of any bookmark to view the associated page in the right window pane (Figure 2.2 gives an example of the Bookmark and Page view).

Links also provide for browsing by subject. Links represent the connections between the current subject and other related subjects in your document (or other documents). Links are as easy to use as bookmarks—clicking on a link takes you to the destination page of the link. Normally the author of the document provides for highlighting the link either by drawing a box around it or by using colored text to set off the link from surrounding text. The Go Back command, described below, is especially useful with links, as it lets you explore linked subjects and easily return to your original place in the document.

Thumbnails are probably less familiar to most users, but they are also quite useful, especially for finding figures and illustrations quickly within a document. They can also help you stay oriented when you are viewing a page at high levels of magnification—a little box on the thumbnail shows you what portion of the page you are viewing. Select Thumbnails and Page view to display thumbnails in the left window pane; if it is empty, your document does not have thumbnails. Vertically scroll down through the thumbnail window pane to see all the thumbnails, and click on one to bring the page into view in the right window pane. Note that documents are not required to have thumbnails, and may not have them for every page (Figure 2.3 shows an example of Thumbnails and Page view). If thumbnails are missing, you will still see blank gray thumbnail icons which serve the same purpose.

Two additional commands are critically important when browsing a document: Go Back and Go Forward. Go Back lets you move back to a previous view of the document (up to 64 views back), acting as a

 **Chapter 2: The Acrobat Reader**

kind of undo command. Go Forward lets you redo the commands that you retraced with Go Back. These commands remember the document, page, and view magnification you were using in the previous display view. The list of commands you can retrace through is called the *navigation stack*. One note: If you use Go Back to return to a previous view, and then you alter the view in any way, you won't be able to use Go Forward to return to your starting point, because the commands are thrown away when you make a change. Actions that terminate the Go Forward list include grabbing and moving the page with the Hand tool, or changing the magnification of the view, as well as any of the navigational commands.

Navigation Stack Commands	Menu Selection	Keyboard Accelerator	Button
Go back to a previous view	View | Go Back	Ctrl/⌘+-	◀◀
Return from a previous view	View | Go Forward	Ctrl/⌘+=	▶▶

Controlling Document View Scaling

Several different factors work together to control the size of the displayed document, including the page size the author used to create the original document and the size of the Reader's display window. These two factors determine how much of the document is displayed at a given scaling factor for the page. Within these constraints the Reader lets you zoom in and out to magnify a portion of the page, and gives you controls to allow easy scrolling through the document at high magnification.

    The table below lists the commands for resizing the page to fit the screen in various ways. Since most computer displays are much too small to display a full letter-size page at a readable magnification level, the View \| Fit Width and View \| Fit Visible commands are

 **Controlling Document View Scaling**

particularly useful. Fit Width displays the page scaled so that its width fits within the bounds of the Reader's window, while Fit Visible does the same thing except it trims the page margins, displaying only that portion of the page that is not blank.

Page Scaling Command	Menu Selection	Keyboard Accelerator	Button
Display the page at its actual size	View | Actual Size	Ctrl/⌘+H	
Fit a full page in the window	View | Fit Page	Ctrl/⌘+J	
Fit the page width in the window	View | Fit Width	Ctrl/⌘+K	
Fit the visible portion of the page in the window	View | Fit Visible	Ctrl/⌘+M	Ctrl/⌘ +

Another set of commands gives you finer control over the scaling of the page display. You can specify a scaling factor with the View | Zoom To command. This command doesn't have an icon on the toolbar, instead it has a graphic control on the bottom border of the Reader window. This control displays the current scaling factor; click on it to bring up a list of scale factors you can select.

You can also use the Zoom In or Zoom Out tools to magnify portions of the document. When you select one of the zooming tools, the cursor changes to a magnifying glass (with a plus sign for Zoom In, and a minus for Zoom Out). You can use these tools in two ways:

- Click the left mouse button to step the page scaling factor in the direction of the tool you have selected. Each click doubles or halves the scaling factor.

- Click and drag a rectangle with the mouse to outline the area you want displayed in the window. When using the Zoom In tool, the area within the box you outlined will be enlarged to fit in the

 **Chapter 2: The Acrobat Reader**

window. The Zoom Out tool also works in this mode; however, the results are not particularly intuitive. What appears to be happening is that the Reader takes the difference between the box you draw and the current window size and inverts it, shrinking the window by that amount (or it may magnify if the box you draw is larger than the screen). If that doesn't make sense to you, don't worry about it; just use the tool by clicking it to zoom out.

The boxes drawn by the Zoom tools have the same aspect ratio (the ratio between the length and height of the box) as the current dimensions of the Reader's window. Change the size of the window and the zoom box will change too.

When you have selected either Zoom In or Zoom Out, you can quickly swap to the other one by pressing the Ctrl/⌘ key and clicking. Doing so inverts the meaning of the current tool, so that Zoom In becomes Zoom Out while the Ctrl/⌘ key is held down, and vice versa. The cursor changes to show this swap. Also, check out the Snap tool described in Chapter 7.

Zoom Command	Menu Selection	Keyboard Accelerator	Button
Set a scale factor	View | Zoom To…	Ctrl/⌘+L	🔍 100%
Enlarge a portion of the document.	Tools | Zoom In	Ctrl/⌘+Shift+2	🔍
Reduce magnification	Tools | Zoom Out	Ctrl/⌘+Shift+3	🔍
Scroll the visible area of the document	Tools | Hand	Ctrl/⌘+Shift+1	✋
Full screen display mode	View | Full Screen	Ctrl/⌘+Shift+L	None

Often you will be working with a document in a magnified view. This eases the strain on your eyes but means the whole document is

 **Full Screen Display Mode**

not visible at once. The Reader provides both the standard mechanisms for scrolling the document (horizontal and vertical scroll bars) and several unique methods for bringing off-screen portions of the document into view. First is the Hand tool which, when selected, lets you click on a portion of the visible page and drag it to bring more of the page into view. The Hand tool is selected by default when you start the Reader. Another method is to use the Page Up and Page Down keys on your extended keyboard. Finally, there's a way to use thumbnails to scroll the document. In Thumbnail and Page view for the current page, when the page is displayed at magnification, the thumbnail shows a box within it that marks the visible area of the screen. You can drag this box around on the thumbnail itself to view different portions of the page, and you can use the resizing corner on the box in the thumbnail to change the size of the box and the magnification of the page (see Figure 2.4 for an example). This works even if you don't have thumbnails in your document (although it is not as useful).

Full Screen Display Mode

The View | Full Screen menu selection actually changes the user interface of the Reader—the entire screen is devoted to the Page Only view of the document (you cannot use this mode to view thumbnails or bookmarks). The menu and toolbars are both removed, along with the window borders and scroll bars—only the keyboard and mouse are active during Full Screen mode. You can use the keyboard accelerators listed in the tables above to navigate through the document, and you can click on links and notes in your document to view them. Exit Full Screen mode by scrolling past the last page of the document or by pressing the Esc key.

24  Chapter 2: The Acrobat Reader

Figure 2.4
Using the Thumbnail view to scroll around on the page.

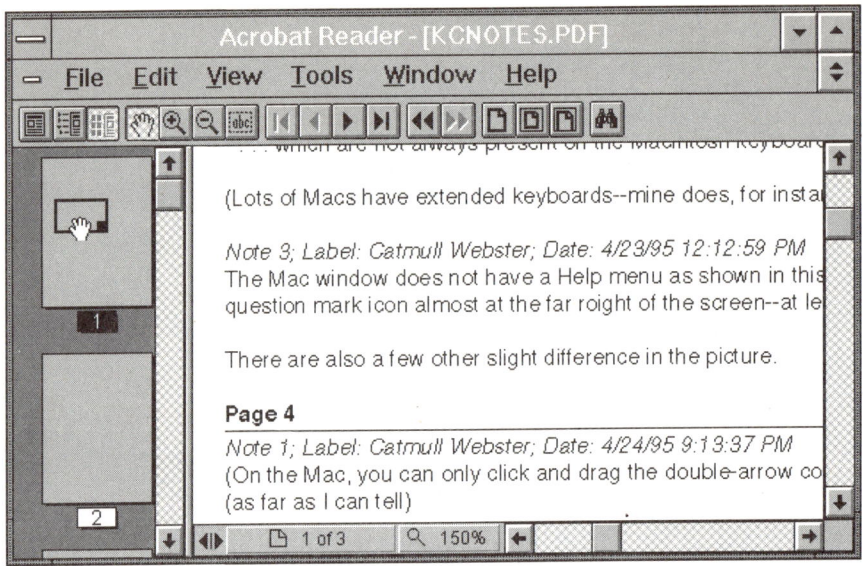

Searching for Text

The Reader provides a straightforward text search capability, similar to that provided in any word processor. Selecting the Find function brings up the dialog box shown in Figure 2.5; the user enters a word or phrase, optionally selects one or more of the options, and presses Find to search for the first occurrence. The user can continue the search with the Find Again function after matching some text with Find. The options to Find are

- *Match Whole Word Only*. This option requires the matching text to start and end on nonalphabetic characters, such as spaces, new lines, or punctuation marks.

- *Match Case*. Selecting this option requires the text to match the capitalization in your search string. The default is to ignore capitalization.

Figure 2.5
Using the Find function to search for text.

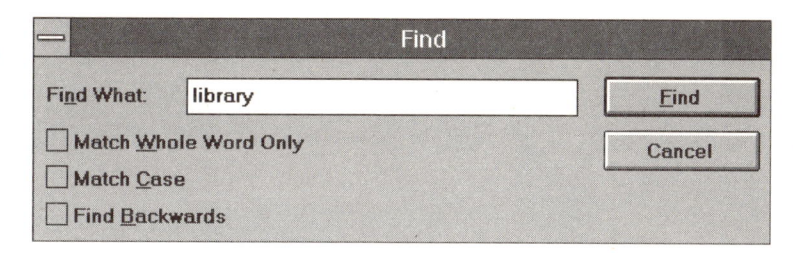

[Find dialog box: Find What: library; Match Whole Word Only; Match Case; Find Backwards; Find; Cancel]

- *Find Backwards.* The search normally proceeds from the current location towards the end of the document, but checking this option causes the search to proceed backward towards the beginning of the document.

Find Commands	Menu Selection	Keyboard Accelerator	Button
Find first match	Tools | Find	Ctrl/⌘+F	🔍
Find next match	Tools | Find Again	Ctrl/⌘+G F3 (PC only)	None

Acrobat Exchange provides more advanced text search procedures using the Acrobat Search plug-in, and you can create search indexes for a collection of PDF documents using Acrobat Catalog. These capabilities are discussed in Chapter 5.

Using Notes

Acrobat Exchange users can add the electronic equivalent of Post-it™ notes to their PDF documents. Figure 2.6 shows such a note displayed in the Reader window. Reader users can view these notes but cannot modify, delete, or add their own notes to the file.

You can move a note around on the page to see what is beneath it, but notes are attached to the page they appear on and can't be

Chapter 2: The Acrobat Reader

Figure 2.6
Unopened notes in the Reader window.

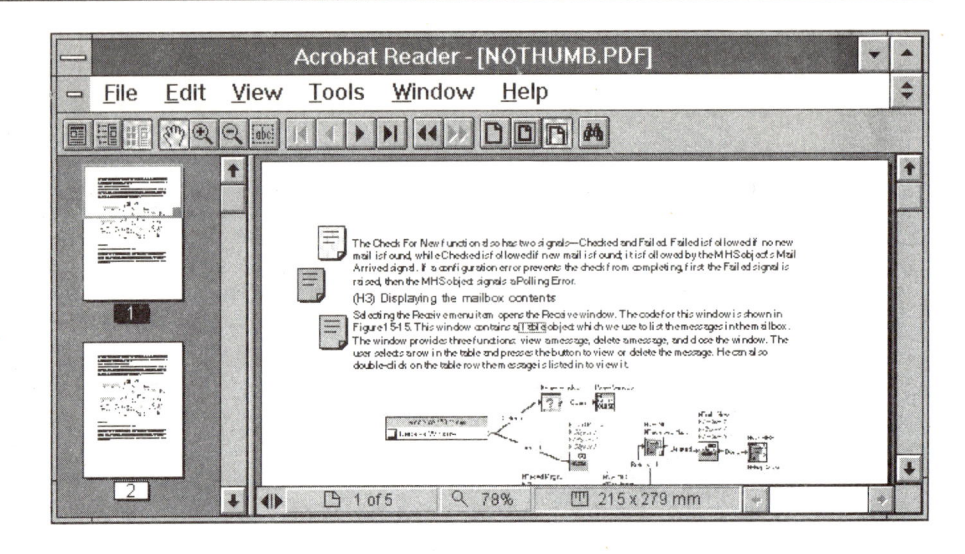

removed from it. Double-click on the unopened note to view its contents (see Figure 2.7 for an example). When opened, the note has a title bar and close box just like any other window. If the text of the note doesn't all fit in the space provided, the window will have a scroll bar you can use to bring the rest of the note into view. Alternatively, you can change the size of the note window by dragging the Macintosh-style resize box in the lower-right corner of the window. While the note is open, you can select text inside the note and copy it to the clipboard using the standard Edit | Copy commands (use Edit | Select All to select all the text of the note). Click on the close box in the upper-left corner of the note to return it to its unopened state.

The Reader provides a command that will take you directly to the next page with a note on it. The menu command is Tools | Find Next Note (the keyboard accelerator is Ctrl+T). The Reader will change the view of the document to display the page where the note is placed, and bring the note into view if possible.

Figure 2.7
An open note

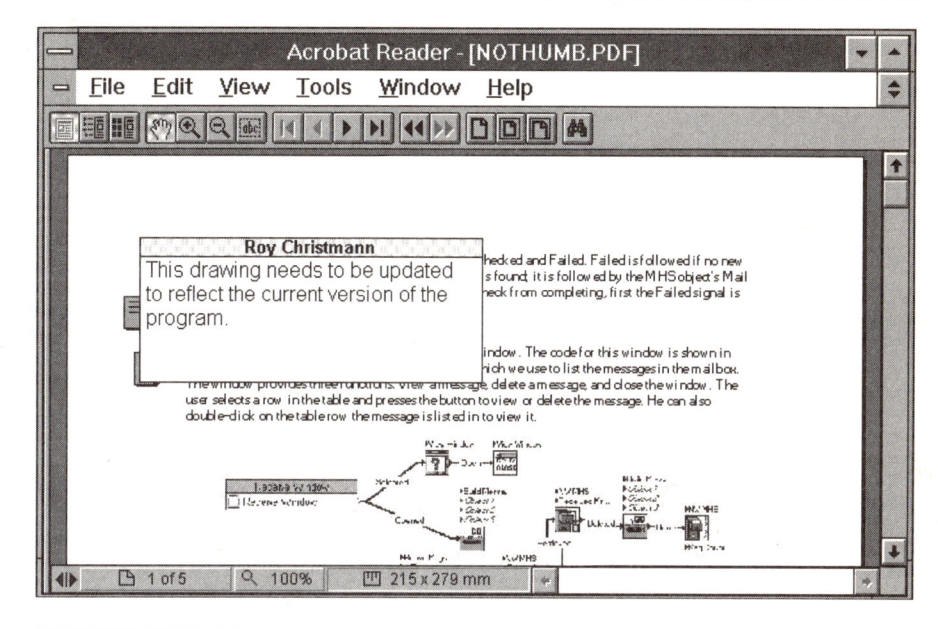

Note: In a full-page view of the document, notes can be moved off of the page itself into the window border displayed around the page. Acrobat still thinks the note is on the page, but when you use Find Next Note it won't change the page view to display the note. If you select Find Next Note and you don't see the note displayed (and you don't get an error message indicating that there are no more notes), switch to View | Fit Page in order to see the note.

Reading Articles

The Reader provides a feature called articles that makes it easy to read columns of text on the page. Articles must be set up by the creator of the document, so they are not present just because the text is in columns (see the next chapter for instructions on creating articles). Articles are especially useful when there are several of them on

Chapter 2: The Acrobat Reader

the same page, such as with a newspaper. An example of an article can be found on the Acrobat CD Sampler in the file EVSTAND.PDF, an electronic version of the *London Evening Standard* newspaper. Figure 2.8 shows what the Reader window looks like when the cursor is over an article. You'll notice two changes. First, the cursor, which was displaying the Hand tool, now displays the Hand with a small downward-pointing arrow within it. This signifies that the cursor is over an article. Second, on the status line at the bottom of the Reader window, where the size of the document is usually displayed, the Reader displays the legend Read Article.

Left-click with your mouse when the article cursor is displayed and the article text will expand to fill the window, making it easy to read. Then, each time you click your mouse, the next unread section of the article text will be displayed. A small black arrow flashes for a second next to the text where you should start reading. As you read, the bottom of the window displays Follow Article. When you reach

Figure 2.8
An article is ready to be viewed.

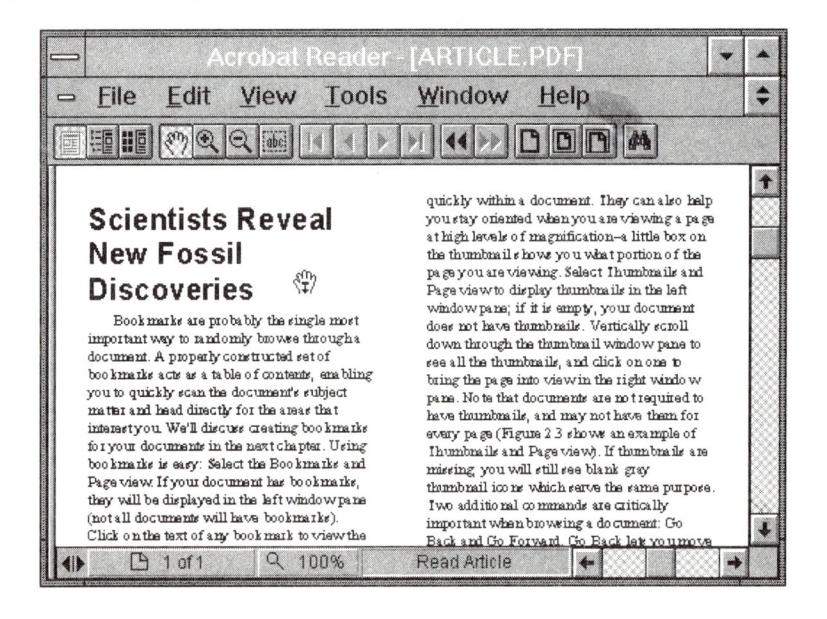

the end of the article, the legend at the bottom of the window changes to Exit Article, and your next mouse click will return you to the view you were in when you started viewing the article.

There are a few other options you can use when reading an article. You can shift-click to go back to the previous view of the article, and Ctrl/Option-click to return to the beginning of the article. To exit an article, you can Shift-Ctrl-click the mouse for Windows, or Shift-Option-click on the Mac. Also any navigational command (such as changing pages) will exit the article.

There is also a menu item View | Articles that will be grayed if there are no articles in your document. If there are articles, you can select this menu item to display a list of the articles (see Figure 2.9). Select one for viewing or select the Info button to see the article's title, subject, author, and any keywords defined for it.

Copying to the Clipboard

The Acrobat Reader supports copying text and graphics to the clipboard, if the document security settings allow it (see the next chapter for a discussion of document security). If they don't allow it, the menu items and toolbar button will be grayed. Selecting text means that the text characters will be transferred to the clipboard as a text

Figure 2.9
The Articles dialog box

item (without formatting). Selecting graphics means that the portion of the document you select (which may include text) is transferred to the clipboard as a bitmap.

After choosing the Select Text tool, the cursor changes to an I-beam with a little bar across the middle of it. Now there are several ways to select text. The first is to hold down the left mouse button and drag the cursor over the text you want to copy. The second is to press the Ctrl/Option key and drag a box around the text you want with the mouse. Either way gives you the same result. Also, if you hold down the Shift key and click the mouse, all the text from the top of the page to your cursor position will be selected. Finally, you can quickly select all the text on the page using Edit | Select All. After making your selection, choose the Edit | Copy command to actually put the text on the clipboard. Now it is ready to paste into your application.

Clipboard Commands	Menu Selection	Keyboard Accelerator	Button
Select text to copy to the clipboard	Tools	Select Text	Ctrl/⌘+Shift+4	abc
Select all the text on the current page for copying	Edit	Select All	Ctrl/⌘+A	None
Select graphics to copy to the clipboard	Tools	Select Graphics	Ctrl/⌘+Shift+5	None
Copy the selection to the clipboard	Edit	Copy	Ctrl/⌘+C	None

Selecting graphics is very similar, though there are not as many options. After choosing the Select Graphics tool, the cursor will change to a crosshair. Use the crosshair to drag a box around the portion of the document you want to copy. Then select the Edit | Copy command to put the selection on the clipboard.

Windows OLE and the Reader

Microsoft Windows provides a technology called Object Linking and Embedding (OLE) which allows you to create *compound documents* (that is, documents that contain data from several different applications). We discuss these capabilities more thoroughly in Chapter 8; however, you should be aware now that the Reader can act as an OLE version 1 server application. This capability allows you to link or embed Acrobat PDF files into other documents and view them with the Reader. The standard way to access these capabilities is through the Insert | Object or Edit | Paste Special menu items in your OLE client application programs (such as a word processor). Adobe does not advertise this fact, preferring to talk about the OLE version 2 capabilites built into Exchange.

On the other hand, note that none of the Acrobat tools can act as an OLE client application. This means that you cannot directly link or embed, for example, a portion of an Excel spreadsheet into your PDF document. Instead, you must construct your compound document in an application that offers these capabilities, and then print from that application to a PDF file using PDF Writer (or print to PostScript and use Distiller). The reason for this is that PDF is intended to be portable to any computer system, while OLE is currently limited to Windows (and is starting to appear on Macintosh systems).

Preferences

The Reader has a number of defaults which users can adjust to their own preference. These items are found in the Edit, Preferences menu item. There are two categories of preferences: General and Full Screen. The General Preference items are a group of miscellaneous options settings for the program, while the Full Screen preferences allow you to configure an autopilot for the Reader's Full Screen display mode, which automatically pages through the document. Each selection brings up its own dialog box, which we'll discuss in turn. For Windows users, these options all have equivalent settings in the ACROREAD.INI file that the Reader creates in the Windows home directory. Figure 2.10 shows the General Preferences dialog box. The preference items are

- *Default Magnification.* This sets the magnification used when a document is opened and the document does not provide for its own private default magnification setting. You can select a numeric value or one of the three "sticky" options: Fit Page, Fit Width, or Fit Visible.

- *Max "Fit Visible" Magnification.* This option sets the maximum magnification level used by the Fit Visible display mode and by the article reading mode. This won't have any effect on normal documents, but if your document consists of a small word or

Figure 2.10
The General Preferences dialog box

image in the middle of a big empty page, this setting will prevent the Reader from enlarging your document excessively.

- *Display Large Images*. Bitmapped images take considerably more time to display than text, and this can really slow you down if you are trying to scan quickly through a document. Turning this option off instructs the Reader to display a gray box on the page instead of the image. To restore images to view, you must return to this dialog box and check this option again.

- *Use Page Cache*. This option reserves a block of system memory to hold recently accessed pages from the document, which can speed up access to those pages if you are flipping back and forth between them. Usually you should leave this option enabled. The Page Cache is not available in 16- and 24-bit color display modes.

- *Greek Text*. If the displayed text is too small to read in your window, then it might as well be Greek to you—hence this option. Text that is smaller than the specified size when rendered in the current view will be drawn as a gray line, which speeds up display of such text. The proper setting depends on your display resolution, but the default is usually fine.

- *Substitution Fonts*. The Reader comes with separate master fonts for serif and sans serif fonts. Using both of these masters allows the most faithful rendering of fonts that are not present on your system; however, it can take up more memory in the printer, causing some printers that don't have much memory to fail to print the page. This option allows you to substitute only one of the two master fonts for both kinds of fonts regardless, thereby freeing up some memory in the printer. If you have problems with PostScript printers running out of memory while printing a page, try selecting either the option for Sans only or Serif only instead of the default Both serif and sans.

- *Page Units.* This option governs which measurement units the Reader uses to display the size of the current page in the status box at the bottom of the Reader window. You may select inches, millimeters or points.

- *Display Splash Screen at Startup.* Selecting this option causes the Reader to display the same graphic image as the Help, About Acrobat menu item as the program starts up. In the Windows version you can insert three lines of your own text into this image by modifying the Reader's .INI file.

- *Display Open Dialog at Startup.* Selecting this option causes the Reader to bring up the File, Open dialog to allow the user to select a file to open.

The Full Screen Preferences dialog box (shown in Figure 2.11) allows you to choose between manual use of Full Screen mode or automatic display of the document in this mode, and to set the background color for parts of the screen not covered by the document. Select a background color from the drop-down list (selecting Custom allows you to create a color other than black or white).

The automatic display option is useful for displaying a PDF document as part of an automated presentation such as a product

Figure 2.11
The Full Screen Preferences dialog box

demonstration or information kiosk. To use the automatic display capability, first select the Change Pages option in this dialog box and select the number of seconds between page changes. If you want the document to loop back to the beginning after it is displayed, also select the Loop option box. With these options selected, when you enter Full Page display mode, the automatic mode will take over (though the keyboard commands continue to work). Press Esc to exit the Full Display mode, as usual.

Summary

In this chapter we've learned how to use the Reader or Exchange to view PDF documents. Of course, you want to use Acrobat to create PDF documents, not just read them. In the next chapter, we discuss the two basic tools for creating Acrobat PDF files: PDF Writer and Exchange. PDF Writer lets you create PDF files from standard Windows and Macintosh applications, while Exchange builds on the capabilities of the Reader by allowing you to modify PDF files as well as view them.

CHAPTER 3

Acrobat Exchange and PDF Writer

Creating PDF Documents

Creating a PDF Document with PDF Writer

PDF Page Setup Options

Using Exchange

Creating PDF Documents

Acrobat Exchange is the entry-level tool for creating and editing PDF documents and is found in every Acrobat commercial package. Exchange really consists of three different components:

- Exchange itself is a PDF document editor, which allows you to modify PDF documents and add advanced PDF features like bookmarks and links to PDF documents created from other sources.

- PDF Writer is a printer driver that allows you to create raw PDF files from any application that prints using the Macintosh or Windows printer driver interface.

- Search is a plug-in tool that provides sophisticated full-text search capabilities for PDF documents that have been previously indexed with Acrobat Catalog.

This chapter covers two subjects: using PDF Writer to create PDF documents, and using Exchange to edit those documents. We discuss the Search capability in Chapter 5, along with the Adobe Catalog application.

Creating PDF Documents

You have three choices for creating PDF documents, presented here in order of increasing difficulty.

- Use PDF Writer to generate PDF files directly from your Macintosh or Windows applications

- Use your application to create a PostScript file using the standard PostScript driver for your software and send the PostScript file through Acrobat Distiller to create a PDF file

- Write your own PDF file directly

You can't use Exchange until you have created a PDF file using one of the above methods. PDF Writer is simple and quick; it should be your first choice for creating PDF files in a Windows or Macintosh environment. PDF Writer looks like any other printer to your system, so you can create PDF files directly from any application that provides a print function. However, there are times when you should use Distiller rather than PDF Writer:

- If you're a Microsoft Windows user who is using Encapsulated PostScript (EPS) images. In Windows, the application program must render the EPS file into a bitmapped image before sending it to the printer driver. This results in a degraded image in the PDF file. Instead, print the document as a PostScript file and use Distiller to convert the file to PDF. Alternatively, consider converting the EPS file to a different file type (such as TIFF) using a conversion program (for example, HiJaak from Inset Systems) and use the converted file with your application and PDF Writer.

- If you use applications that produce lower quality font representations on non-PostScript printers, such as CorelDraw, Micrografx Designer, and Harvard Draw.

- If you use applications that rasterize their output to non-PostScript printers, such as Harvard Graphics and Adobe Illustrator.

- If you use images which include patterned fills (either monochrome fill patterns or dithered colors). PDF Writer substitutes a solid color for such patterns.

- If you're using one of the many high-end graphics applications that will allow you to do things with PostScript that it doesn't support in other formats. This list includes Pagemaker and Quark XPress as well as the applications listed above.

Of course, if you already have PostScript files to work with, you should use Distiller. If you've written an application that creates PostScript directly, you can usually modify your application to write a PDF file as well; see Chapter 10.

There is one occasion where you may want to use PDF Writer instead of Distiller: when you are using unusual TrueType fonts (particularly ornate fonts or those based on non-Latin character sets). PDF Writer will embed TrueType fonts in your PDF file; but Distiller will convert those fonts to PostScript Type 1 fonts and embed the converted font instead. This may not work well for all fonts.

Creating a PDF Document with PDF Writer

When you install Exchange, it installs the PDF Writer printer driver as one of the standard printer drivers on your system. Then, when you want to create a PDF file, select PDF Writer as your printer using the standard method on your system:

- On Windows systems, you select PDF Writer in the Control Panel Printers applet. Most Windows applications also allow printer selection as an option from their File | Print menu item.

- On Macintosh systems, you select PDF Writer in the Chooser. You can also select PDF Writer temporarily for the current job by pressing the Command (⌘) key while choosing Print from the File menu of your application (⌘ + File | Print). Windows users don't have this second option.

Once you've selected PDF Writer as your printer, just print the file using your application's standard print function. Macintosh users will see a PDF Writer dialog box immediately when they select Print (see Figure 3.1), while Windows users will see their application's standard Print dialog box.

Figure 3.1
PDF Writer dialog box (Macintosh version)

```
Acrobat™ PDFWriter                                    2.0    [  OK  ]
Page Range: ● All    ○ From: [    ]  To: [    ]           [ Cancel ]
□ View PDF File
□ Short (DOS) File Names          ☒ Prompt for Document Info
Print Pages:   ● All   ○ Odd Pages Only   ○ Even Pages Only
Section Range: From: 1      To: 1       □ Print Selection Only
□ Print Hidden Text    □ Print Next File
```

On either system, when this dialog box is completed, PDF Writer brings up a standard Save As dialog box for you to enter the name of the PDF file. Macintosh users should consider whether they need to choose a name that matches MS-DOS file naming conventions (no more than 8 uppercase alphanumeric characters for the file name, a period, and the extension *PDF*). Use MS-DOS file names if any of the following are true:

- You are distributing the files to users on more than one platform (Macintosh, Windows, UNIX).

- You are distributing the files on CD-ROM.

- You are indexing the files with Acrobat Catalog.

- You will use hypertext links between the documents.

Macintosh users can select the Short (DOS) File Names option in the PDF Writer dialog box to truncate file names automatically.

PDF Writer provides two options when creating a file. Due to the differences described above, these options appear in the PDF Writer dialog box on the Macintosh (Figure 3.1), and in the Save As dialog on Windows (Figure 3.2):

- *Prompt for Document Info*. Enabling this option brings up the Document Information dialog box, allowing you to enter some

Figure 3.2
PDF Writer Save As dialog box (Windows version)

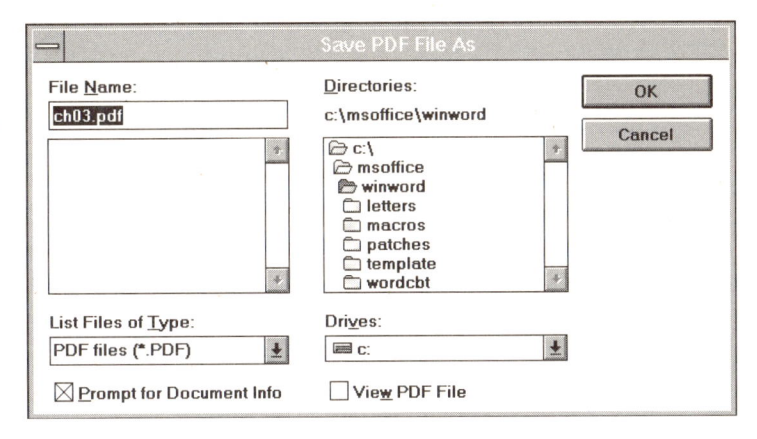

additional information that is stored in your PDF file (see Figure 3.3). You can specify a document title, subject, author, and keywords associated with your document. This information can be referenced by Acrobat Search and exported to other applications, such as Lotus Notes.

Figure 3.3
Document Information dialog box

- *View PDF file.* Enabling this option causes PDF Writer to open Exchange with the newly created PDF file once the file is created. This is useful for checking how PDF Writer handled your document.

PDF Page Setup Options

When you select PDF Writer as your printer, you should also review the Page Setup options that PDF Writer provides.

- In Windows systems, you set these options in the File | Print | Printer | Options dialog box, shown in Figure 3.4 (beware of confusing this with the File | Print | Options dialog box).

Figure 3.4
PDF Writer Options dialog box (Windows version)

- In Macintosh systems, you set these options in the dialog box brought up by ⌘ + File | Page Setup (see Figure 3.5).

We'll give you some guidelines on how to make these choices in the pages that follow. The available options are:

- *Page size.* You can select from a set of standard paper sizes, a Screen size which is ideal for online viewing, or you can specify a custom page size.

PDF Page Setup Options 43

Figure 3.5
PDF Writer Page Setup dialog box (Macintosh version)

- *Page orientation.* Select either portrait or landscape orientations.

- *Resolution.* A real printer has a physical limit on how many dots per inch (dpi) it can print to the page. PDF Writer does not have any such limit, but it still must tell any application that asks what its resolution is. This field allows you to set the value that PDF Writer reports to the application. Normally this is not used unless the application program is *rasterizing* its own output (converting its output to a bitmapped graphic). If that is the case, you will likely get better results with Distiller than PDF Writer. The default value of 300 is usually fine here.

- *Compression.* Select the Compression button to change the type of compression PDF Writer uses to create the PDF file.

- *Font.* Select the Font button to change the way fonts are embedded in your PDF file.

TIP: *The Page Setup options apply to the entire document that you generate; however, you may not want to use the same options throughout your final document. For example, you may want most of your pages in portrait orientation, but you have several pages that work better in landscape mode. You may want to adjust other options such as compression types on a per page basis. Instead of* *trying to write the entire document in one pass, consider writing separate PDF files, each with its own optimized page setup options. Then use the page composition features of Exchange (described later in this chapter) to create your final document from the separate pieces.*

Guidelines for Selecting Page Size

The optimal page size for your document depends on what you intend to do with it. If your primary purpose in creating PDF files is to transmit, archive, or allow electronic browsing of pre-existing paper documents, then you want to use a PDF page size that matches your original document. However, if the primary use of your document is going to be electronic viewing (such as an online help facility, computer-based training, online catalog, and so on), you should seriously consider a page layout using the PDF Writer's smaller Screen page size option instead. The reason is simple: most computer users do not have very large screens. A typical 14-inch monitor can comfortably display only about half of an 8½-by-11 inch page. In contrast, book readers usually see two full pages at once. Diagrams and section headings visible to a book reader are hidden by the online viewer's small screen size, making it more difficult to skim through the online version of a paper document. The most effective and usable online documents embrace the limitations of the medium in their basic design—Acrobat's help files are a good example.

Compression Options

PDF Writer provides several different options for compressing the data in your PDF file. Pressing the Compression button on the Page Setup options dialog box brings up the dialog box shown in Figure 3.6. This dialog box gives you compression choices for three different kinds of document data:

PDF Page Setup Options

Figure 3.6
PDF Writer Compression Options dialog box

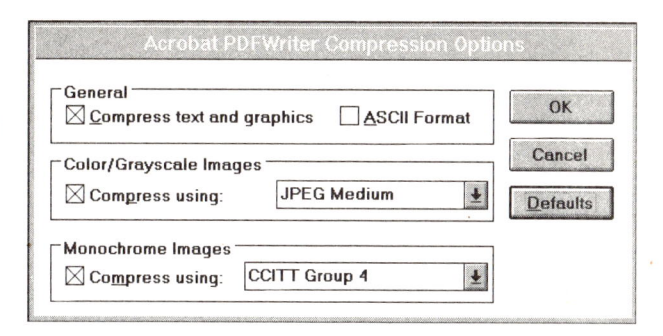

[Acrobat PDFWriter Compression Options dialog box:
General — ☒ Compress text and graphics, ☐ ASCII Format
Color/Grayscale Images — ☒ Compress using: JPEG Medium
Monochrome Images — ☒ Compress using: CCITT Group 4
Buttons: OK, Cancel, Defaults]

- *General.* This selection covers text and line art in the PDF file. If you don't select any compression here, the page description in the PDF file will be readable ASCII (the PDF headers are ASCII regardless). If you select Compress text and graphics, the page description will be compressed with the Lempel-Ziv-Welch compression algorithm (LZW). This is a variation of the same algorithm used in disk compression programs like Stacker and utilities like PKZip. If you also select ASCII Format, the output of the LZW algorithm will be encoded in Adobe's ASCII base-85 format, which converts the binary LZW data to pure seven bit ASCII.

- *Color/Grayscale Images.* This selection covers images included in your file that have more than one bit per pixel. There are two basic options for including color/grayscale images in a PDF file: whether to use a compression method that preserves all the data in the image (LZW) or a "lossy" compression method (Joint Photographic Experts Group or JPEG). The JPEG algorithm attempts to reduce file size by splitting the image into blocks and encoding only some of the image data in each block. PDF Writer provides a JPEG implementation with five different degrees of compression as well as an LZW compression option.

- *Monochrome Images.* This selection covers images in your document with only one bit per pixel, such as a fax image. PDF Writer provides LZW, Run Length, and CCITT Group 3 and Group 4 compression algorithms.

WARNING: *We were unable to include color images in our PDF files without choosing some form of compression for them. If we didn't have Color/Grayscale compression enabled, we got a solid black blob in the file where the image should have been.*

Guidelines for Selecting Compression Options

You will almost always benefit from using the General compression option. For example, a two-page, text-only document generated in Microsoft Word produced the results shown in Table 3.1.

Table 3.1 Comparison of the Effect of Different General Compression Options

File	File Size (bytes)	Percent of Original Word File
Original MS Word .DOC file	18,944	—
PDF file with no compression	27,522	145 percent
PDF file with General ASCII compression	20,660	109 percent
PDF file with General binary compression	17,907	95 percent

The only reason you might not want to use General compression in PDF Writer is if you intend to compress the resulting PDF file independently. Since General compression doesn't compress the PDF file headers, font encodings, and trailers, you may be able to produce an even smaller file using an external compression program. However, the result will no longer be a PDF file recognizable by Reader or Exchange—you'll have to decompress it yourself.

The final question is whether or not to check the ASCII Format button when you use compression. Leaving this option unchecked is the recommended setting, and it results in the best compression ratio for the file, as shown above. However, some antique communication methods won't support a binary file. If you must, for example, send your file over a 7-bit modem connection (without using a file transfer protocol), then you want to select the ASCII Format option.

TIP: *Parts of the internet are pretty old, including the original mail service, which requires all data to be 7-bit ASCII. PDF files written with the ASCII Format option can be sent successfully as Internet mail (without having to resort to uuencode).*

Color and Grayscale Image Compression Options

The question of which compression algorithm to use for color image data is less straightforward. There is usually a trade-off between the size of the file PDF Writer generates and the quality of the resulting image, but the optimal selection for a given image can only be determined by experimentation. Consider Figure 3.7, a grayscale image captured from a computer screen (similar to most of the pictures used in this book). This image contains a lot of white space, which makes it ideal for LZW compression. Figure 3.8 shows what the resulting PDF image looks like at 800 percent magnification for each of four compression algorithms: LZW, Low JPEG, Medium JPEG, and High JPEG.

The LZW and JPEG Low images are largely indistinguishable, but in the JPEG Medium and especially the JPEG High compression pictures, you can see where the compression method adds noise that is not present in the original image. Even more telling are the file sizes produced by PDF Writer (see Table 3.2); not only does LZW produce the best image but it is much smaller than any of the JPEG files.

48 Chapter 3: Acrobat Exchange and PDF Writer

Figure 3.7
Sample grayscale image

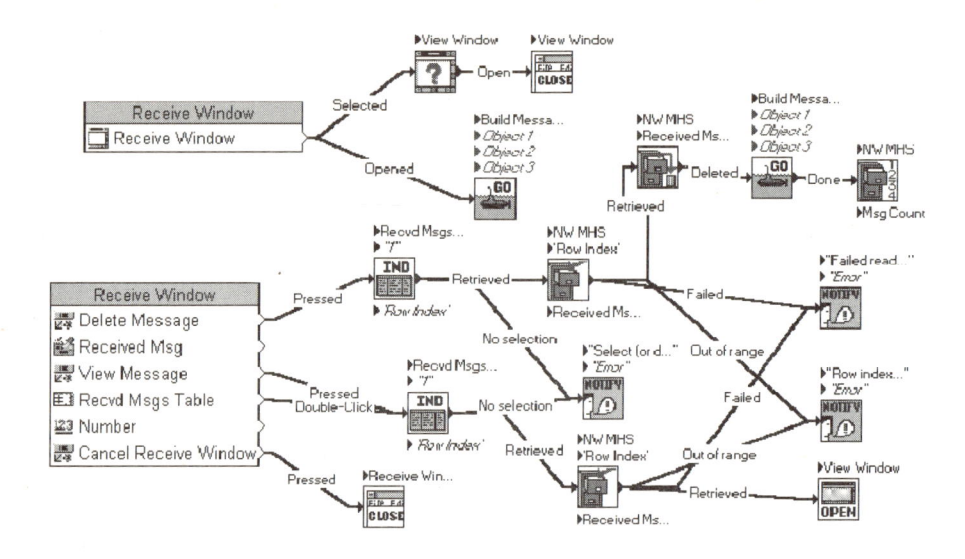

Figure 3.8
PDF Writer compression results for sample image, magnified 800 times

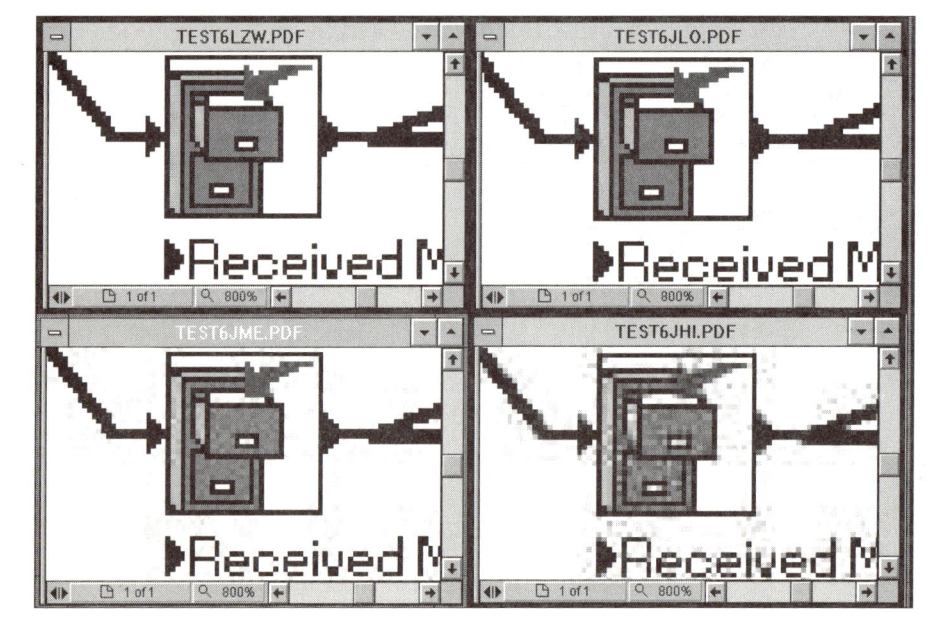

Table 3.2   **Comparison of Different Compression Options on a Grayscale Image**

Compression Type	File Size (bytes)	Percent of Original File Size
Uncompressed Word source file	322,560	—
LZW	19,840	6 percent
High JPEG	42,930	13 percent
Medium JPEG	66,663	21 percent
Low JPEG	100,028	31 percent

Clearly JPEG is not always the optimal choice. However, these results will differ considerably for a full-color image, such as a scanned photograph. We cannot reproduce such images in this book, but we can tell you that the situation described above is reversed for a full-color image with lots of detailed color in it. In this case, LZW may produce a file that is larger than the original image, while JPEG will be much smaller but not necessarily much poorer in quality. We discuss these results for color images in Chapter 4. The important point is that for optimum image quality (and minimal file size) you'll have to try the different options yourself and compare the results on an image by image basis (at least until you are familiar with the types of images you work with).

Monochrome Image Compression Options

With monochrome images, the only issue is the size of the PDF file produced by PDF Writer, since none of these compression algorithms affects image quality. Again, the answer to this depends entirely on your image. Generally, LZW and CCITT Group 4 give the best results, but if file size is an important criterion, you will have to experiment with your images.

Font Embedding Options

PDF Writer makes decisions about how to represent fonts it finds in your document. The font may be embedded in the PDF file or it may be generated from within Reader or Exchange when your PDF file is displayed, using one of the built-in fonts or Adobe's multiple master font technology. The Fonts options dialog box, shown in Figure 3.9, gives you a chance to modify PDF Writer's default font embedding behavior.

Figure 3.9
Font Embedding dialog box

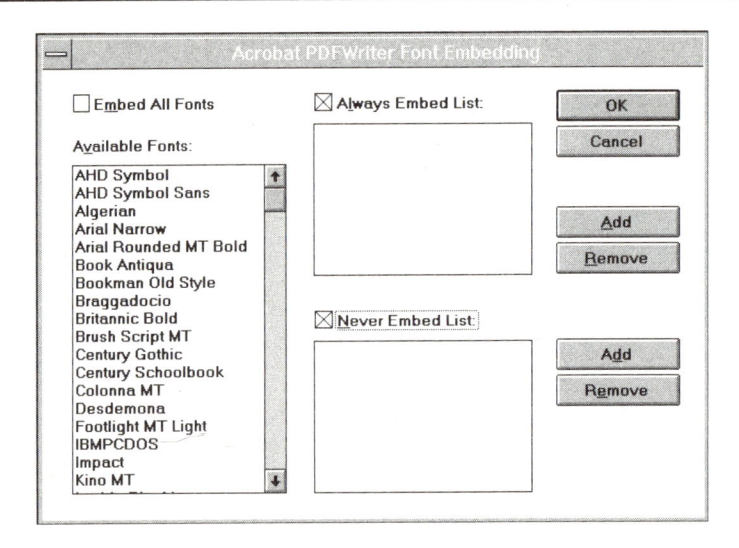

The Embed All Fonts option in the upper-left corner specifies that all fonts used in the source document should be placed in the PDF file. Alternatively, you can specify that only certain fonts should always be embedded in the PDF file, by checking the Always Embed List check box and entering the fonts into the list box. Conversely, you can specify that certain fonts should never be embedded by checking the Never Embed List check box. Use this in combination with the Embed All Fonts check box to embed all fonts but those you specify here.

PDF Page Setup Options 51

If either the Always Embed List or Never Embed List check boxes are enabled, the list boxes beneath them become active. Select a font in the Available Fonts list and click the Add button to add the selected font to the list. Remove fonts from the list by selecting them and pressing the Remove button.

Guidelines for Selecting Font Embedding Options

There are many different types of fonts that PDF Writer may encounter in your source documents:

- PostScript Type 1
- PostScript Type 3
- TrueType (Macintosh and Windows)
- PCL bitmap
- PCL outline
- Windows bitmap
- Windows vector

Acrobat has a default for handling each type of font that it finds; these are listed below in Table 3.3 for Windows and Table 3.4 for Macintosh. All of the different fonts are handled in one of four ways:

- The font name is placed in the PDF file. This method is used for PostScript Type 1 fonts provided with Acrobat, including fonts in the Helvetica, Times, and Courier families, as well as Symbol and Zapf Dingbats. These fonts are also called, collectively, the Base 14 fonts. They are a standard part of every PostScript printer.
- The entire font is embedded in the PDF file.
- A multiple master font descriptor is placed in the PDF file.

- The font is rasterized and put in the PDF file as a bitmapped graphic.

Table 3.3   **PDF Writer's Default Font Handling (Windows)**

Font Is Embedded in PDF File.	Multimaster Font Is Used.	Font Is Rasterized.
PostScript Type 1 (all except ISO Latin)	PostScript Type 1 (ISO Latin)	TrueType Symbol
PostScript Type 3	Windows TrueType (except Symbol)	Windows bitmap and vector

Table 3.4   **PDF Writer's Default Font Handling (Macintosh)**

Font Is Embedded in PDF File.	Multimaster Font Is Used.	Font Is Rasterized.
PostScript Type 1 (all except ISO Latin and Symbolic)	PostScript Type 1 (ISO Latin)	PostScript Type 1 Symbolic
	Adobe Multiple Masters (ISO Latin and Expert)	Macintosh TrueType Symbolic
	Macintosh TrueType (except Symbolic)	PostScript Type 3
	Adobe Cyrillic	Macintosh bitmap

Adobe uses its multiple master font technology to re-create fonts used in the PDF document but not embedded in the document or present on the Acrobat viewer's host system. Whether this works or not depends on the font used—and primarily on the character set used in the font. English and other languages that use the Roman alphabet are usually expressed in the ISO Latin 1 character set; consequently a lot of fonts exist which use it. The multiple master fonts that ship with Acrobat are based on the ISO Latin 1 character set, and they are designed to replicate the look of any other font that also uses ISO Latin 1. This works quite well if the original font is not too stylized or decorative, and it is adequate for communication even if the original font is very elaborate. However, it doesn't work at all for fonts that use other character sets—the wrong characters are generated.

If absolute fidelity to the original document is your goal, then you should always embed all the fonts that you use (unless you only use fonts from the so-called Base 14 set described above that are guaranteed by Acrobat to be available). You must also embed any TrueType fonts that use a character set other than ISO Latin 1, or Acrobat will substitute the ISO Latin multiple-master font for it, and probably garble your message. Any decorative font, such as a script font, must also be embedded to achieve identical results on a system without these fonts already installed.

If the smallest possible file size is your goal, there are several steps you should take. The first is to minimize your use of different fonts. Use outline fonts (such as PostScript or TrueType) instead of bitmapped fonts. Avoid using fonts that must be rasterized or embedded. Use fonts that can be represented by a multiple-master font (see Tables 3.3 and 3.4 above). You can reduce the size of a file containing embedded fonts by using Acrobat Distiller instead of PDF Writer; Distiller can generate font subsets in your file that include only the characters used in your document.

Using Exchange

Now that we've created some raw PDF files to work with, we can turn our attention to enhancing those files with Exchange. Exchange allows us to add PDF features like bookmarks, links, notes, and document security features, as well as manipulate pages in the PDF file.

Exchange uses much the same user interface as the Reader. All of the basic navigational techniques described in Chapter 2 work in Exchange as well, and we won't repeat them here. Exchange's capabilities can also be extended by the use of plug-ins, such as Acrobat Search. Plug-ins can augment Exchange's user interface by providing additional menus and toolbar buttons (and by suppressing standard Exchange features). If you see differences between your version of Exchange and our displays, they may be due to the presence of additional plug-ins in your Exchange setup. We discuss plug-ins in Chapter 7.

Versions of Exchange

Adobe provides two versions of Exchange. The full-featured retail version of the program is a part of every Acrobat package you purchase. Another version, called Exchange LE, is available only to developers who want to redistribute it with their products. The LE version fills a gap between the Reader, which is freely available but lacking in important features (like full plug-in and IAC capabilities), and the full-featured Exchange program that is much more expensive. Exchange LE allows the use of Acrobat Search, Weblink, Movie Player and any other Exchange-compatible plug-ins, and it supports IAC functions including AppleScript on the Macintosh and OLE 2 in Windows. The one crucial thing missing from Exchange LE is the ability to change a PDF file and write it back to disk. Exchange LE is a value-added viewer you can include, for example, with your document collections on CD-ROM (after indexing them with Acrobat Catalog).

Adobe does not allow you to redistribute Exchange LE for free—a small per-copy licensing fee is required. You can obtain more information from Adobe's agent for Acrobat program licensing:
R. R. Donnelley, 77 West Wacker Drive, Chicago, IL 60601, or at (312) 326-7674.

Full versus Short Menus

Exchange provides an option on the Edit menu to choose either full menus or short menus. Selecting Short Menus removes menu items

Using Exchange

for bookmarks, links, pages, articles, thumbnails, and notes from the Edit and Tools menus and the toolbar. This makes Exchange into a glorified version of the Reader. Make sure you do not have Short Menus selected when you try to use the commands in the rest of this chapter, because most of them will not be present (however, keyboard accelerators for these commands work even when Short Menus are in effect).

With Full Menus selected, Exchange adds several new buttons to the toolbar. Two buttons are added in the tools button group on the left side of the toolbar; these are shown below (no button is provided for creating articles). Four more buttons are added on the right side of the toolbar; these buttons support Acrobat Search and we describe them in Chapter 5. We describe these tools in detail in the sections that follow.

Tools	Menu Bar Command	Keyboard Accelerator	Button
Note tool	Tools | Note	Ctrl/⌘+Shift/Option+6	📄
Link tool	Tools | Link	Ctrl/⌘+Shift/Option+7	🔗
Article tool	Tools | Article	Ctrl/⌘+Shift/Option+8	None

Properties

Exchange lets you add bookmarks, links, and other annotation objects to a document. Each of these objects have properties that control their behavior. Some of them have special commands which allow you to quickly change some of the object's properties; but the general purpose way is to select the object you want and then select the Edit | Properties menu item (or press Ctrl/⌘+I). We'll discuss the properties of each object in this chapter.

Saving Files

Exchange provides the standard File | Save and File | Save As functions, but these functions have a nonstandard side effect due to the way PDF files are structured. Save stores the changes you've made to the PDF file as an incremental update to the existing file, while Save As writes an entirely new file. The result is that Save As will often give you a more compact file than Save, since unneeded items are eliminated from the new file written by Save As. For example, if you delete a page, the Save command doesn't actually remove the page from the file; it simply marks the page as deleted. Save As will write a new file without the deleted page in it. Save As is also required to change the security options on a file (see the next section).

Document Security

Exchange gives you the option to control access to the contents of your PDF document with its security options. You can

- Require a password to open the file for viewing
- Disallow printing the document
- Disallow changing the document
- Disallow copying text or graphics to the clipboard
- Disallow adding or changing notes

Access the security options from the File | Save As menu item. The Save As dialog box has a Security button; press it to bring up the dialog box shown in Figure 3.10. To establish new security for a PDF file, you must save it as a new file using File | Save As; you cannot change the security options for an existing file and save it. You can set two security passwords in your PDF file: a password to open the file for viewing, and a password to allow changing the security options of the file. You don't have to use them together—if you want to allow anyone to view the file but not change it, you need use only the second password (and check the box to disallow changing the document).

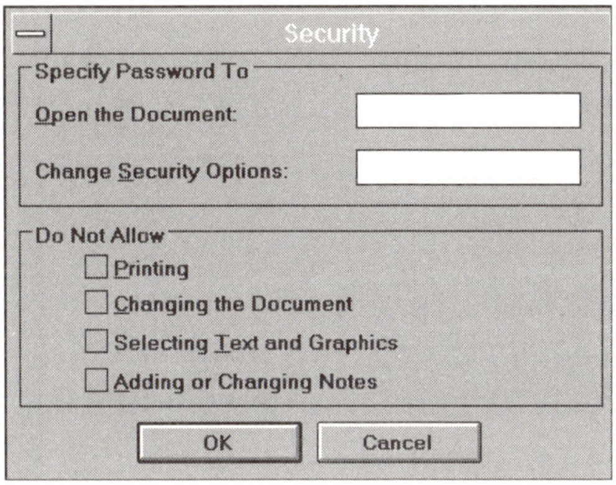

Figure 3.10
Security dialog box

WARNING: *If you set security options for the file, but don't establish a password for them, then any Exchange user can change the security options and write the file back out again, circumventing your security effort.*

On the other hand, sometimes it is useful to set security options but not set a password to protect them. For example, you may want to distribute a PDF document to others in your workgroup and require them to save any changes to a new file. You can do this by checking the Do Not Allow Changing the File checkbox in the Security dialog box, but not setting a password for Change Security Options. The result is that other users cannot change your file, but they may make a new copy of it using the File | Save As menu command and by resetting the security options in the new file they can make changes to it.

When you select a password for viewing the PDF document, Acrobat encrypts the contents of the text in the new file so that it cannot be viewed even by using another application. Both the Document Information you enter (such as title, author, and keywords) and each page's description are encrypted.

The effect of selecting one of the four Do Not Allow options is to disable the viewer's menu items and toolbar buttons that provide that function. For example, if printing is disabled in the Security dialog box, then the File | Print option will be disabled when this document is viewed.

TIP: *Acrobat can keep your PDF files secure, but only if you select a good password. All the usual rules apply: don't choose a word in the dictionary, or the name of your dog or your children, or something else someone could easily guess. Your password should be at least six characters long (preferably longer), with a mixture of uppercase and lowercase characters, numbers, and punctuation marks. If you are password protecting documents you intend to distribute publicly, make sure you use the maximum length password string (20 characters). The longer the password, the more difficult it is for a password cracker to guess the right answer. Also, don't forget to delete the original unencrypted files from your hard disk after you save the password protected version.*

Thumbnails

Thumbnails provide users a way to get a quick look at all the pages in your document. They can be helpful in browsing because they draw attention to figures and tables that change the look of the page. Thumbnails are even more useful when you are editing with Exchange. You can select and drag thumbnails both within and between documents to add or replace pages.

Create thumbnails in your PDF file by selecting the Edit | Thumbnails | Create All menu item. When you save the file, the thumbnails will be saved along with the file. Since thumbnails can expand the size of your file substantially, you can delete thumbnails using the Edit | Thumbnails | Delete All menu item. There are no options for creating or deleting individual thumbnails. If you compose a PDF document from other document pieces, thumbnails will be merged if they exist.

You can use thumbnails without actually creating them. Both the Macintosh and Windows platforms draw blank thumbnail pages when the file doesn't contain a thumbnail for the page. Windows users have another option: They can cause Exchange to display thumbnails even if they are not present in the file. Edit ACROEXCH.INI with your text editor and find the entry named DrawMissingThumbs. By default it is set to zero, but if you set it to one, thumbnails will be drawn for each page even if they are not present in the file. The thumbnails are created and drawn "on the fly" by Exchange. Unfortunately this feature doesn't exist on the Macintosh versions. Don't be confused when you delete thumbnails with this option enabled—the thumbnails will still be drawn on screen but they are removed from the file. Effectively, this option eliminates the need to store thumbnails in a PDF file for Windows Exchange users.

Pages

The page is the basic unit that Exchange works with—you can add or delete pages from within Exchange, but you cannot change what is printed on a page. Exchange usually provides two different ways to work with pages: using menu commands or using thumbnails. The menu commands ask you to specify the page number(s) you want them to operate on, while the thumbnails operate visually. The following table summarizes the page commands:

Page Editing Command	Menu Bar Command	Keyboard Accelerator	Button
Insert pages from one PDF file to another	Edit | Pages | Insert	Ctrl/⌘+Shift/Option+I	None
Replace pages in a PDF file with pages from another PDF file	Edit | Pages | Replace	Ctrl/⌘+Shift/Option+R	None
Delete pages from a PDF file	Edit | Pages | Delete	Ctrl/⌘+Shift/Option+D	None
Copy pages to a new PDF file	Edit | Pages | Extract	Ctrl/⌘+Shift/Option+E	None
Crop the margins of a page	Edit | Pages | Crop	Ctrl/⌘+Shift/Option+C	None
Rotate pages by 90 degrees	Edit | Pages | Rotate	Ctrl/⌘+Shift/Option+O	None

IMPORTANT NOTE: *Acrobat maintains its own page numbers independent of any page numbers that may be printed on the pages of your document. Acrobat page numbers start with one and go sequentially to the end of the document. When entering page numbers in an Exchange dialog box, always use Acrobat page numbers; don't get confused and enter your page numbers or you may change the wrong pages.*

Inserting Pages

It can be useful to compose your final document out of individually crafted pieces of PDF. Different people may be contributing pages, or you may want to combine different page sizes into your document.

Exchange gives you several ways to insert or add pages from one PDF document to another.

The easy way to insert individual pages is to use thumbnails. Figure 3.11 shows how you can open two documents in Exchange and drag pages from one to the other (in this figure, the thumbnails are blank because they don't actually exist—but we use them anyway, for their page numbers). Drag the page you want to insert by clicking and dragging it by its label (beneath the thumbnail). In our picture, the window on the left is providing the source for the page, and the selected page's thumbnail has a border around it. The cursor changes to a page icon as the page is brought over. In the right window, as we move the cursor up and down the thumbnail view, a heavy black bar shows us where the insertion point will be. Don't drop the page onto an existing thumbnail's label or you will replace that page instead of inserting. Release the mouse button when the insertion point is beneath the thumbnail you want to insert your page after.

You can insert an entire file using the method above, but it may be a lot of work. Instead, in Windows you can drag a PDF file from the File Manager and drop it into the thumbnail view where you want it inserted. Again, the insertion point is indicated by a black bar in between two of the thumbnails. Release the mouse, and a confirmation dialog box appears. Click on OK and you are done. You can also drop the file on the document view pane rather than the thumbnail pane of the Exchange window. In this case Exchange displays the Insert dialog box to find out exactly what you want to do with the file (Figure 3.12). Select where you want the file inserted and press OK.

Another way to insert an entire file is through the Edit | Pages | Insert menu item. This command brings up a standard Open File dialog box, allowing you to select the file you want to insert. After you choose a file, the Insert dialog box is displayed. Select where you want the file inserted and press OK.

62   Chapter 3: Acrobat Exchange and PDF Writer

Figure 3.11
Using thumbnails to insert pages in a document

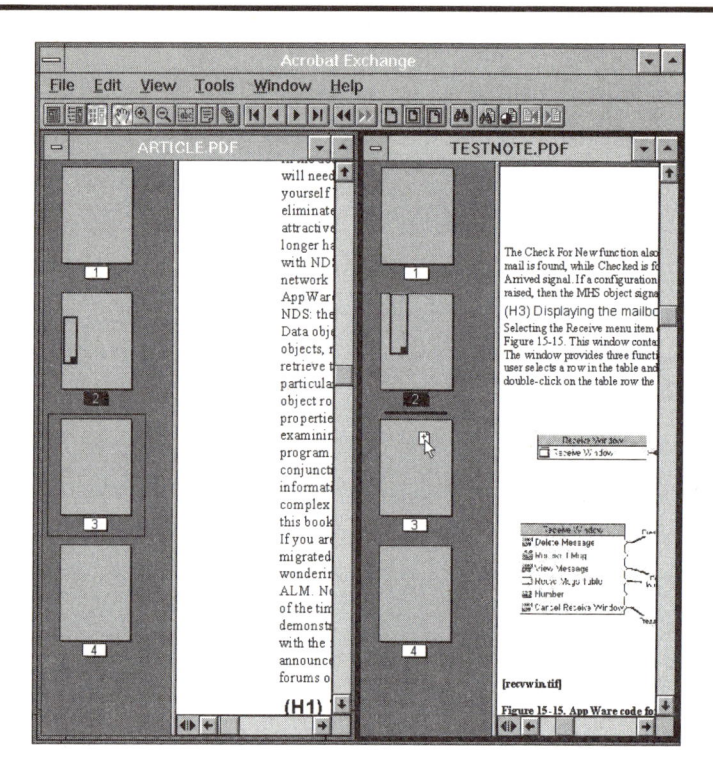

Figure 3.12
The Insert dialog box

When you insert a file, all the contents of the file are inserted: bookmarks, notes, thumbnails, links, and so on. Bookmarks are inserted into the bookmark list in the proper order, but bookmarks from the inserted document are all made subordinate to a new bookmark that contains the name of the file you inserted. You probably don't want this bookmark, so you'll have to delete it (unindent the subordinate bookmarks first—see "Creating a Bookmark Hierarchy" later in this chapter).

Replacing Pages

Replacing pages in a PDF file is a useful alternative to re-creating the file from scratch when you have to make a correction. This is especially true if you've already added bookmarks and links to your document, since replacing pages won't change them.

Replacing pages is easy using thumbnails. With both documents in view, drag the new page over and drop it onto the label of the thumbnail you want to replace. When the cursor is over the label, the entire thumbnail will be displayed in reverse video, indicating that it is selected for replacement (see Figure 3.13). The cursor will display a small capital *R* indicating replacement.

You can also replace pages in the document you are viewing using the menu command Edit | Pages | Replace. Selecting this command brings up the Open File dialog box. Choose the file which contains the replacement pages. The Replace Pages dialog box (shown in Figure 3.14) then appears. Select the page or range of pages you want to use as new pages, and the first page in the original document to replace. Press OK and a confirmation dialog appears; press OK again to commit the change.

Deleting Pages

You can delete pages you no longer want in your document using either thumbnails or the menu commands. When you delete pages, you also delete any notes on that page. Bookmarks and links associated with the deleted page no longer work, although they are still present. To actually remove deleted pages from your PDF file, you must save the file using the File | Save As menu command. If you use File | Save instead, the pages are marked as deleted but the data is

64   Chapter 3: Acrobat Exchange and PDF Writer

Figure 3.13
Replacing pages using thumbnails

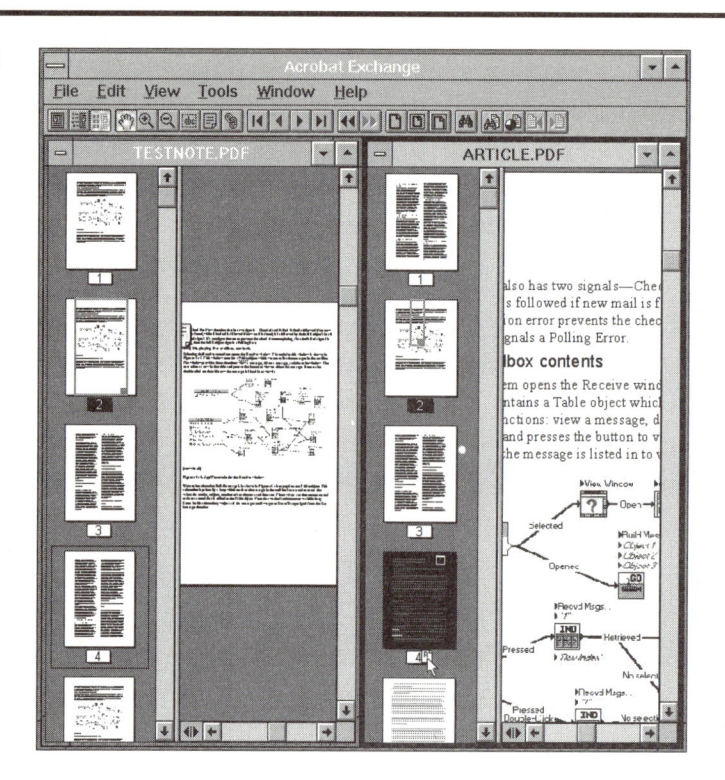

Figure 3.14
The Replace Pages dialog box

still present in the file. Regardless of which save command you use, you cannot undo the Delete Page command.

To delete using thumbnails, select the thumbnail you want to delete by clicking on its label (you can select more than one by shift-clicking each one) and either press the Delete key or select the Edit | Clear menu item.

Alternatively, select Edit | Pages | Delete. This brings up the Delete Pages dialog box (Figure 3.15). Enter the page number or range of numbers for the pages you want to delete; the default is the current page. Press OK and OK again in the confirmation box to delete the page.

Figure 3.15
The Delete Pages dialog box

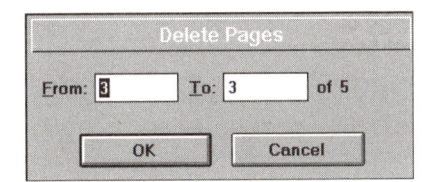

Extracting Pages to a File

The Extract Page command copies one or more pages to a new PDF file. If any document security option is enabled, the Extract command is disabled. Extract will copy notes on the pages and links between pages you extract, but it won't copy bookmarks or articles defined on those pages, or links that connect to pages you are not extracting.

Use the Edit | Pages | Extract command to bring up the Extract Pages dialog box (see Figure 3.16). Enter the page number or a range of pages to extract; the default is the current page. You can automatically delete the pages after extraction by checking the Delete Pages After Extracting check box. Press OK when you are ready, and OK again in the confirmation box.

Figure 3.16
The Extract Pages dialog box

Cropping Pages

Exchange lets you crop the margins of individual pages or all of the pages in your document. Cropping doesn't actually remove image data from the file—it simply reduces the amount of the page that Exchange will display. You can use cropping to achieve the same effect as the View | Fit Visible command, removing white space around the borders of a page. Like cropping a photograph, you can also use it to remove unwanted parts of the document from view. However, unlike cropping a photograph, you can "uncrop" or restore the page to its original state.

When you select Edit | Pages | Crop, the Crop Pages dialog box appears (see Figure 3.17). Use the mouse to move it over so you can see the page. You can manually enter the new dimensions for the page, or use the arrows to change the page interactively. Exchange previews the new margin by drawing a red line on the page when you click an arrow or enter a value for one of the four margin values. Select all pages or a page range to change; by default only the current page is affected. Select OK and a confirmation box appears; press OK again and the page is cropped.

You can always restore the page to its original dimensions by using the Crop command and setting the margin values to zero. The uncovered page borders will not display properly in preview, but the margins will be restored when you select OK.

Figure 3.17
The Crop Pages dialog box

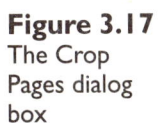

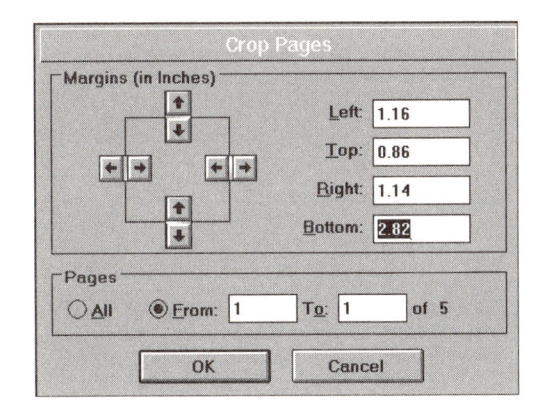

Adobe recommends that if you are going to crop, rotate, and insert pages into your document, that you do so in that order. For best results, don't insert the pages and then crop and rotate them.

Rotating Pages

Some applications print pages in landscape mode and then they expect you to turn the page around sideways to view it properly. You won't get your neck bent out of shape looking at Acrobat documents if you use the Edit | Pages | Rotate command to flip the rebellious page on either its left or right side (see Figure 3.18). Select all pages or a page range to change; by default only the current page is affected. The Rotate command only offers 90 degrees of rotation, but you can repeat the command to turn the page upside down or restore its original orientation if you want.

Figure 3.18
The Rotate Pages dialog box

Articles

If you are publishing a document like a newspaper that has several different articles in columns on the same page, you can define a special view for each article using Acrobat's article capabilities. The Acrobat notion of an article allows the user to start with a view of the document the way it would look on paper, but provides the ability to zoom in on a particular article and follow the thread of that article down columns and across the pages of the document. Additionally, the user can select the View | Articles menu item to see a list of articles defined in the document. Article viewing is described in Chapter 2; here we will describe how to create articles.

Articles are implemented as a sequence of blocks of text (sometimes called a thread). During article creation, each block of text in an article is numbered so that you can see the flow of the article through your document. Articles themselves are also assigned numbers starting with one for the first article you create. Articles are listed in the Article Selection dialog box in the order in which you define them.

Creating Articles

To create an article, begin by displaying the document page where the article starts. Use a page view that allows you to see the whole article on that page. Select the Tools | Article menu item to start defining an article. The cursor changes to a cross hair (+). Any previously defined articles are also displayed with boxes surrounding their text.

Drag a box around the first full column of the article text. When you are finished, your screen should look something like Figure 3.19. At the top of the box is a label which identifies the article number and the number of this text block within the article. The corners of the box contain resizing handles which you can use later to adjust the box if you need to (first, though, you must finish defining the article). Near the bottom-right corner of the article box is a small black

Using Exchange

box with a plus sign in it; this is called the *plus tab*. The plus tab allows you to insert a new box into an existing article thread.

Figure 3.19
An article box just after creation

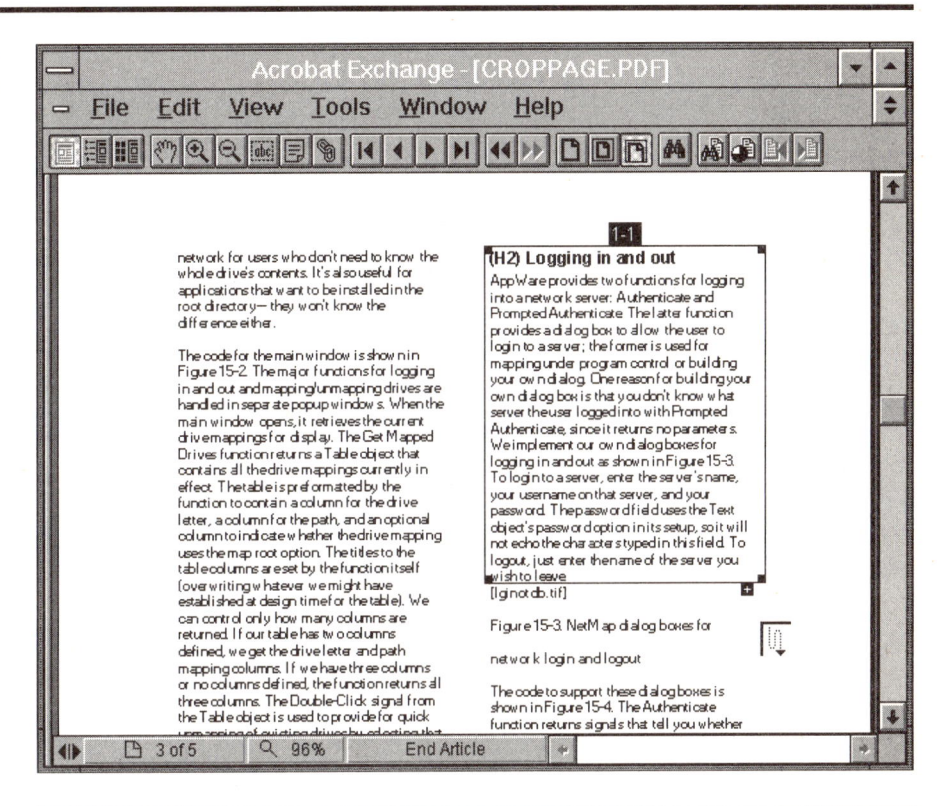

After you've selected the first text box in an article, the cursor changes to display the Article Flow cursor (shown in Figure 3.20). Proceed to the next column of the article and draw a box around that text, continuing until you have defined the entire article. When you are finished, click the End Article button at the bottom of the Exchange window. The End Article button displays in the space normally occupied by the dimensions of the current page (see Figure 3.21).

Figure 3.20
The article flow cursor

Figure 3.21
The End Article button

Selecting, Inserting, and Deleting Articles

Select an article by first selecting the Tools | Article menu item. The cursor will change to a cross hair outside the boundaries of any existing articles, but will change to the standard selection arrow when it is over a previously defined article box. Click on the article box to select it. Once selected, you can resize the box and move it around on the page.

NOTE: *The Article tool stays active until you select another tool.*

To insert a box into an existing article, first select the article box that comes just before the new article box you want to add. Then click the plus tab at the bottom of that box; the cursor will change to the article flow cursor. Draw the new box. When you release the mouse button after dragging the box, the remaining boxes in the article (if any) will be renumbered to follow the new box.

Delete a box in an article or the entire article by selecting it and then selecting Edit | Clear (or press the Delete key). The confirmation dialog will ask you whether to delete the selected box or the entire article. Select one and press OK.

Bookmarks

You can use Exchange to create bookmarks to take you quickly to a view of any page in your document, or another document, or even start another application. Bookmarks are always available for viewing anywhere in the document by selecting the Bookmarks and Page view. The commands for creating and manipulating bookmarks are shown in the following table:

Bookmark Editing Command	Menu Bar Command	Keyboard Accelerator	Button
Create a new bookmark	Edit | Bookmarks | New	Ctrl/⌘+B	None
Reset a bookmark's destination	Edit | Bookmarks | Reset Destination	Ctrl/⌘+R	None

Bookmarks can be arranged hierarchically, like an outline, with indenting for subordinate-level bookmarks. A small triangle appears to the left of the bookmark's page icon to show that subordinate bookmarks exist beneath it. When the triangle points to the right, the subordinate bookmarks are hidden; click on the triangle to alternately display or hide them.

Creating a Bookmark

Create a bookmark by selecting the menu item Edit | Bookmarks | New (or by pressing Ctrl/⌘+B) and a bookmark with the name Untitled is created. Enter a new name for the bookmark by simply typing it in while the bookmark text is selected (if the cursor is moved over the bookmark, it will change to an I-beam that you can use to select text). You can also paste text from the clipboard directly into the bookmark; this makes it easy to copy a heading directly from your document (see "Selecting and Editing Bookmarks").

Before you create your bookmark, arrange the page view to look the way you want it to when the bookmark is selected. You don't have total control over this, because the end user viewing the document controls the size of the viewer window. However, each bookmark remembers what point on the page was at the top of the window when the bookmark was created, and it restores this position in the document when the bookmark is selected again. Use this feature to position the bookmark precisely so that users don't have to scroll or resize their windows to see what you intended them to see.

The same principle applies to the scale factor in effect when the bookmark is displayed—it will be saved with the bookmark. For example, select View | Fit Visible before creating the bookmark and the bookmark will restore the page to the Fit Visible scale factor when it is chosen by the user.

Creating a Bookmark to Another Document or Application

Bookmarks can take you from one PDF document to another or to a completely different application if you desire. To create this type of bookmark, begin by creating a bookmark as described above (but don't worry about how the page looks). Now select the new bookmark's page icon (just to the left of the bookmark title). Select the Edit | Properties menu item (or press Ctrl/⌘+I); this brings up the Bookmark Properties dialog box (shown in Figure 3.22). The first field, Type, controls what other options appear in the dialog box. The built-in types are

- *Go To View.* Changes focus to a view of the PDF file saved when the bookmark was created. The file doesn't have to be the current one.

- *Open File.* Opens the named file or starts an application. The file must be either an application program itself or a data file that belongs to a registered application.

Figure 3.22
Bookmark Properties dialog box with initial view of Go To View options

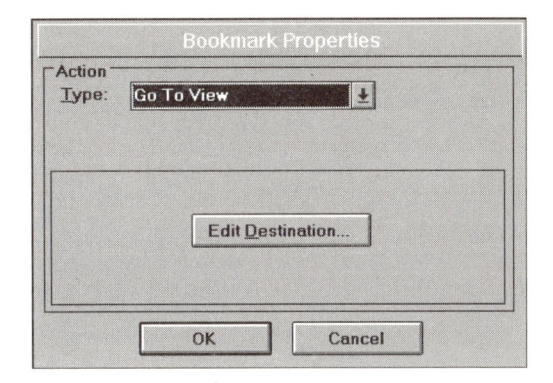

- *None.* Allows you to have bookmarks that display text but don't do anything. These are useful for adding more information to an existing bookmark or for adding white space to a bookmark collection.

You may see other types listed as well; additional types are provided by plug-ins you may have added to your configuration (see Chapter 7). By default, the bookmark will have the type Go To View. Press the Edit Destination button, which changes the dialog box to that shown in Figure 3.23. The Bookmark Properties dialog box will float on top of the Exchange window even when it is not active, allowing you to see the PDF file beneath it. Move it off to the side if you need to see what's underneath. Use your mouse to go back to the Exchange main window and open the PDF document you want to link the bookmark to (if it is already open, just display it). Select the page in the new document and arrange it as described in the last section (or you can use the Magnification options in the dialog box—see below for instructions). When you have the new document displayed the way you want it, press the Set Action button in the Bookmark Properties dialog box to save the new destination for the bookmark.

Figure 3.23
Bookmark Properties after pressing Edit Destination

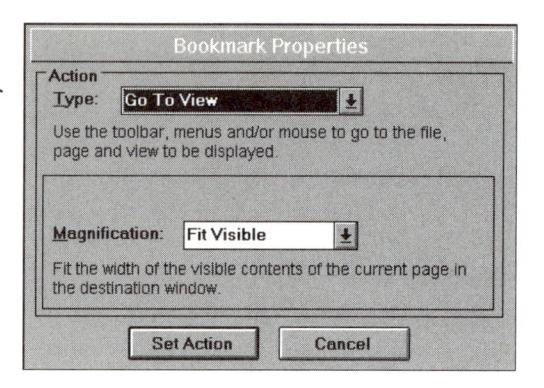

> **NOTE:** *Exchange shows you the path it is using for the destination file in the Bookmark Properties dialog box. Remember that the files and paths you select must be arranged in the same places on your client's system or the bookmark will fail. Additionally, Macintosh users should use MS-DOS file names for PDF documents (or other files) when you create bookmarks or links between them.*

To create a bookmark that starts another application, change the Type of the bookmark to Open File in the Bookmark Properties dialog box (shown in Figure 3.24). The dialog box changes to display the Select File button. Pressing this button brings up the standard Open File dialog box. Use the dialog box controls to select a file to open (remember the file must be on the same disk drive for portability). The file may be a PDF document, a document file registered to another application, or an executable file (in Windows, a .EXE, .COM, or .PIF file).

If the file you select is not executable, then there must be a registered application on your system that can open and display the file, or you will get an error when the bookmark is selected. For example, in Windows if you select MYFILE.DOC, Windows will open the application registered with the system to handle the .DOC file type (usually Microsoft Word). If you don't have an application that is

Figure 3.24
Bookmark Properties after selecting the bookmark action type Open File

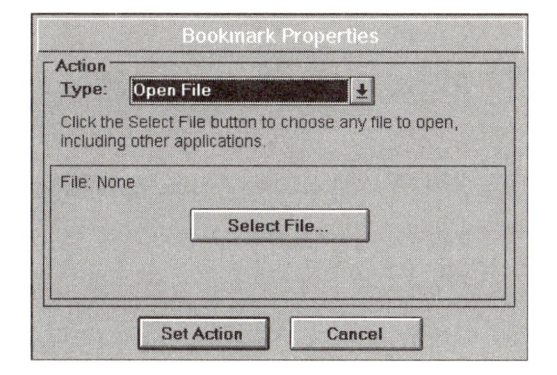

registered to handle .DOC files, the bookmark will generate an error. Macintosh versions of Acrobat provide a similar capability using standard Macintosh file types to find the application program to run.

Magnification Options for Bookmarks and Links

A bookmark or link of type Go To View allows you a lot of flexibility to control the view of the page the reader sees. Since the window your readers use may be larger or smaller than the one you are using to edit the document, Acrobat supports options that let you specify how to set the view independent of any scaling you are currently using. You may select one of the following magnification options for display when the page is viewed by a user of the document (called the viewer's window below):

- *Fixed*. The page magnification of the viewer's window is set to the level used by your current view of the page (current when you create the bookmark, that is).

- *Fit View*. The boundaries of your current view as you create the bookmark are scaled to fit in the viewer's window.

- *Fit Page*. The page is scaled to fit entirely in the viewer's window.

- *Fit Width.* The page is scaled so that its width will fit in the viewer's window.

- *Fit Height.* The page is scaled so that its height will fit in the viewer's window.

- *Fit Visible.* The page is scaled so that its visible width will fit in the viewer's window.

- *Inherit Zoom.* The magnification of the page is not changed—it is whatever the viewer is using when he selects this page.

You should use a magnification option that allows the user to see what you want them to see when you established the bookmark, without having to change the magnification themselves.

Selecting, Editing, and Deleting Bookmarks

Click on the little page icon to the left of a bookmark to select it for editing. The entire bookmark will change color to show the selection. If the bookmark has subordinate bookmarks, they will be selected too. This is great when you want to move the whole set of bookmarks somewhere else, but you can't edit the properties of the bookmark while its subordinates are also selected. Click on the text of the bookmark to restrict selection to just that one.

After selecting the bookmark, you can edit the text by moving the cursor over the text of the bookmark; the cursor will change to an I-beam. Click on the text with the I-beam cursor to begin editing it. When you start editing the bookmark using this method, all of the text is selected for replacement. Anything you type will replace the bookmark, or you can paste text from the clipboard to replace the bookmark.

If you just want to modify the text, use the arrow keys to move through it to the point you want to change. Type the characters to insert, or use the Delete key to remove characters. When you are finished editing, click in the far left column of the bookmark window pane to deselect the bookmark.

Delete a bookmark by selecting it and then pressing either the Delete key or using the Edit | Clear menu item. Select OK in the confirmation dialog box. If the bookmark has subordinate bookmarks, they will all be deleted too.

TIP: *It is easy for casual Exchange users to accidently select a bookmark when they are simply trying to use it. This can be confusing and annoying because the bookmark stops working normally while it is selected. Using the Short Menus option to remove the bookmark editing functions does not help; even with Short Menus selected, the bookmark can still be edited. To disable bookmark editing, set the document security option to disallow changing the document (see "Document Security" earlier).*

Creating a Bookmark Hierarchy

Once you have created a bookmark, you can make it subordinate to a bookmark above it. Click and drag the bookmark's page icon to the right about half an inch; you will see a dark black line appear at the bottom of the text of the bookmark above. Release the mouse button and the bookmark will be indented underneath the one above it.

To unindent a bookmark, select the page icon and drag it to the left and down a line; you will see the dark line at the bottom of the bookmark above move back to the left. Release the mouse button and the bookmark is no longer indented.

NOTE: *Unindenting is a little tricky. If you don't drag the page icon downward as well as to the left, you won't see the black line and the bookmark won't move. Don't move it too far downward, though, or you will move the bookmark to a new line.*

You can move bookmarks around in the bookmark list by selecting them and dragging them to the new location in the list. The thick black line is used to mark the new position. Release the mouse button when the black line is resting on the bookmark you want above the one you are moving. When you move a bookmark that has subordinate bookmarks, all the subordinate bookmarks move with it. If you don't want them to move, unindent them first, as described above.

Changing a Bookmark's Destination

There are two ways to change the destination of a bookmark of type Go To View: by using the Edit | Bookmarks | Reset Destination command (or Ctrl/⌘+R), or by editing the bookmark's properties using Edit | Properties (or Ctrl/⌘+I). Use Reset Destination to make a small change, such as adjusting the view of the document; use the Properties dialog box to change the bookmark to view a different document entirely (see "Creating a Bookmark to Another Document or Application" earlier). To use either method, you must first select the bookmark by clicking on its page icon.

To use Reset Destination, select the bookmark and then arrange the viewer page view as you want it (see the guidelines mentioned in Creating a Bookmark). Then select the menu option or, even easier, press Ctrl/⌘+R. Exchange asks if you are sure you want to change the destination; press the Yes button and the change is made. Note that if you use the Reset Destination command on a bookmark with a different action type (such as Open File), the type will be reset to Go To View. You must edit all other bookmark action types using the Edit | Properties menu command.

Guidelines for Creating Bookmarks

Bookmarks are a valuable way to give the user quick access to the contents of your document. If your document already has chapters or sections with headings and subheadings, these make natural bookmarks. Arrange the bookmarks hierarchically to match the structure of your document.

Bookmarks can also be used to provide an alternate organization for the document. You can create bookmarks to draw attention to specific places in the document that the reader may otherwise spend a lot of time trying to find. This is not a general-purpose technique, but it can be useful when you are working closely with other people who are already familiar with the document, or where familiarity with the entire document is not desired. Used in this way, bookmarks become a kind of annotation to the document, similar to a note, but more visible.

Links

Acrobat's links are very much like bookmarks—they take you from your current position in the document to a new one (in the same document, a different document, or another application). The primary purpose of a link is to connect together information that is located in disparate places in your documents. Use links to provide access to:

- Definitions for unfamiliar terms
- Detailed information about a subject
- Cross-references to related subjects, perhaps in other documents
- Information in other media (such as sound or video)

Like bookmarks, links have action types including the basic Go To View type. We speak of these links as having a *source* and a *destination*. Such links are one-way trips; they take you to a new place in the document but they don't automatically take you back. To get back, the Acrobat viewers provide the navigation stack and the View | Go Back menu item (discussed in Chapter 2). Not all link action types change the view of the document, and the ones that don't also do not change the navigation stack.

Creating Links

Select the Tools | Link menu item, or click the Link tool button on the toolbar, to activate link editing in Exchange. The cursor changes to a cross hair (+). Move the cursor to the beginning of the area of the document you wish to use for the source of the link, and drag a box around it (Note: You aren't limited to text when creating a link). Release the mouse button and the Create Link dialog box is displayed (see Figure 3.25).

Figure 3.25
The Create Link dialog box

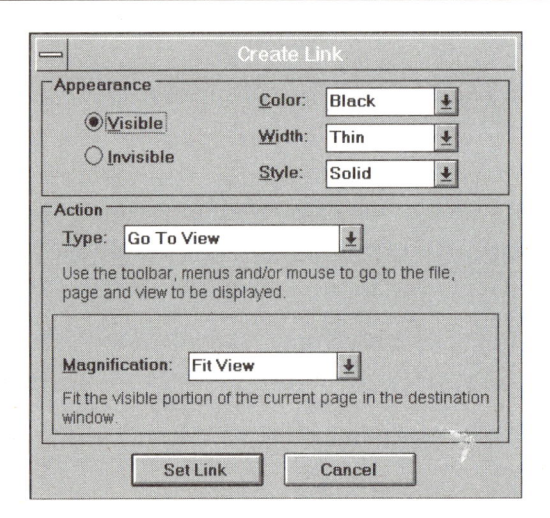

This dialog box is split into two halves labeled Appearance and Action. The Appearance section lets you specify whether the link will be visible or not, and if it is, how it will look. We discuss setting the appearance of the link in the section on link styles below. We are already familiar with the Action section of the dialog box because link actions are the same as bookmark actions. If this book were a PDF document, we would provide you with a link to that topic here. Instead we'll summarize what you need to do to establish an action for the link. To create a link to another spot in your document or another PDF document using the default Go To View action type, follow these steps:

1. Once the Create Link dialog box is displayed, use Exchange to display the link destination in the page view window pane. The Create Link dialog box will float on top of your document view (you can move it aside if you need to without closing it—but don't close it unless you are canceling the link).

2. Arrange the page view to look exactly the way you want it to look when the user selects the link. By default the link uses the Fit View magnification option, which remembers what portion of the document is visible when you create the link (see "Magnification Options for Bookmarks and Links"). Press Set Link when the page view is satisfactory.

To create a link that opens a different file, select Open File as the action type in the Create Link dialog. Press the Select File button and select the file you want to open when the link is pressed. The file may be an application program or a data file that belongs to a registered application program. Press Set Link when you are finished.

You may see other link action types listed in the Link Properties dialog box. These come from plug-ins added to your Acrobat setup; we discuss a few of them in Chapter 7.

Link Styles

An Acrobat visible link consists of the hollow box you've traced with the Link tool. You can select a different color for the box, and you can specify whether the box is drawn with a solid or dashed line. Figure 3.26 shows an example of a visible link. To be effective, a link must somehow be visible, but you may not want to use the Acrobat method of indicating links.

Use an invisible link when the document itself already highlights the link area. For example, you may use invisible links to turn

Figure 3.26
An example of a visible link

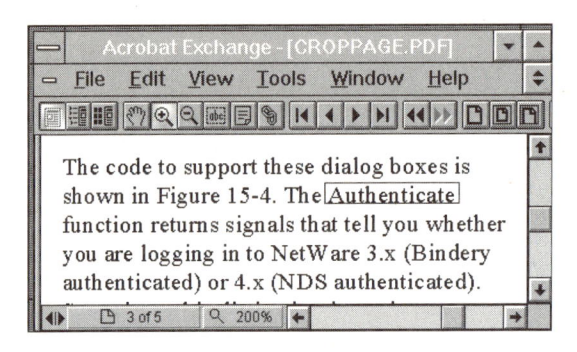

pictures or elements of pictures in your document into link buttons. Alternatively, if everything on the page is a link (and you inform the user of that, perhaps with a note), you may not need to highlight the link itself. A table of contents at the start of your document is an example—take each entry and make it a link to the page it specifies (do the same for a list of figures).

Acrobat's help files demonstrate what is probably the best technique for creating links. The files use invisible links, but the text of the link source is drawn in a different color to make it stand out. These files were written with links in mind—they were planned as an integral part of the file. The result is easy to read (no distracting boxes around words in the text) but the link is readily apparent, inviting the reader to use it.

You may not have the option of designing links into your PDF document's sources. Discreet use of the visible link option can be very effective in highlighting important ideas and themes in your document, as well as providing the link itself. Choose a color and line style for the box that demurely calls attention to itself. Stay away from using custom colors; your document may be viewed on a monochrome or 16-color laptop computer where your extra work will have unpredictable results.

If you use different kinds of links, use different colors to indicate what they do. For example, links that provide word definitions might be in one color, while links that play video clips could be in another. You can choose the colors arbitrarily, but be consistent in your use of them (especially important in document collections with more than one editor involved).

Selecting, Editing, and Deleting Links

Select an existing link for further operations by first selecting the Link tool either from the Tools menu or by pressing the Link toolbar button. Press Ctrl/Option while selecting the Link tool and it will stay set until you select another tool; by default it switches back to the Hand tool after you use it once.

With the Link tool selected, single-click inside the link's box to select it for moving or resizing. Drag the entire box to move it around, or drag one of the resizing boxes on the border to resize the box. Double-click the link to bring up the Link Properties dialog box (which is just another name for the Create Link dialog box—see the discussion above).

To delete a link, select it and press the Delete key, or select the Edit | Clear menu item. Click OK in the confirmation dialog box.

Changing a Link's Appearance or Destination

You can change both the appearance of a link and its destination by editing the link's properties. Select the link you want to change (see above). Double-click the link or select Edit | Properties to bring up the Link Properties dialog box. Make the changes you want (see the discussion under Create a Link).

Guidelines for Using Links

It's impossible to do justice to the subject of good hypertext document design in a few paragraphs. We list a few guidelines below; for more in-depth discussion, see the sources listed in "Further Reading" at the end of this book.

- Make the link obvious, but not obtrusive. The link has to call attention to itself but not be so loud as to make reading difficult. The text or picture within the link should provide a good clue of what lies at the destination of the link.

- Use links only for associations that are important to the topic being discussed. Avoid making links out of all the casual relationships in your document.

- If your document has a table of contents, list of figures, or an index, turn them into links.

Notes

All of the features we've described so far are designed to aid the document publisher in organizing the document. Notes can be used to add commentary to a document, but they are most useful for communication between readers and back to the originator of the document. Notes make it possible to use Exchange as a workgroup tool.

Creating Notes

To create a note, first select the Tools, Note menu item or press the Note toolbar button. The cursor will change to a cross hair (+). Click anywhere in the document to create a note. If you just click, you'll get a note in the default size (2 by 3 inches). Drag the cursor to create a note in a different size.

Just start typing to enter text into your note. While editing, you can use any of the standard text editing commands on the Edit menu: Undo, Cut, Copy, Paste, and Clear. Use the cursor keys to move around in the note to insert or delete text. When you are finished, click the note's close box to return it to icon size.

Selecting, Editing, and Deleting Notes

A note can exist in four different states:

- *Iconized and not selected*. The note icon is drawn in the color assigned when the note was created.

- *Iconized and selected*. The note is drawn in gray.

- *Open and not selected*. The title bar of the note is drawn in the assigned color.

- *Open and selected*. The title bar acquires a close box, and the window also displays a vertical scroll bar.

Select a note by single-clicking it. You can move it around on (or even off) the page (you can put the icon anywhere in the page window pane and it will stay there—it doesn't have to be on the page itself). Delete the note by pressing the Delete key or selecting Edit | Clear in the menus.

Double-click on the note icon to open it. The text cursor is at the start of the note in the upper-left corner. Use any of the standard editing commands to modify the text. When you are finished, click on the close box to close and deselect the note.

You can resize an open note by dragging the resize box in the lower-right corner of the note. Notes have a maximum size of 4 by 6 inches.

Notes Properties and Preferences

To edit a note's properties, either select the note and then select Edit | Properties, or double-click on the title bar of an open note. The Note Properties dialog box, shown in Figure 3.27, lets you change the title text of the dialog box or the color assigned to the note.

Figure 3.27
The Note Properties dialog box

You can establish default values for notes you create by selecting the Edit | Preferences | Notes menu item. This brings up the dialog box shown in Figure 3.28. Changing the Default Label or Default Color field affects any future notes you create. Changing the font and point size affects all notes in the document—they are displayed in the new font and size as soon as you select OK in the dialog box. All notes, regardless of origin, are always displayed in the default font and size you select.

Figure 3.28
The Notes Preferences dialog box

Importing and Exporting Notes

Suppose you sent a PDF document to others in your workgroup, and they sent back annotated copies of the document. Now you want to merge the notes you have received from the different copies and redistribute the document for review. You can do this by opening the document you want to use as the master document and selecting the Edit | Notes | Import menu item. The Select Import dialog box is displayed, allowing you to select a file for import (see Figure 3.29). Select the file you want to copy the notes from and press Select. Exchange will copy just the notes from the selected file into the same pages of your current file.

Figure 3.29
The Select File Containing Notes dialog box

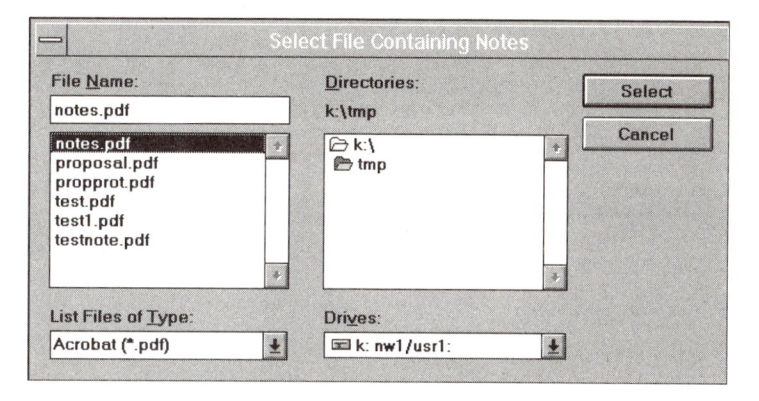

You can also copy just the notes from a PDF document to a new, blank PDF document by using the Edit | Notes | Export menu item. Selecting this item brings up the dialog box shown in Figure 3.30. Enter the name of a new file to save the notes in. The new file will have a blank page for each page of the original document, with only the notes present in the file. The notes will be attached to the Acrobat pages they were originally created on.

TIP: *You don't have to export notes from one file before you import them into another. Just import the original PDF file directly; everything but the notes will be ignored.*

Figure 3.30
The Export Notes dialog box

Summarizing Notes

You can take all the notes from a file and convert them from notes into regular text in a new PDF file using the Tools | Summarize Notes command. Figure 3.31 gives an example of the result.

Figure 3.31
Sample document produced by Tools | Summarize Notes command

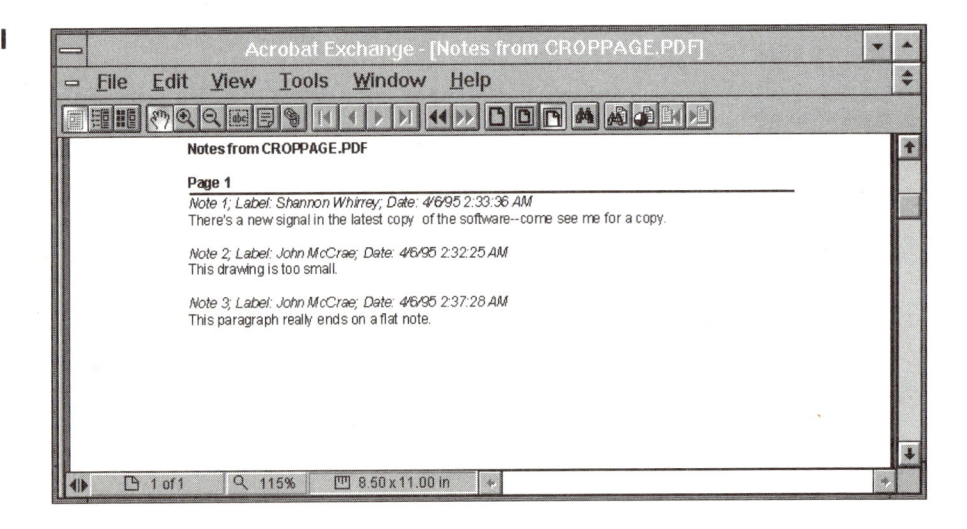

Summary

We've covered a lot of ground in this chapter. At this point you should be able to

- Create PDF files from your standard Windows or Macintosh applications using PDF Writer.

- Control font embedding and image compression in PDF files you create.

- Add bookmarks, links, and notes to your PDF files using Exchange.

- Insert, replace, and delete pages from your PDF files.

- Control who can read or change your files using Adobe's built-in document security functions.

In the next chapter, we will look at a more sophisticated tool for creating PDF files: Acrobat Distiller.

CHAPTER 4

Acrobat Distiller

Guidelines for Choosing Distiller over PDF Writer

Using Distiller in Single-User Mode

Generating PostScript Files from Your Applications

Distiller Configuration

Guidelines for Using Distiller as a PDF Server

Distiller Error Logging

Combining Several PostScript Files into a Single PDF Document

In Chapter 3 we described the easy way to create PDF documents, using the PDF Writer printer driver that comes with Exchange. In this chapter we introduce Acrobat Distiller, which also creates PDF documents. Distiller works by taking an existing PostScript file and converting it to a PDF file. Distiller is really a PostScript interpretor, just like the one in your PostScript printer. To use Distiller, you first print from your application to a file using a PostScript printer driver; the resulting file is passed to Distiller for conversion to PDF.

So why have two ways to create PDF (and why might you want to pay extra for a copy of Distiller rather than just using PDF Writer)? There are three good reasons why Distiller is necessary:

- Some applications (like high-end graphics and publishing programs) do not even attempt to produce their best output except through their own PostScript drivers. This is because PostScript has more capabilities than the native graphics libraries used by Macintosh and Windows.

- PostScript is the page description language of choice for most high-end printers and imagesetters. Using Distiller, publishers can be assured of producing the same output in PDF as they do on paper. Since PDF Writer is not a PostScript interpreter, it can introduce minor differences in positioning that can cause text to "walk" or move to a different page. If you are trying to produce an electronic version of a printed document, even minor differences are unacceptable.

- Distiller can generate PDF from PostScript created on other computers not supported by PDF Writer (UNIX, VAX, etc). Distiller provides a server mode of operation that can provide automatic PDF file generation to a pool of users on a network.

In this chapter we describe how to use Distiller as both a single-user program to create PDF files on a personal workstation and as a PDF server, providing its services to a network of computer users. We'll describe the configuration options for Distiller, and for Windows users, how to use Distiller Assistant to help you to generate PDF files almost as easily as you can using PDF Writer.

Guidelines for Choosing Distiller over PDF Writer

You should always choose Distiller over PDF Writer if either of the following apply to you (these reasons were also mentioned in Chapter 3):

- You are using any of the following applications: CorelDraw, Micrografx Designer, Harvard Draw, Harvard Graphics, Adobe Illustrator, Adobe Pagemaker, or Quark XPress. These applications only produce their best output on a PostScript device.

- You are printing Encapsulated PostScript (EPS) images as part of your document with a Windows-based program. These images must be rasterized to be sent through the Windows printer interface, which reduces the image quality.

If you have the choice of using Distiller or PDF Writer, which should you choose? Distiller offers some advantages over PDF Writer:

- Distiller can embed fonts in a PDF file more compactly than PDF Writer. Distiller can embed only the characters used in the document, resulting in considerable savings in file size.

- Distiller provides you with the option of *downsampling* image data. Downsampling reduces image resolution, hence reducing file size. While not always desirable, this capability is available only in Distiller.

- Distiller provides more flexibility in assigning compression options to image data than PDF Writer does.

PDF Writer offers one capability that Distiller does not: PDF Writer can embed a TrueType font in a PDF file. Distiller actually never sees a TrueType font when you use them in your documents—your PostScript printer driver will convert them to PostScript fonts for you, and Distiller will see the PostScript fonts. Usually the difference is not noticeable, as in the example we give later in this chapter. However, if you have an unusual TrueType font and you have problems with its representation in Distiller-generated PDF files, try using PDF Writer instead and embedding the font in the file. Alternatively, check with your font vendor for a PostScript Type 1 version of the font.

Using Distiller in Single-User Mode

Distiller doesn't require or provide an extensive user interface. See the later sections on Distiller Configuration for information on how to setup Distiller. The Distiller main window is shown in Figure 4.1. The window has a Cancel Job button you can use to cause Distiller to abandon the current job and move on to the next one. The Pause button suspends a job in process or keeps Distiller from looking for more work to do if it is not currently busy. Its name changes to Resume when pressed; press it again to resume file processing.

There are two ways on the Macintosh to start processing a PostScript file to produce PDF, three in Windows systems:

- You can simply drag a PostScript file from a folder (Mac) or the File Manager (Windows) and drop it onto the Distiller window or icon, and Distiller will process the file to produce PDF.

- You can also use Distiller's File, Open menu command to process a file.

Figure 4.1
The Distiller main window

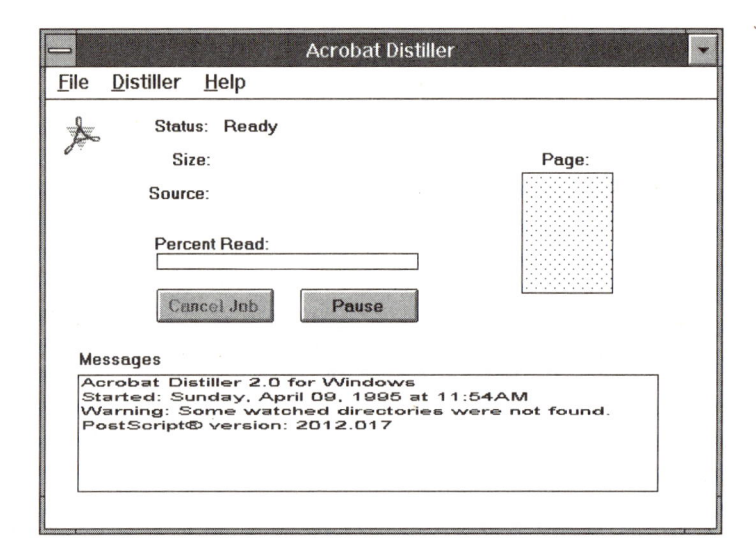

[Screenshot of Acrobat Distiller main window showing Status: Ready, Size, Source, Percent Read, Cancel Job and Pause buttons, and Messages area with text:]

Acrobat Distiller 2.0 for Windows
Started: Sunday, April 09, 1995 at 11:54AM
Warning: Some watched directories were not found.
PostScript® version: 2012.017

- In Windows, you can use Distiller Assistant to process the file for you. Distiller Assistant works much like PDF Writer—it provides a special printer driver you select before printing.

Generating PostScript Files from Your Applications

Before you can use Distiller, you must produce a PostScript file containing the text and images used in your document. With Macintosh and Windows personal computers, this is usually done by telling your application to print the file on a PostScript printer, but to save the output to a file rather than send it to the printer directly. You do not need to own a PostScript printer to use this method.

The standard convention for naming PostScript files is to give them the file extension .PS. As distasteful as it may be to Macintosh users, they, as well as Windows users, should follow this convention both to reduce document name confusion and for portability's sake in a network of mixed computer types.

Using Windows Distiller Assistant

The easiest way for a Windows user to generate PostScript for Distiller to work with is to use Distiller Assistant, which is installed with Distiller. Distiller Assistant is a small utility program that runs as an icon (it does not have a window). You include Distiller Assistant in the Startup group of the Windows Program Manager so that it is always running. Then, when you want to print to a PDF file using Distiller, select the printer named \DISTASST.PS in your Print Setup dialog box. Your application will automatically write a PostScript file which Distiller Assistant will hand off to Distiller itself. You do not have to check the Print to File option in the Print dialog box to make this work. Also, the Distiller Assistant printer driver properly handles color in your document.

Distiller Assistant has three options you can set to customize its behavior. You access these options by single-clicking on the Distiller Assistant icon at the bottom of your screen to bring up the icon's system menu. The options appear as menu items at the bottom of the menu. When one is enabled, a check mark appears next to it.

- *View PDF File* will start Exchange to view the results after Distiller is finished with your file.

- *Exit Distiller When Idle* causes Distiller Assistant to kill Distiller when it is not in use. Since Distiller is a big program, this can free more memory for your use when you are not printing—at the cost of taking a few more seconds to distill your file.

- *Ask For PDF File Destination* allows you to specify the output file name and directory where Distiller will put the resulting PDF file. By default, the file is left in the same directory the PostScript file was in, and it has the same name as your original document, but with a .PDF extension.

Using Windows PostScript Print Drivers

Windows comes with a set of standard PostScript printer drivers, but you must first install one of them if you haven't done so already. Printers are installed from the Windows Control Panel application (see your Windows documentation for a full explanation of how to install a printer driver). You will need to have your Microsoft Windows installation disks handy. If you are using color in your document and you want that color to carry through to your PDF file, make sure you select a color PostScript printer driver; otherwise the driver will likely convert color in your documents to black and white in the PostScript output. We had good results using the QMS ColorScript 100 printer driver (chosen primarily because we knew it was a color printer—most PostScript printers use the same driver with different parameters set by the manufacturer).

When you are ready to print, select File | Print from your application's menu. Make sure your chosen PostScript printer is selected. Check the Print to File check box in the Print dialog box. When you press OK to start printing, Windows will ask you to name the output file. The standard convention is to use the same name as the source document but to substitute the .PS extension. When your program is finished, pass the file to Distiller either by using the Distiller File | Open menu or dragging the PostScript file from the File Manager window and dropping it on the Distiller window (or icon).

If you are using Distiller in server mode (described below), you can save yourself an extra step by having the printer driver write the PostScript file directly into one of Distiller's watched directories.

Using Macintosh Print Drivers

The Macintosh supports a number of different PostScript printers. Adobe recommends selecting the LaserWriter or PSPrinter printer driver, though you can use any printer driver that can generate a PostScript file. If you want to produce color documents you must enable color/grayscale in the printer driver. Select File as the destination instead of the printer. Also, check the Font Inclusion menu (if present) and select the All But Standard 13 menu item; this causes fonts other than the ones provided by Acrobat to be embedded in the PostScript file directly.

Using Adobe PageMaker or Quark XPress

Acrobat comes with a Printer Page Description (PPD) file which is used to configure PageMaker and Quark XPress for a print job. This file is installed in the correct location for these two programs if they are installed on the machine where you are installing Distiller. The ACROBAT.PPD file is also available in the Distiller XTRAS directory or folder; you should copy this file to the appropriate Quark Xpress or PageMaker directories on other machines where you will be preparing files for Distiller. See the Distiller online help file for specific instructions on how to print from different versions of PageMaker or Quark XPress.

Distiller Configuration

Distiller provides for several alternative means of configuration. There are PostScript files read from the Distiller Startup directory when Distiller begins executing; these are described below. The **setdistillerparams** PostScript operator can also be used to change the configuration of Distiller, even during a job (such as specifying compression options for an image). Then there are the configuration dialog boxes; these establish defaults for Distiller's operation and represent its current state. Some of the configuration items are general purpose, while others apply only to the server mode of operation. All of the following Distiller configuration items are located under the Distiller menu.

Preferences

The Distiller | Preferences menu item brings up the Preferences dialog box (Windows version shown in Figure 4.2). The three preference items all affect Distiller's behavior in the event of an error.

Figure 4.2
The Preferences dialog box (Windows version)

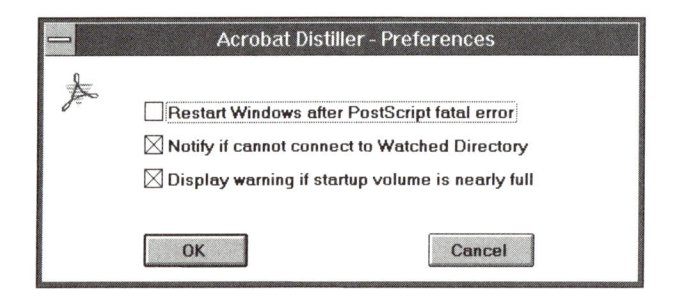

Restart Windows after PostScript fatal error is an option that will reboot Windows—so it's not something you want enabled when you are doing other things with your computer. It is really only useful when Distiller is used on a dedicated server machine. Restarting Windows has the effect of restoring network connections, memory configurations, and other similar variables that could be the source of a PostScript fatal error.

Distiller Configuration

The Macintosh version of Distiller has a similar option that restarts Distiller in the event of an error. This is much less dangerous than restarting Windows, and can be used safely on any machine.

The Notify if cannot connect to Watched Directory option generates an error message notification if a directory in the watched directory list cannot be found (see below for how to setup watched directories). This can result from a network error (such as a server being down) or because someone has deleted the directory. When this option is enabled and Distiller starts up and cannot find all of the named directories, it displays the dialog box shown in Figure 4.3.

Figure 4.3
The Watched Directory Alert dialog box

Acrobat Distiller - Watched Directory Alert

Some watched directories could not be watched because the directories were not found.

[Open List] [OK]

The final option is Display warning if startup volume is nearly full. The startup volume is the volume where Distiller is installed (for Windows users, the startup volume is the disk volume named in the Startup Directory property in the Program Manager's icon for Distiller). This option does not check whether the disk volumes where watched directories are kept are nearly full. If those volumes fill up, error messages are logged (if possible) and Distiller service is stopped on those volumes until the Watched Directories dialog box is opened and closed.

Job Options

The Job Options dialog box (accessed via the Distiller | Job Options menu item and shown in Figure 4.4) is where the default parameters for converting PostScript to PDF are set. These parameters are an expanded set of the options available in PDF Writer. This dialog box establishes the job option defaults used by Distiller, but these defaults can be overridden in two ways:

- By using a special job option configuration that applies only to a specific watched directory (see Watched Directories below).
- By special commands added to the PostScript file.

We'll discuss each part of the Job Options dialog box in the sections that follow.

Figure 4.4
The Job Options dialog box

General Options

Compress (LZW) text and graphics stores all of the text and line drawing commands generated by Distiller to describe each PDF page in a compressed format. This option does not affect bitmapped images, which are governed by the options below. In Chapter 3 we compared files sizes using this compression method against an uncompressed PDF file, a PDF file compressed using LZW with the ASCII Format option, and the original source file. The file produced by selecting this option was the smallest of the four files. We recommend you use this option unless you need to read the text stored in the page descriptions.

Generate Thumbnails allows you to automatically generate a thumbnail sketch for each page of the PDF file you create. Thumbnails are useful for finding tables and figures in your documents as well as for editing in Exchange. However, they add to the size of the file, 1,000 to 3,000 bytes per page of PDF generated, and they take more time to generate.

Make Font Subsets is a valuable feature if you use a lot of embedded fonts. When you embed a font, PDF Writer always stores the entire font in your PDF file, and so does Distiller if this option is not checked. A font subset consists only of the characters that you actually use in your document. Since the character set size for a font is usually 256 characters, you can realize considerable savings using this option. Table 4.1 gives a dramatic illustration of the savings. The file FONTTEST.DOC (shown in Figure 4.5) contains a handful of characters from 12 different TrueType fonts. The table shows the resulting file size when the original document is converted to PDF using different font embedding options.

An important fact to note about this sample document is that it will not print correctly without embedding at least some of the fonts used. The two fonts at the bottom of the page, Nahkt and Pars Ziba, do not use the Roman character set. However, the PDF Writer default

Table 4.1 File Sizes Produced by Different Font Embedding Options for Sample Document

Font Embedding Option	File Size (Bytes)	Percentage of PDF Writer Default
PDF Writer default (no embedding)	27,686	—
PDF Writer with Embed All Fonts enabled	602,839	2,177 percent
Distiller with Make Font Subsets enabled	20,301	73 percent

Figure 4.5 Sample document for font comparisons

TrueType Font Test

Font Name	Sample
AvantGarde	ABC123
Braggadocio	**ABC123**
Century Schoolbook	ABC123
Desdemona	ABC123
Algerian	ABC123
Brush Script	ABC123
Symbol	ABX123
Nahkt	(hieroglyphs)
Pars Ziba	(Arabic script)

for these TrueType fonts substitutes a multiple master font in the PDF file. The result is that Exchange will display random Roman alphabetic characters on systems that do not have the original fonts installed. So at least some embedding of fonts is necessary to make this document work at all. As the table shows, Distiller can produce a correct document that is actually smaller than the incorrect result produced by PDF Writer.

Downsampling

Distiller can optionally perform downsampling on each image in the file. Downsampling can be used with any image compression method. Downsampling means reducing the number of samples (or pixels) in the image. For example, an image scanned at 300 dpi (dots per inch) might be downsampled to 150 dpi. This downsampled image has only one quarter of the number of pixels that the original image had (it has half as many in the X direction, and half as many in the Y direction as well). The downsampling process replaces four pixels with one pixel that contains the average color of the original four. Any details that were only one pixel wide in the original image are now blurred or missing entirely in the reduced image.

The result is a smaller image file, only one quarter of its original size. Whether the resulting picture is acceptable or not depends as much on how the image will be viewed as it does on the image itself. If the image will be seen primarily on a computer monitor screen (at a typical resolution of 72 to 96 dpi), then any extra resolution is mostly redundant data that can be thrown away. On the other hand, a detailed 300 dpi image downsampled to 75 dpi will be noticeably blurry when printed on a 600 dpi printer.

Specifying Downsampling Options to Distiller   In the Job Options dialog box, first check the Downsample to ___ dpi check box. When choosing a target resolution for downsampling, it helps to know what the resolution of your original image is. Distiller will always downsample your image by a power of two; that is, it will take the original resolution of the image and divide it by 2 or by 4 (but not by 3 or 1.5). The number you enter as the target resolution for the image is just a guideline to Distiller; the result may not be the resolution you enter. Instead, Distiller takes the resolution of the original image and repeatedly divides it by two until it finds a resolution smaller than the one you requested; then it backs up one step, using the resolution value that is just larger than what you specified.

For example, if your document is sampled at 300 dpi, and you have specified a downsampling resolution of 72 dpi, then Distiller will downsample the image to a resolution of 75 dpi (which is 300 ÷ 4).

Guidelines for Using Downsampling

If file size is not a concern in your application, don't bother using downsampling. However, this is rarely the case. You should try to preserve enough resolution to display or print the image accurately at the magnification level and resolution you need. Keep in mind the typical use of your image. Often, loss of resolution in the image is not bothersome unless the image is viewed at high magnification. Images that are merely decorative can be downsampled to the resolution of the device they will be displayed on (75–100 dpi for a computer screen). However, if you expect to view the image at 2× magnification, you need to have twice the number of dots per inch that you would otherwise require; four times as many for 4× magnification, and so forth. This generally rules out downsampling for these images.

You can experiment with different combinations of compression and downsampling to find a good trade-off between file size and image quality. Try comparing a downsampled image compressed using JPEG Low compression with the normal image compressed using JPEG Medium or High (see the discussion of compression options below). JPEG compression also results in a loss of image resolution, but the results are not as predictable as downsampling, so take the time to experiment.

Guidelines for Compressing Color Images

Distiller provides the same two options for compressing color images that PDF Writer supports: LZW and JPEG compression. However, Distiller offers a lot more flexibility than PDF Writer:

- As discussed above, Distiller will optionally downsample images to reduce their resolution and size.

Distiller Configuration

- Distiller distinguishes between color images and grayscale images and lets you compress them differently (PDF Writer treats them all the same).

- Distiller lets you apply JPEG compression to 16- and 24-bit color images and LZW compression to 8-bit color images.

- Distiller version 2.1 offers a new feature, Automatic Filter selection, which can examine your images and automatically choose the best compression algorithm for each one.

- Distiller recognizes special PostScript operators you can use to customize the compression of each image in your file.

In the following paragraphs we provide a description and a few notes about each type of compression. Following this is a table which compares how the compression types performed with an RGB full-color image taken from a Kodak PhotoCD.

JPEG Compression   Distiller provides five levels of JPEG compression. JPEG Low provides the least compression, and JPEG High the most. JPEG works by splitting the image into small blocks and compressing each block independently. A sophisticated mathematical algorithm is used to determine how to compress each block. At higher levels of compression, the blocks can become visible, especially when viewing the image at 2× or greater magnification. This is because smooth color blends in the original image end up in different blocks which are compressed differently. This is quite noticeable at high magnification levels, but may not be very noticeable at normal viewing levels.

Even if you select JPEG compression for color images, Distiller does not use JPEG for every color image. Images using 8 or fewer bits to represent a color are compressed using LZW even when JPEG is selected. This allows you to pick a suitable JPEG compression level for your large full-color images, without compromising the quality of your smaller, 8-bit color images.

LZW and LZW 4-Bit Compression LZW compression works differently from JPEG. LZW finds patterns in the image data and compresses those patterns. This can work well for images with large blocks of solid color, such as those produced by paint programs. Unlike JPEG compression, LZW compression preserves the color value of each pixel in the original image, so all the detail in the image is retained in the compressed version. Images compressed with LZW do not deteriorate at high levels of magnification.

Distiller offers an LZW compression option not provided by PDF Writer: Called LZW 4-bit, it reduces the color space to 4 bits, then compresses the resulting image using the LZW algorithm. This compression option can produce a much smaller image file than standard LZW, at the cost of a severe limitation in colors (4 bits yields only 16 colors). The 16 colors are carefully chosen to best represent the actual colors used in the image, but fine detailed shadings are lost when using this algorithm. Most limiting is the fact that the LZW 4-bit algorithm doesn't allow a pure white color—pure white is changed to a shade of light gray. This algorithm is suitable for simple drawings like bar and pie charts that paint large areas of the picture using a small number of colors, but it won't do as well as JPEG does for photo-quality images.

In Table 4.2 we compare the results of using several of the above compression methods. The original image is a detailed close-up color photograph of a bouquet of flowers. The original image was saved as a PostScript EPS file; this file was distilled to produce a PDF file of the image. We also note two other factors that may affect your decision to pick a given compression algorithm: the time it takes to distill the file and the time it takes to display the resulting image in Exchange. Both the distillation time and the display time are roughly proportional to the size of the PDF file (except that JPEG images require more computation to prepare the image for display, slowing down JPEG somewhat).

Table 4.2 **Comparison of Color Image Compression Methods**

File	Size (Bytes)	Percent of Original Size	Distill Time (Seconds)	Display Time (Seconds)
Original EPS	9,594,877	—	—	—
PDF: LZW	4,752,503	50 percent	121	18
PDF: LZW 4-bit	907,779	10 percent	46	7
PDF: JPEG Low	471,631	5 percent	29	11
PDF: JPEG High	75,097	< 1 percent	21	5

The AutoFilter Option   Distiller version 2.1 offers a new option for handling color images: the AutoFilter option. You enable this option using the setdistillerparams operator described later in this chapter. When enabled, this option lets Distiller examine your image data and make its own decision about how to compress the image. Distiller tries to identify color and grayscale images that would be good candidates for LZW compression, and it uses that compression algorithm on those images, regardless of what you have established as the default. To use the AutoFilter option, set your color image compression option to the version of JPEG you want to use (Low through High). Then, following the example in the Distiller Startup directory section below, set the AutoFilterColorImages parameter to true in the Distiller startup file.

Guidelines for Compressing Grayscale Images

Unlike PDF Writer, Distiller lets you handle grayscale images differently from color images. The same compression options are available, but you don't have to apply the same option settings to both kinds of image. This is quite useful if you are combining high resolution color images with lower resolution screen shots in the same file. Distiller also lets you downsample grayscale images to further reduce file size; see the discussion above. Grayscale images have their own version of the AutoFilter option described above for color images; see "The Distiller Startup Directory and the **setdistillerparams** Operator" later in this chapter for an example of how to enable it.

JPEG Compression   Distiller lets you specify JPEG compression for grayscale images; however, it doesn't apply JPEG to every grayscale image. Only 8-bit grayscale images are compressed with JPEG when it is selected. 4-bit and 2-bit grayscale images are compressed using LZW when JPEG is selected. JPEG only works well when there are very fine shading details and gradual blends of color (or gray) in an image. The 4- and 2-bit images don't offer enough detail for JPEG to work effectively. Often, an 8-bit grayscale image does not compress well with JPEG either.

LZW Compression   Distiller offers the standard (and familiar) LZW compression scheme, as well as the LZW 4-bit compression algorithm introduced for color images above (see the discussion there for more explanation). The 4-bit algorithm makes a lot more sense for a grayscale image than it does for a full-color image. It was the best performing compression algorithm for the test image we used below.

Figure 4.6 shows a sample page containing a grayscale image taken from a screen capture program. In Figure 4.7 we present a comparison of grayscale compression algorithms using this image. This comparison shows a portion of the image blown up 800 times. Even at this level of magnification, the images are almost identical, with only the JPEG High compression algorithm showing any deterioration in the image. However, Table 4.3 shows that the JPEG algorithms don't compress this kind of sparse grayscale image very well. JPEG compression algorithms do not reduce the file nearly so much as the much simpler LZW algorithms do. The JPEG Low compression algorithm actually produced a file larger than the original PostScript file it was distilled from. These comparisons were done without performing any downsampling; since the image came from a screen shot, it was not a high resolution image to begin with.

Distiller Configuration

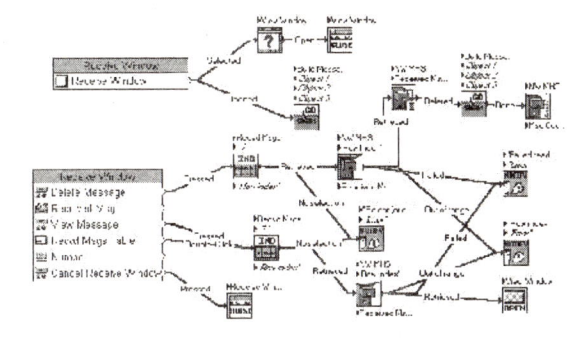

Figure 4.6
Sample document containing grayscale image

Table 4.3   **Comparison of Grayscale Compression Methods**

File	Size (Bytes)	Percent of Original Size	Distill Time (Seconds)	Display Time (Seconds)
Original Word Document	646,656	—	—	—
PostScript file	90,848	14 percent	—	—
PDF: JPEG Low	100,544	16 percent	27	2
PDF: JPEG High	49,381	8 percent	29	4
PDF: LZW	16,823	3 percent	26	1
PDF: LZW 4-bit	15,528	2 percent	26	1

Figure 4.7
Comparison of grayscale image compression results at 800× magnification

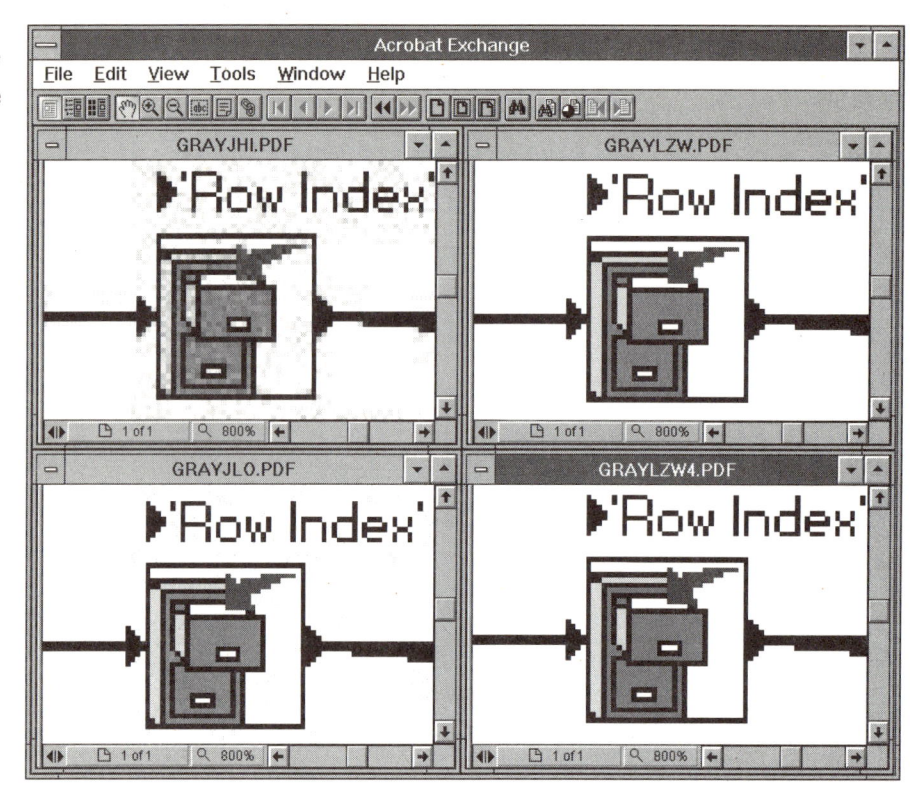

Monochrome Images

Distiller provides the same four compression choices for monochrome images that PDF Writer does:

- CCITT Group 3—the original fax compression standard
- CCITT Group 4—the new, improved fax compression standard
- LZW—our friend from color and grayscale compression
- Run-length—probably the earliest known image compression algorithm

Distiller Configuration

None of these compression methods cause a loss of image quality, so any of them can be used safely. CCITT Group 4 and LZW give the best results over a large range of monochrome images. Either represents a good first choice, but the best compression method for a given image has to be determined by experimentation. There is no AutoFilter option for monochrome images. Monochrome images are not as widely used as they were only a few years ago, so the choice is less of an issue to many users.

Font Locations

In general, Distiller needs to see the actual fonts you are using in your documents when it distills them. There is a select group of fonts which Distiller knows about and can handle on its own:

- Adobe Type 1, Base 14 fonts. These are the basic 14 fonts found in every PostScript printer: the Helvetica, Courier, and Times font families, Symbol, and Zapf Dingbats.

- Many Adobe Type 1, ISO Latin 1 fonts. Descriptions for these fonts come with the version of Adobe Type Manager that ships with Acrobat. However, not all Type 1 ISO fonts are known to ATM, so it is best to provide them to Distiller.

A second group of fonts Distiller can handle on its own are the fonts that are embedded in the PostScript file as part of the print job (downloaded or soft fonts). For example, properly configured Windows and Macintosh PostScript printer drivers will embed synthesized versions of TrueType fonts directly in the PostScript files they create (see "Macintosh PostScript Driver Font Handling" and "Windows PostScript Driver Font Handling").

If your PostScript file names a font that is not included in the file or with ATM, you must own the font and give Distiller access to it. You do this in the dialog box activated by the Distiller | Font Locations menu command (shown in Figure 4.8). This dialog box contains a list of the directories where Distiller will look for fonts.

Figure 4.8
The Font Locations dialog box

To add directories to the font list, click the Add Directory button; this brings up the dialog box shown in Figure 4.9. Use this variation on the standard file opening dialog to select a directory; press OK, and the directory is added to the list. To remove a directory from the list, select the entry in the list you want to remove, and click the Remove button.

If Distiller cannot find the fonts you use in your document somewhere, it will generate a PostScript findfont error, which will be reported in the error log for the job. Distiller will usually substitute Courier for the font it couldn't find, but in some cases it will fail to complete the job, issuing error messages in the log file instead (see "Distiller Error Logging" later in this chapter).

Font Embedding

Both Distiller and PDF Writer follow a set of default rules for determining how to handle fonts. The rules specify which fonts use the Adobe-provided multiple master fonts, which are embedded in the

Figure 4.9
The Add Directory dialog box

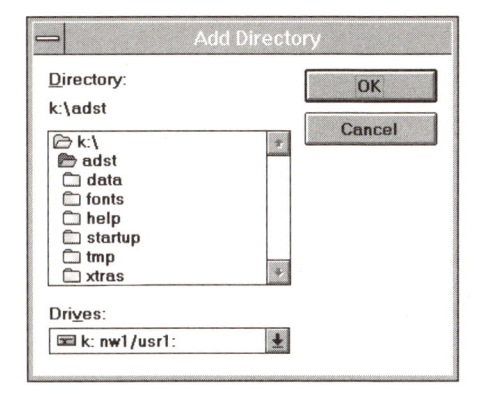

document, and which are rasterized directly. However, Distiller and PDF Writer differ in some of their rules. Distiller lives in a somewhat sheltered environment, and it will never see a TrueType font, Windows or Macintosh bitmap font, or a PCL font, because the PostScript driver will handle these fonts when the PostScript file is written.

Macintosh PostScript Driver Font Handling

If you are using a PSPrinter or LaserWriter 8 printer driver, open the Font Inclusion menu in the File | Print dialog box and make sure you select All But Standard 13. This causes the driver to include the necessary fonts in the PostScript file. The LaserWriter 7 driver already includes the correct fonts.

By default, the Macintosh uses two kinds of fonts: bitmap fonts and TrueType fonts. In both cases, the fonts are usually handled correctly for Distiller by the PostScript driver. A Macintosh bitmap font is converted to an Adobe Type 3 font, and this font is embedded in the PostScript file. Macintosh TrueType fonts are converted to synthetic Type 1 fonts and, depending on the font, either the font description or the entire font is placed in the file. Symbolic TrueType fonts are embedded, while normal TrueType fonts use font descriptors.

Windows PostScript Driver Font Handling

Windows programs may use TrueType, bitmap, or PCL fonts, all of which have to be converted to something a PostScript printer will understand. Bitmap fonts are converted to Adobe Type 3 fonts just like the Macintosh fonts, while PCL fonts are converted to TrueType fonts. The result is that usually by default you will be using TrueType fonts. The standard Windows PostScript driver provides options to allow you to specify exactly what to do for each TrueType font. Check these options by selecting File | Print. In the Print dialog box select the Printer button, and with a PostScript printer driver selected, press the Options button. The PostScript printer driver's main Options dialog box will display. What you see next will depend on which version of the PostScript driver you have installed. Most Windows 3.1 users will see an older-style flat dialog box with a row of buttons down the right side. Select the Advanced button in the Options dialog box. You should see a dialog box like that in Figure 4.10. A newer PostScript driver (version 3) has a gray background using the now-popular 3-D look, and tabs along the top of the dialog box. Choose the Fonts tab as shown in Figure 4.11.

In either case, at this point you should see at the top of your dialog box a combo box control with choices for handling TrueType fonts in the PostScript output. The correct selection for this item depends on which version of Distiller you are using. Distiller version 1 requires you to choose Type 3 fonts; it cannot handle TrueType fonts converted to Type 1. Distiller version 2 fixed this problem and it allows you to choose either, but you will get better results by choosing Type 1 fonts instead of Type 3.

NOTE: *If you are using very small TrueType characters in your document, the PostScript driver will substitute Type 3 fonts in the PostScript file for those fonts even if Type 1 is selected. Adobe specifies that the driver uses the Type 3 substitution when the TrueType*

Distiller Configuration 115

Figure 4.10
The Windows PostScript Printer Advanced Options dialog box

Figure 4.11
Choosing the Fonts tab

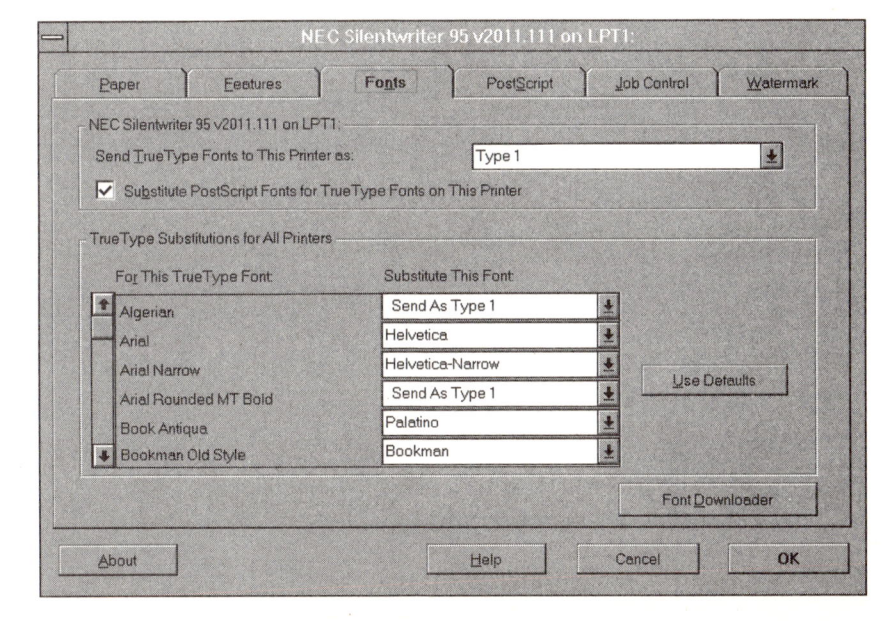

font size would draw the em-dash character (—) less than 16 points wide.

You do not have to convert every TrueType font to a PostScript font; you can save time and space by substituting PostScript fonts for equivalent TrueType fonts. If your dialog box looks like Figure 4.10, check the Use Substitution Table box and click on the Edit Substitution Table button to see what substitutions are being made. If you are using the newer driver, check the Substitute PostScript Fonts for TrueType Fonts on This Printer box; in this case the substitution table is already displayed at the bottom of the current dialog box.

Many TrueType fonts are designed to be similar to PostScript fonts; for example, the standard PostScript Palatino font can be substituted for TrueType Book Antiqua. This dialog box contains all the standard substitutions between TrueType fonts and the larger set of standard PostScript fonts. Pressing the Default button (or Use Defaults) will restore these standard substitutions if you have changed them. To change the substitution for a particular TrueType font, scroll in the left list box (titled For TrueType Font) to display the font you want. In the older version of the driver, when you select a font name from the left list, the right list box (titled Use Printer Font) shows you what substitution is in effect for that font. Each entry in the left list box can have a separate selection on the right. Fonts that don't correspond to any of the standard PostScript fonts should have the entry Download as Soft Font chosen for them in the Use Printer Font list. The new driver shows the current substitution selection for each font in a combo box. Select Send As Type 1 to cause the driver to synthesize a Type 1 font, or select a PostScript font from the list provided.

Distiller Font Embedding

Finally, this brings us to a discussion of the Distiller | Font Embedding dialog box (shown in Figure 4.12). This box is very similar to the one used in PDF Writer. At the top is the option to Embed All Fonts; the other two options in this dialog allow you to control on a font-by-font basis which fonts are embedded. Fonts listed in the Never Embed List are not embedded regardless of whether Embed All Fonts is checked. If you do not have the Embed All Fonts option checked, fonts listed in the Always Embed List will be embedded.

Figure 4.12
The Font Embedding dialog box

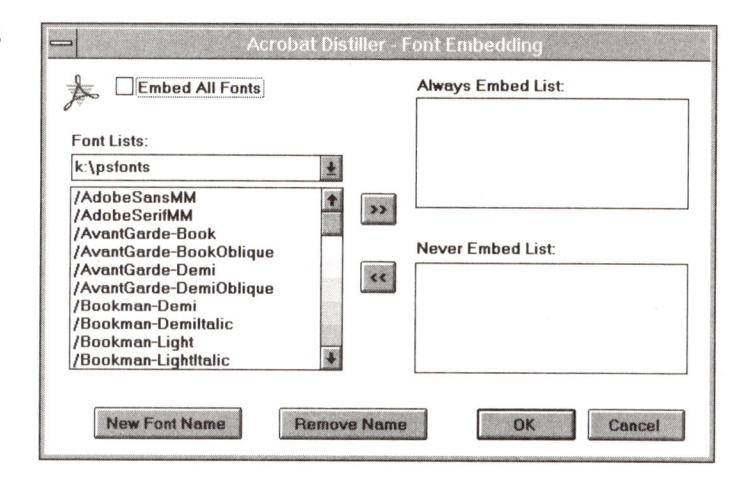

You can enter fonts into these two lists by one of two methods: select a font from the Font Lists list box, or press New Font Name to type in a font name. The Font Lists box allows you to select and display any of the font directories you have entered in the Distiller | Font Locations dialog box (see above). You must use the New Font Name option to enter names for fonts that are not installed on your system but were synthesized and embedded by the PostScript driver. In other words, you don't have to embed a font in your PDF file just because it was embedded in the source PostScript file.

To select an installed font, first select the directory it is installed in from the Font Lists combo box. Select the name of the font by clicking on it. You may then press one of the double-arrow buttons to copy the name to the appropriate list.

To remove a font from one of the embedding lists, click the name with the cursor to select it. Press Remove Name to delete the name from the list. You can also copy the name back to the Font Lists box using the double-arrow (note that the arrow changes direction when one of the entries in Always Embed or Never Embed is selected).

To enter a name for a font that was embedded in the PostScript file, press the New Font Name button. The Add Font Name dialog box is displayed (see Figure 4.13); enter the name of the font you wish to add. Select either the Always Embed List or the Never Embed List, and press the Add button. The dialog box stays open, allowing you to add more than one font name. Press Done when you are finished.

Figure 4.13
The Add Font Name dialog box

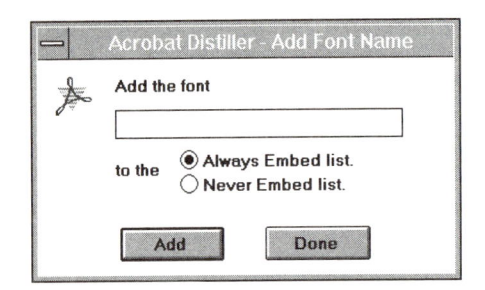

To determine what font name you need to use to make Distiller embed it, create a document using the font (a single-word document will suffice) and use PDF Writer to produce a PDF file from the document (Distiller will not produce the correct font listing unless the font in question is a Type 1 font). Display the file using the Reader or Exchange. Open the File | Document Info | Fonts dialog box (shown in Figure 4.14). All the original names of the fonts used in the document are shown in the leftmost column.

Distiller Configuration

Figure 4.14
The Exchange Doc Info, Fonts dialog box

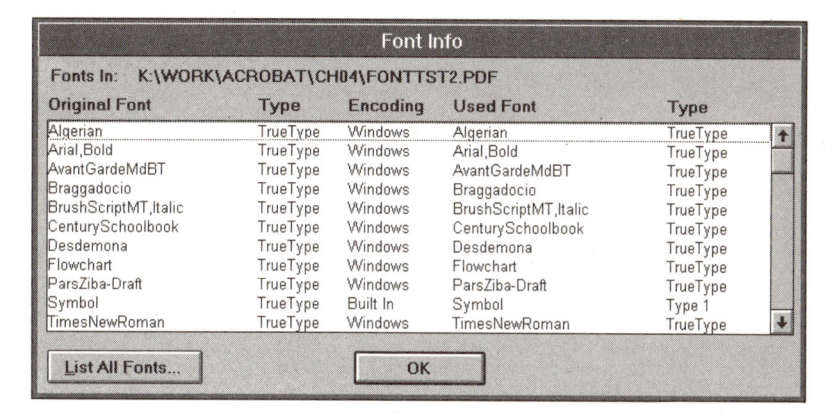

Font Info

Fonts In: K:\WORK\ACROBAT\CH04\FONTTST2.PDF

Original Font	Type	Encoding	Used Font	Type
Algerian	TrueType	Windows	Algerian	TrueType
Arial,Bold	TrueType	Windows	Arial,Bold	TrueType
AvantGardeMdBT	TrueType	Windows	AvantGardeMdBT	TrueType
Braggadocio	TrueType	Windows	Braggadocio	TrueType
BrushScriptMT,Italic	TrueType	Windows	BrushScriptMT,Italic	TrueType
CenturySchoolbook	TrueType	Windows	CenturySchoolbook	TrueType
Desdemona	TrueType	Windows	Desdemona	TrueType
Flowchart	TrueType	Windows	Flowchart	TrueType
ParsZiba-Draft	TrueType	Windows	ParsZiba-Draft	TrueType
Symbol	TrueType	Built In	Symbol	Type 1
TimesNewRoman	TrueType	Windows	TimesNewRoman	TrueType

[List All Fonts...]   [OK]

Guidelines for Choosing Font Embedding Options

Embed All Fonts is always a safe option to use as it guarantees your PDF file will contain all the information needed to reproduce the fonts used in your original document. In PDF Writer, using this option can produce very large PDF files because the entire font is embedded regardless of which characters are used, but with Distiller this is not a problem. Just make sure that the Make Font Subsets option is checked in the Distiller | Job Options dialog box (discussed above), and Distiller will only embed the characters you actually use in your document, rather than the entire font. Table 4.1 (shown previously) illustrates the difference this option can make.

You may not need to embed all fonts, but you may have a problem font that needs embedding. This can occur with Adobe or TrueType fonts using character sets other than ISO Latin 1. If a font isn't displaying properly, use Exchange's File | Doc Info | Fonts dialog box to determine how the font is being handled. Embed only this font by adding it to the Always Embed List in the Font Embedding dialog box.

On the other hand, you may not want to embed a font which Distiller embeds by default. You may be able to require your users to have certain fonts installed on their computers, which eliminates the need to embed them. In this case, enter the names of these fonts in the Never Embed List.

Use the Never Embed List in combination with the Embed All Fonts option to embed all fonts but those you specify. This allows you to make an exception for fonts you know will be present on the viewer's host system instead of having to specify all the fonts that won't be present.

Watched Directories

The Distiller | Watched Directories Options dialog box (shown in Figure 4.15) is used to configure Distiller's server mode of operation. In this dialog box you can specify a set of directories for Distiller to watch. Distiller creates two subdirectories underneath the directory you specify: the *name*\IN subdirectory and the *name*\OUT subdirectory. The IN subdirectory is where you put PostScript files you want Distiller to convert. Distiller puts the resulting PDF files in the OUT subdirectory when they are finished. When Distiller is running, it will check these directories for new files at the interval you specify here. When a new PostScript file is found, Distiller will go right to work converting it to PDF, without any intervention on your part. You can also specify options for how to dispose of both PostScript and PDF files generated automatically by Distiller.

NOTE: *Distiller can perform as a server and as a local application at the same time. You can use Distiller to process a PostScript file you specify using the standard means of handing a file off to Distiller (File menu, drag and drop, or Distiller Assistant) even while Distiller is monitoring the watched directories. These files will have processing priority over files from the watched directories. If watched directories are specified, whenever Distiller is running it will monitor them in a round-robin fashion.*

Distiller Configuration

Figure 4.15
The Watched Directories Options dialog box

[Acrobat Distiller - Watched Directories Options dialog box showing: Check watched directories every 10 seconds; After Distilling, the PostScript file should be: Deleted / Moved to the "Out" directory (selected); Delete files in "Out" directory older than 10 days; Watched Directories List with Add Directory, Remove Directory, Edit Options, Clear Options, OK, and Cancel buttons]

The first field in the dialog box allows you to specify the number of seconds that elapse before Distiller checks for new files in the watched directories. During normal operation, you should set this to a fairly large value—like 60 seconds—to avoid needless overhead on your network. Since the process of generating a PDF file isn't interactive in this mode anyway, there's usually no reason to check more often.

The next field lets you specify whether to delete the PostScript file after distilling or move it to the OUT directory along with the PDF file. The third field lets you delete PDF files in the OUT directory that are older than a certain number of days. These options allow you to maintain a production environment without having to go in and clean up the directories manually.

To add a directory to the watched directories list, press the Add Directory button. A dialog box lets you pick the disk drive and directory you want to add.

Distiller allows you to establish different job options for each watched directory. To set the job options for a particular directory, select the directory in the Watched Directories List, then press the Edit Options button. This brings up the standard Distiller Job Options dialog box (discussed above). The options you specify in this dialog box apply only to the files that are placed in the IN subdirectory of this directory.

To restore the watched directory to use the current Distiller default job options, select the directory in the list and press the Clear Options button. By default, the job options used for a particular watched directory are those in effect when you specify the directory to Distiller.

Distiller puts a special file in the OUT directory to record the options in effect, named DTIME.TXT. When the directory is being watched, Distiller writes to this file on the order of once a minute (times may vary depending on the watch interval you specify and how busy Distiller is). You can examine the modification time of this file to determine when Distiller last looked at the IN directory associated with this OUT directory. While this file can be edited by hand, it is best to use Distiller to make any changes; this ensures that you won't inadvertently enter an erroneous value.

The Distiller Startup Directory and the setdistillerparams Operator

The Distiller Startup directory or folder contains PostScript files that are read by Distiller as it begins operation. By default, the Startup directory contains the file EXAMPLE.PS on Windows, Example.ps for Macintosh; these files contain examples of startup PostScript code. While you can load any PostScript program into Distiller from one of these files, a primary use for them is to add Distiller initialization parameters using the PostScript **setdistillerparams** operator. Most of these parameters are also available using the Distiller configuration dialog boxes described in the preceding

Distiller Configuration

sections. However, using **setdistillerparams** to initialize Distiller does give you some unique capabilities:

- Set a default page size for Distiller to use. This parameter has its own operator (see below).
- Enable or disable the automatic selection of compression types for images (Distiller version 2.1 and greater).
- Enable or disable antialiasing of downsampled images.
- Enable or disable the conversion of CMYK color images to RGB.

All of the parameters discussed in this section are set with the **setdistillerparams** operator except one: the page size is set with the PostScript **setpagedevice** operator. The procedure, though, is the same: edit the Startup directory file and add the following line to it:

```
<</PageSize [ width height]>> setpagedevice
```

The *width* and *height* parameters specify the dimensions of the page in points. There are 72 points to the inch in PostScript, so a standard 8½-by-11 inch page has a width of 612 points and a height of 792 points. Your PostScript files may also include this operator; that value will only be in effect while the current job is being processed.

As you can tell by its name, the **setdistillerparams** operator is only used for changing the configuration of Distiller. When used in a file read from the Startup directory, the **setdistillerparams** operator affects every PostScript file subsequently processed by Distiller. However, you can also include any of these parameters within a PostScript file you convert to PDF with Distiller. When used within a PostScript file processed after initialization is complete, the operator only affects the current file.

Setdistillerparams takes a PostScript dictionary containing key-value pairs; Distiller saves the dictionary internally and consults it as the PostScript file is processed to determine how to proceed.

Some of the parameters, such as image compression parameters, can be changed in the middle of the PostScript file to cause Distiller to change its output. Others are only examined before Distiller starts processing the file. PostScript dictionaries and programming techniques are thoroughly described in the *PostScript Language Reference Manual, 2nd Edition.* The **setdistillerparams** operator has the following syntax:

```
dict setdistillerparams -
```

The trailing dash indicates that setdistillerparams has no output values. A *dict* can be represented as a key-value pair enclosed within double angle-brackets. This is an example of a dictionary used with **setdistillerparams** that enables the automatic filter feature found in Distiller 2.1:

```
<< /AutoFilterColorImages true
/AutoFilterGrayscaleImages true >> setdistillerparams
```

You can find more examples in the EXAMPLE.PS file located in the Startup directory.

There is a corresponding operator called **currentdistillerparams** that returns a copy of the PostScript dictionary containing the current parameter values. If you are knowledgeable about writing PostScript programs, you can use this operator to create a PostScript program that checks and/or saves the current values of Distiller's parameters before setting new ones with **setdistillerparams.** The proper syntax for **currentdistillerparams** is:

```
- currentdistillerparams dict
```

Table 4.4 lists the key names and value types recognized by **setdistillerparams** for Distiller 2.1. For detailed technical information on **setdistillerparams,** see Adobe's *Technical Note #5151, Acrobat Distiller Parameters.* For more details on programming image compression parameters, see *Technical Note #5116, Supporting the DCT Filters in PostScript Level 2.*

Distiller Configuration

Table 4.4   setdistillerparams Key Values

Key	Value Type	Definition
CoreDistVersion	Integer	Returns the version of Acrobat Distiller. Version 2.10 is returned as the value 21xx, where xx is a minor release number.
SetOutputFile	String	Specifies a path and file name for Distiller's output PDF file. The name must be a Macintosh path name for Mac Distiller, or a DOS path name for Windows Distiller. Example: (c:\document\mydoc.pdf). Parenthesis are required. Can only be used on a per-job basis, not as a start-up default.
DoThumbnails	Boolean	True to cause thumbnails to be rendered and stored in the PDF file. This parameter is checked for each distilled page, allowing you to control thumbnails on a per-page basis.
LZWEncodePages	Boolean	True to use LZW compression on text and line graphics. Must be set at the beginning of the PostScript file.
ASCII85EncodePages	Boolean	True to encode binary (compressed) data in the PDF file into ASCII. Must be set at the beginning of the PostScript file.
EncodeColorImages	Boolean	True to cause color images to be compressed using the algorithm specified in ColorImageFilter (or selected by Distiller if AutoFilterColorImages is true). Can be changed for each image in the file.
AutoFilterColorImages	Boolean	True to enable Distiller to determine the compression algorithm to use for each color image automatically. Only present in Distiller 2.1 and later. Used only if EncodeColorImages is true.

ColorImageFilter	Name	The name of the compression algorithm to use for color images, unless AutoFilterColorImages is true. Valid names are:
		    DCTEncode for JPEG compression.
		    LZWEncode for LZW compression.
		Can be changed for each image in the file.

ColorImageDict	Dictionary	A dictionary containing parameters for JPEG compression. See the references for more information. Can be changed for each image in the file.
DownsampleColorImages	Boolean	True to downsample color images. Can be changed for each image in the file.
ColorImageResolution	Integer	Minimum downsampling resolution in dpi. Can be changed for each image in the file.
AntiAliasColorImage	Boolean	True to apply antialiasing to color images. Can be changed for each image in the file.

Table 4.4   setdistillerparams Key Values (continued)

Key	Value Type	Definition
ColorImageDepth	Integer	Specifies the number of bits to use to represent color in an image. Values are –1, 1, 2, 4, or 8, where –1 means do not change the image depth from the original. Can be changed for each image in the file.
EncodeGrayImages	Boolean	True to cause a grayscale image to be compressed using the algorithm specified in GrayImageFilter (or selected by Distiller if AutoFilterGrayImages is true). Can be changed for each image in the file.
AutoFilterGrayImages	Boolean	True to enable Distiller to determine the compression algorithm to use for each grayscale image automatically. Only present in Distiller 2.1 and later. Used only if EncodeGrayImages is true.

GrayImageFilter	Name	The name of the compression algorithm to use for grayscale images, unless AutoFilterGrayImages is true. Valid names are:
		    DCTEncode for JPEG compression.
		    LZWEncode for LZW compression.
		Can be changed for each image in the file.

GrayImageDict	Dictionary	A dictionary containing parameters for JPEG compression. See the references for more information. Can be changed for each image in the file.
DownsampleGrayImages	Boolean	True to downsample grayscale images. Can be changed for each image in the file.
GrayImageResolution	Integer	Minimum downsampling resolution in dpi. Can be changed for each image in the file.
AntiAliasGrayImages	Boolean	True to apply antialiasing to grayscale images. Can be changed for each image in the file.
GrayImageDepth	Integer	Specifies the number of bits to use to represent the grayscale in an image. Values are –1, 1, 2, 4, or 8, where –1 means do not change the image depth from the original. Can be changed for each image in the file.
EncodeMonoImages	Boolean	True to cause monochrome images to be compressed using the algorithm specified in MonoImageFilter. Can be changed for each image in the file.

MonoImageFilter	Name	The name of the compression algorithm to use for monochrome images. Valid names are:
		    LZWEncode for LZW compression.
		    CCITTFaxEncode for Group 3 or Group 4 compression.
		    RunLengthEncode for run length compression.
		Can be changed for each image in the file.

Table 4.4 setdistillerparams Key Values (continued)

Key	Value Type	Definition
MonoImageDict	Dictionary	Dictionary of compression parameters used for the CCITTFaxEncode algorithm. See the references for more information. Can be changed for each image in the file.
DownsampleMonoImages	Boolean	True to downsample monochrome images. Can be changed for each image in the file.
MonoImageResolution	Integer	Minimum downsampling resolution in dpi. Can be changed for each image in the file.
AntiAliasMonoImages	Boolean	True to apply antialiasing to monochrome images. Can be changed for each image in the file.
MonoImageDepth	Integer	Specifies the number of bits to use to represent a pixel in a monochrome image. Values are −1, 1, 2, 4, or 8, where −1 means do not change the image depth from the original. Note that this parameter can turn a monochrome image into a grayscale image. See *Technical Note #5151* for more information. Can be changed for each image in the file.
AlwaysEmbed	Array of font names	Specifies a list of fonts that are added to the current list of fonts that are always embedded in the PDF file. The list is restored to its default after each PDF file is complete. This parameter must be set at the start of the file.
NeverEmbed	Array of font names	Specifies a list of fonts that are added to the current list of fonts that are never embedded in the PDF file. The list is restored to its default after each PDF file is complete. This parameter must be set at the start of the file.
EmbedAllFonts	Boolean	True to specify that all fonts except those in the NeverEmbed list should be embedded in the PDF file.
SubsetFonts	Boolean	True to enable font subsetting (embedding only the characters used in a font, rather than the whole font).
MaxSubsetPct	Integer	The percentage of glyphs in a font that can be used before the font is embedded entirely, rather than a subset.
OutputCSD	Boolean	True to output a device-independent color space descriptor into the PDF file. Default is true.
ConvertCmykImagesToRGB	Boolean	True to convert color images using the CMYK color space to RGB, false to leave them alone. Conversion reduces the file size. This value is true by default.

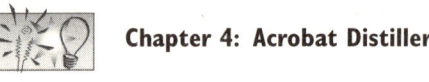

Guidelines for Using Distiller as a PDF Server

With Distiller's watched directories feature, you can use a single copy of Distiller running on a network to convert files to PDF for many different users automatically. Users can simply copy PostScript files to the IN subdirectories of the watched directories you specify. They can set up their applications to print their PostScript files directly into these directories. You should dedicate a machine as the Distiller server in this mode of operation, as the load that Distiller puts on a computer would make it unwelcome as a background task on someone's desktop computer.

You can establish different job options for each watched directory you use, including disposition of source PostScript files placed in the IN directory and PDF files in the OUT directory. The best way to do this is to use the Edit Options button in the Watched Directories dialog box described above.

Note that the computer running Distiller must have read/write access to all of the watched directories you specify. Users must have write access to the IN subdirectory, and read access to the OUT subdirectory. To make the watched directories easier to use, you may want to set up mapped network drives (Windows) or aliased folders (Macintosh) for your users. You may want to secure the Distiller server machine alongside your network servers to avoid both changes to Distiller's setup and unauthorized use of the server to access other network resources.

Distiller Error Logging

Distiller writes a log file in its home directory that contains status and error messages describing each file it processes. This file is called MESSAGES.LOG, and it is a standard text file. All messages that display in the Distiller main window are also printed in this file.

You can monitor this file to find out what happened to jobs that failed and to measure the performance and utilization of Distiller.

The MESSAGES.LOG file is automatically limited in size to 30KB. When the file reaches this size, Distiller erases the first 10KB of the file and continues writing the file. You may want to archive this file on a daily basis (or more frequently if Distiller is very busy) to provide a record of Distiller's activity.

Distiller also writes a log file for individual distilled files that produce errors in processing. The file is written to the same directory where Distiller writes the PDF file for this job. The file is named *filename*.LOG, where *filename* is the name given to the PDF output file. If you are using Distiller in a server mode of operation, these log files are essential for users to find out what happened to their PDF files (which may not exist if there were PostScript errors).

Combining Several PostScript Files into a Single PDF Document

Sometimes you will be creating a PDF file from PostScript generated by several different applications, different users, or at different times. You can always use Exchange to combine PDF files, but Distiller gives you the option to combine PostScript files directly in the input to Distiller, saving you the extra step of editing the PDF file. This also has the advantage of using fewer font subsets in your files.

To combine PostScript files, you must create your own PostScript program that includes the other PostScript files you want to combine. Adobe provides an example PostScript file you can modify and use: XTRAS\RUNFILEX.PS on Windows, Xtras:RunFileEx.ps on Macintosh. Copy this file to a private directory and rename it to reflect the project you're working on (since the PDF file name will usually be the same as the main PostScript input file name). Edit this file with a text editor such as NotePad (Windows) or TeachText (Macintosh). The file contains the definition of a PostScript procedure called prun. You must call the prun procedure for each file you want to include, in the order you want their pages to display. The sample file you copied has several lines of examples (all ending with the word *prun*), and instructions in a comment at the end of the file. Replace the sample lines with the names of the files you want to include. Save the file (as a plain text file if you have the option) and exit the editor. Now you can submit this file to Distiller to process, and it will in turn process each of the files you have named.

Make sure you specify a full path to each file, and that you use the proper file name syntax for the version of Distiller you are running. In other words, if you are using a Macintosh version of Distiller (perhaps running on a server machine), you must specify a Macintosh path and file name, even if you are a Windows user yourself. Of course, Distiller must also have read access to all of the files you specify.

There is another example in the XTRAS subdirectory: RUNDIR-EX.TXT (Windows) or RunDirEx.txt (Macintosh). This file contains a PostScript program similar to RunFileEx, except that it searches a directory or folder and processes all the files it finds there. This file needs to be altered to accept the name of the directory/folder you want to process; then submit this file to Distiller and all the files in the named directory will be processed.

Summary

In this chapter we've introduced Acrobat Distiller, its configuration, and its use as both a stand-alone program and as a server program on a network. We've also introduced the **setdistillerparams** PostScript operator which you can use to change Distiller's configuration at start-up or on the fly from your own PostScript programs. In the next chapter, we discuss the Catalog program, which lets you combine a group of PDF documents together and perform full-text searches on the contents of those files.

CHAPTER 5

Indexing and Searching PDF Documents

Full-Text Search Capabilities
Using Acrobat Search
Using Acrobat Catalog
Choosing a Graph Type

Indexing and Searching PDF Documents

One of the chief advantages of using electronic documents instead of paper ones is the ability to use the computer to search directly for the information we need. Studies show that this is usually the way we read documents anyway. Most of the time we'll pick up a book and look through its table of contents or index to find the specific information we seek, rather than read from the beginning—that is, if the document gives us the option by providing them. Usually an index is only available for documents that are actually bound, published, and sold, which leaves out most of the documents we create and use every day.

Acrobat provides the ability to index and do a full-text search of any PDF document or collection of documents. Publishers who wish to provide search capability for their documents use Acrobat Catalog to create a full-text search database. Distributing this database with the documents it indexes allows any Acrobat Exchange user to perform a full-text search of the entire document collection using a plug-in module distributed with Exchange called Acrobat Search.

NOTE: *Documents that have not been indexed with Catalog cannot be used with Acrobat Search. Furthermore, in Acrobat version 2.0, Acrobat Search capability is not provided with the Acrobat Reader. At our publication time it appears that a version of Search may be provided for the new version 2.1 Reader. This version will not support the IAC capabilities described in Chapter 8, but it is otherwise identical. Unless and until this version arrives, the low-cost solution for providing Search capability is to distribute Exchange LE (rather than Reader). Contact the Adobe Developer's Association for current details.*

Full-Text Search Capabilities

The search capabilities of Acrobat are built on a full-text search engine provided by Verity Corporation. Similar versions of this search engine are also used in other products, such as Lotus Notes, so you may have encountered it before. The search engine provides the following capabilities on all searches:

- Find a single word or phrase, regardless of letter case. This is similar to the capability provided by the Find command, but Find does not use the search indexes created by Catalog.

- Use wildcard characters to match parts of words. Acrobat's wildcard capability is very similar but not identical to that provided by the UNIX grep command (that is, a regular expression).

- Use AND, OR, and NOT as Boolean operators to construct searches combining more than one word or phrase (for example, "tax" AND "spend").

- Use the Proximity option with the AND operator to find words that are used in close proximity to each other (within 100 words, before or after).

- Use Match Case to limit the scope of the search to exactly match the capitalization of the search terms you supply. The default is to match regardless of capitalization.

The search engine also provides other capabilities that can broaden your search:

- Word Stemming finds words built on the same root as the word you specify. For example, if you specify *matching*, Search will also find *match* and *matches*.

- Thesaurus finds words that have similar meanings to the word you are searching for.

■ Sounds Like finds words that bear some phonetic resemblance to the search term you entered.

Using Acrobat Search

Search, when properly installed, adds a new menu item and several buttons to the Exchange tool bar (see Figure 5.1). Note that Exchange still provides the Find function on the Tools menu as well as the new Search functions. Tools | Find is the same simple text matching function found in the Reader and does not use indexes to find words.

Figure 5.1
The Search menu in Exchange

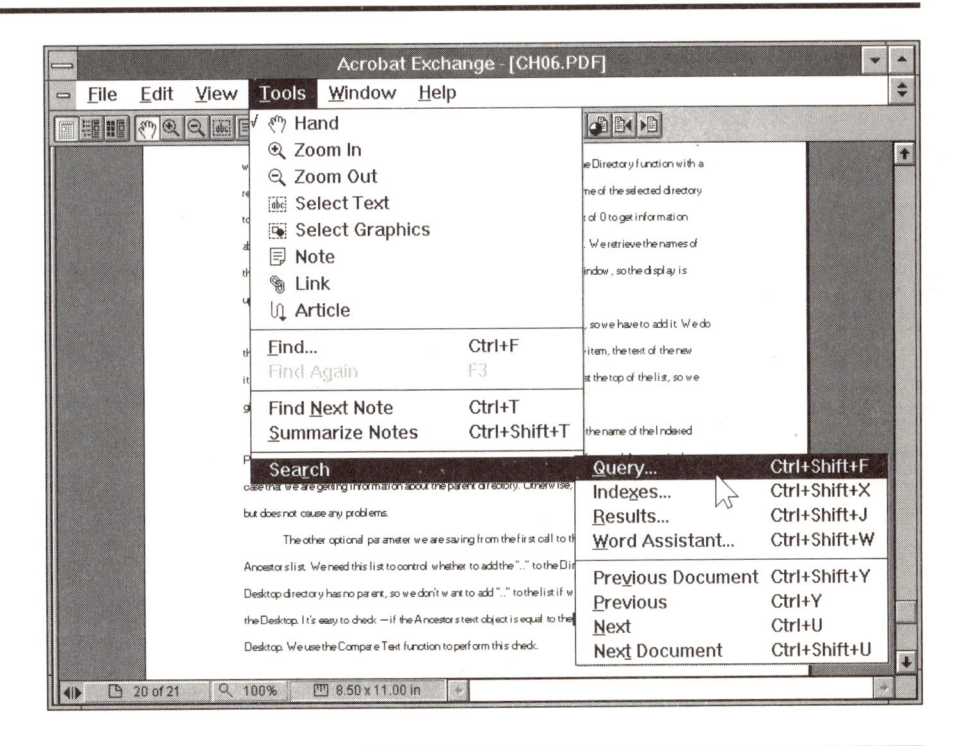

Search Preferences

By default, Acrobat Search presents a very simple dialog box for initiating a search. The first thing you should do is change this to allow yourself the full use of Search's capabilities. Select the Edit | Preferences | Search menu command to bring up the dialog box shown in Figure 5.2.

Figure 5.2
Acrobat Search Preferences dialog box

The first box at the top of the Preferences dialog box, labeled Query, governs the options available when you first initiate a search by making a query of the search database. Show Fields refers to the Document Info fields stored in each PDF file; you can allow searches of the contents of these fields by checking this box. Show Date allows you to restrict the search to documents created or modified before or after a specific date. Show Options lets you select from the different kinds of matching algorithms that Search provides: Word Stemming, Thesaurus, Sounds Like, Match Case, and Proximity. Power users will want all of these boxes checked to make these capabilities available.

The Hide on Search option hides the Search dialog box after the user presses the Search button in the Search dialog box. The Search dialog box is *modeless,* meaning it can stay open in conjunction with the main Exchange window, floating over or beside it. This allows you to easily refine a search by adding new search criteria. You can also refine your search if you set the Hide on Search button, but you must reopen the Search dialog box yourself.

The Results section of the Search Preferences dialog box specifies how many different documents you can track as the result of a query and in what order the matching documents should be listed. The default value of 100 documents is fine for casual use, but if your search returns more documents than this number, they will be silently dropped from the results list. Search gives you nine different sorting options for listing documents with matches. Eight of them correspond to Document Info fields in the PDF file:

- *Author*—an editable Document Info field
- *Created date*—the date the PDF file was first created
- *Creator*—the user's ID (usually a network user name) from the machine where the PDF file was created
- *Keywords*—an editable Document Info field
- *Modified*—the date the PDF file was last modified
- *Producer*—the name of the program that produced the PDF file
- *Subject*—an editable Document Info field
- *Title*—an editable Document Info field

The ninth, Score, is used by default. Search scores each document based on how relevant it thinks the matches found in that document might be. The score (Adobe also calls this the relevance ranking) is determined by how many matches occurred in the document. Documents with more words that matched the query are given a higher score. If the query contains an OR operator, documents that meet both criteria receive a higher ranking, as do documents that match a search combining an AND operator and the proximity option.

The Hide on View option works similarly to the Hide on Search option described above, except that it hides the Search Results dialog box. This dialog box is modeless, so you can keep it open while reading a document in the main Exchange window. The user can bring up the Search Results dialog box at any time by selecting Tools | Search | Results or pressing the Results button on the toolbar (see Table 5.1 below). On small monitors, this should generally be enabled.

The final preference item concerns how to display matches. Search gives you three options for highlighting the results of your search query:

- *No highlighting*—Search takes you to the page where the match occurred but doesn't highlight the match for you.

- *Highlight by page*—All the matching words on the current page are highlighted. Each time you use the Next or Previous commands, a new page is displayed. If the whole page isn't visible at your current magnification, you may not see all the matches. Pressing Next or Previous will not scroll the hidden matches into view—they take you to another page where there are matches. This is the quick way to view matches when there are many of them on the page at once.

- *Highlight by word*—Each match is highlighted individually. When you select the Next or Previous commands, they take you to the specific matching text, not just the page it is on. This option assures you of seeing all the matches individually.

Search Commands

Search provides three toolbar commands you can use from the main Exchange window to search a document. Shown in Table 5.1 with their associated menu items, these commands let you initiate a search and then browse the resulting list of pages.

Table 5.1   Search Commands

Search Command	Menu Bar Command	Keyboard Accelerator	Toolbar Button
New Search	Tools | Search | Query	Ctrl+Shift+F (Win) ? (Mac)	
Next Match	Tools | Search | Next	Ctrl+U (Win) ? (Mac)	
Previous Match	Tools | Search | Previous	Ctrl+Y (Win) ? (Mac)	
View Search Results	Tools | Search | Results	Ctrl+Shift+J (Win) ? (Mac)	
Next Document with Matches	Tools | Search | Next Document	Ctrl+Shift+U (Win) ? (Mac)	Ctrl+Shift+
Previous Document with Matches	Tools | Search | Previous Document	Ctrl+Shift+Y (Win) ? (Mac)	Ctrl+Shift+

Starting a new search brings up the dialog box shown in Figure 5.3. This is the version that appears if you have selected all the query options in the Edit | Preferences | Search dialog box. If you have not selected all the options, the corresponding sections of the dialog box will be missing.

At the top of the dialog box is a text field labeled *Find Results Containing Text.* You must enter a search expression in this text box. In its simplest form, a search expression is just a word or phrase to find in the document. We discuss all the options available for writing a search expression below. If you have the full version of the Search dialog box enabled, you can also enter search text in the

Figure 5.3
Search dialog box (full version)

Document Info fields, specify a date for the document's creation with the Date Info fields, or select one of the search algorithm options.

NOTE: *The search options are always selectable, even if the search database was not set up to support the option when it was created.*

Press the Search button in the dialog box when you have created the search expression you want. Acrobat performs the search and brings up a dialog box that lists the documents that contain matching text to your query (see Figure 5.4). Select a document from the list and press Info to see the Document Info fields for that file, or press View to take a look at the first match in the file itself.

Each time you perform a new search, the list of matching words in your documents are temporarily saved. The Tools | Search | Next and Tools | Search | Previous commands let you browse the matches individually or page-by-page, depending on the setting of the

Using Acrobat Search 141

Figure 5.4
The Search Results dialog box

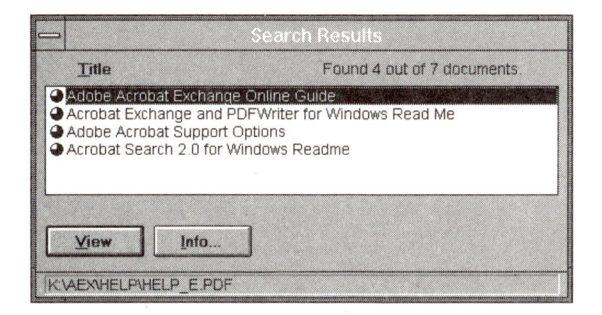

Highlight Display item in the Search Preferences dialog box. If more than one document contains text matching your query, you can go back to the Search Results dialog box and select another document, or you can use the Next Document and Previous Document commands to skip any remaining matches in this document and start directly with the first match in the next document

Selecting Indexes for a Search

Before you start a search on a new document, you must make sure that the index for the document is listed in the Index Selection dialog box (shown in Figure 5.5). Access this dialog box by pressing the Indexes button on the main Search dialog box, or select Tools | Search | Indexes from the menu. The Index Selection dialog box shows you all the indexes that are currently registered with Search. When you want to add a new set of documents with their own index, use the Add button found here to add the new index to the search list. Add brings up a standard File Open dialog box. Acrobat index files have MS-DOS file names that end in the extension .PDX. Select the file and press OK; the title of the index will appear in the Index Selection dialog box.

Figure 5.5
The Index Selection dialog box

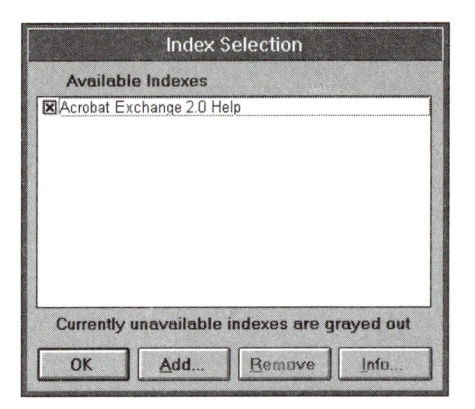

When you use Search, it will search all the search indexes listed in this box on every search. You can select an index with the mouse and click the Remove button to delete the index from the search. This does not delete the index from the disk, so you can add it back again. However, there is no way to temporarily disable or deselect an index for a given search. You can get a look at the index description by selecting an index and pressing the Info button.

Stopwords

When an index is created with Catalog, the creator may specify that certain words, called *stopwords*, not be indexed. Stopwords reduce the size of the index files Catalog creates. A typical list of stopwords would include small "helper" words like *a*, *an*, and *the*. It is important to know what stopwords were used with your index, because you cannot include a stopword in a search phrase. Since a stopword is not in the index, it cannot be found by Search, which means a phrase with that word in it cannot be found either. Typically a list of the stopwords is included with the index description specified by the creator of the index. Use the Info push button in the Index Selection dialog box to view the index description.

Guidelines for Forming Search Expressions

The basic search expression is a word or phrase, optionally in double quotes, but there are certain characters and words that cannot be part of a search expression:

- The double quote character (").

- The words AND, OR, and NOT, in uppercase or lowercase, and their single-character abbreviations (see below). Search uses these words to form Boolean expressions. If you must include these words in your search expression as text to search for, the phrase containing them must be enclosed in double quotation marks.

- Punctuation marks (periods, commas, hyphens, question marks, and so on). Punctuation marks—along with the space character—serve to identify and separate words when indexes are built, and they are not indexed themselves. For example, a hyphenated word will appear as two separate words in the index. Search ignores punctuation marks you put into phrases within double quotes in your search expression, except for wildcard characters. Outside of quoted phrases, some punctuation marks have special meaning in a search expression.

- Stopwords declared for the index. Search will not find stopwords because they are not in the index (we discussed stopwords in more detail above). Phrases containing stopwords will not be found. Instead of looking for a phrase containing likely stopwords (words like *the*), use a Boolean search expression to find the major words in the phrase. For example, instead of searching for "rename the directory," try the search expression "rename" AND "directory," and use the proximity option to restrict the search to locations where those words are close by each other.

- Numbers. When the index is created, numbers can be eliminated or included in the index. If they are not included, they will not be found in a search.

Using Boolean Expressions

A Boolean expression has at least two words or phrases to search for, joined together by one or more of the Boolean operators AND, OR, and NOT. The operators have the following effect:

- *Text1 AND Text2*—Both Text1 and Text2 must be found in the same document for the document to be added to the search results list. Text1 and Text2 may be words or phrases; they don't have to be in quotes unless they contain one of the Boolean operators as a literal. If the proximity option is set in the Options section of the Search dialog, then Text1 and Text2 must be found within 100 words of each other, not just in the same document. You can also use the ampersand character (&) instead of the word AND to form a Boolean AND expression.

- *Text1 OR Text2*—If either Text1 or Text2 or both are found in the document, it is added to the search results list. You can also use the comma (,) or a vertical bar (|) to form a Boolean OR expression.

- *NOT Text1*—Finds all documents that do not contain the specified text. You can also use the exclamation point (!) to form a Boolean NOT expression.

You can combine the Boolean operators to form more complex expressions. For example, you could specify the search expression:

```
Text1 AND NOT Text2
```

This expression finds all documents containing Text1 but not Text2. The Boolean operators in such an expression are evaluated left to right, but you can use parentheses to change the order of evaluation. For example, the expression

```
Text1 AND Text2 OR Text3
```

is evaluated as though it reads

```
(Text1 AND Text2) OR Text3
```

This expression finds all documents containing both Text1 and Text2, or Text3. Using parentheses you can change the order of evaluation to obtain the expression:

```
Text1 AND (Text2 OR Text3)
```

This expression finds all documents containing Text1 and either Text2 or Text3. You could also rearrange the search expression to put the OR clause first and achieve the same result.

One use for Boolean expressions is to find words that are separated by stopwords. You can't find the phrase *paint the boat* if *the* is a stopword; but you can search for *paint AND boat* which will find the phrase you're looking for. Use the proximity option to restrict the search to words that are close together in the document.

WARNING: *AND, OR, and NOT are always recognized as Boolean operators unless they are contained within double quotes. The same is true of the punctuation characters defined as Boolean operators (the ampersand, the comma, the vertical bar, the exclamation point, and parentheses).*

Using Wildcards

You can specify a pattern for Search to match in the text. The pattern may contain alphanumeric characters and any combination of two wildcard characters:

| ? | Matches against any single character |
| * | Matches zero or more characters |

For example, if you search the Acrobat Catalog help files for *cat*, Search will find all instances of the word *Catalog*, but also the name *acrocat.ini*. You can use wildcards in phrases and they are recognized even within double quotes. You can combine wildcards arbitrarily to produce complex expressions. If the expression gets too complicated or there are too many matches found, Search will display an error message. For example, you can search for *cat* file, which returns *indicated file* and *application file*, but you cannot search for *cat* * (though you can search for *cat* ?). You cannot search for the question mark or asterisk characters themselves, even when quoted—they always function as wildcards.

Searching Document Info Fields

You can use the contents of Document Info fields stored in your PDF file in searches to reduce the number of matches you find. Acrobat provides four key fields: Author, Title, Subject, and Keywords. Some document collections may have additional custom fields defined (check with the provider). To match something in one of the default Document Info fields (Author, Title, Subject, or Keywords), specify a literal piece of text in the field you want to match (note that to see this option, you must have this section enabled in the Search Preferences dialog box). You can specify the exact text, a wildcard expression, or a Boolean expression in the Document Info text boxes. Figure 5.6 shows an example that will match against all the Acrobat help files except Acrobat Catalog.

You can also specify search values for Document Info fields in a Boolean expression along with your other search text using a special set of operators that only work with Document Info fields. The operators are listed in Table 5.2. For example, you could specify

```
Falstaff AND Author ~ Shakespeare
```

Figure 5.6
Specifying Document Info search expressions

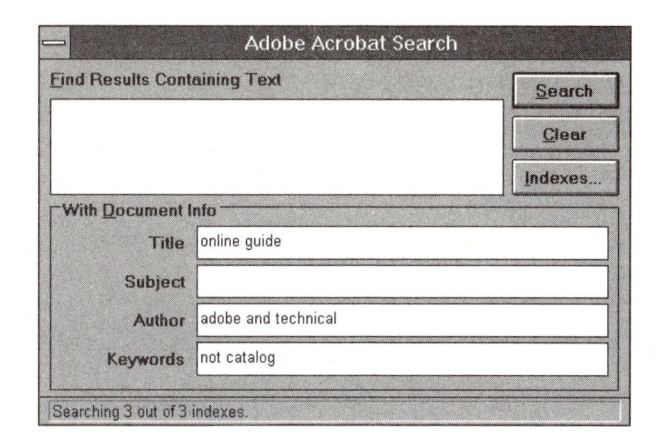

Figure: Adobe Acrobat Search dialog with "Find Results Containing Text" field, Search/Clear/Indexes buttons, and With Document Info section showing Title: "online guide", Subject: (empty), Author: "adobe and technical", Keywords: "not catalog". Status: "Searching 3 out of 3 indexes."

This will find all documents containing the string *Falstaff* and with the name *Shakespeare* in the Author Document Info field. If there are custom Document Info fields in your PDF files, you can use their contents in a search by specifying them in this manner. Use the name of the custom field just like one of the built-in fields with the operators in Table 5.2.

Table 5.2 Search Operators Used with Document Info Fields

Operator	Meaning
=	Exact match of the text
~	Contains the text as part of the field value (text fields only)
!=	Does not contain the text in the field
<	Is less than (for numeric or date fields only)
<=	Is less than or equal to (for numeric or date fields only)
>	Is greater than (for numeric or date fields only)
>=	Is greater than or equal to (for numeric or date fields only)

NOTE: *The four standard Document Info fields (Title, Subject, Author, and Keywords) are text fields. By default there are no date or numeric fields.*

Using the Word Assistant with Search Options

You may not find the information you are seeking with your first stab at using Acrobat Search. If your search does not return the information you expect, you may want to try broadening your search by relaxing your requirements for a match. Consider, for example, redoing the search using only parts of the words you are looking for combined with wild cards.

If you need to broaden your search, Acrobat provides a handy feature called Word Assistant (available from the Tools | Search | Word Assistant menu command). Word Assistant is a dialog box (shown in Figure 5.7) that will tell you what words Search will find using the search option and the word you specify. This gives you an opportunity to try out a search word without actually performing a full search.

Figure 5.7
The Word Assistant dialog box

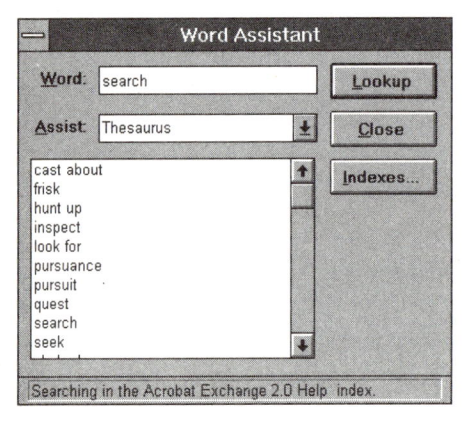

The Word Assistant is a modeless dialog box—it will stay open allowing you to switch back and forth between it and the Search dialog box. Looking at the results of using a word in the Word Assistant dialog box can give you an idea of how to refine your search, without forcing you to wade through every match that the search option would find in your documents. You can then construct a search expression using the interesting words you found with Word Assistant.

NOTE: *Word Assistant can only return words from indexes built with the Word Stemming and Sounds Like options enabled. If some of the indexes you are using were not built with support for Word Stemming or Sounds Like, then Word Assistant will not be able to return words from those indexes. Word Assistant always supports the Thesaurus option.*

To use Word Assistant, first select the type of search you want to perform. You can select from Word Stemming, Sounds Like, or Thesaurus. Enter the word you want to search for and press the Lookup button. The results are displayed in the list box. If there is only a single entry (the word you are searching for), the index may not have been created with support for the search option you specified. In that case, you cannot use Word Assistant.

The Thesaurus is always available for your use in Word Assistant. To use it effectively, use only the root of the word you are searching for. For example, the word *looking* does not turn up any results in Word Assistant, but *look* finds many matching entries in the Thesaurus.

Using Word Stemming

The Word Stemming option works a lot like a wildcard pattern based on the root of the word you specify in the search expression box. Word Stemming finds plurals, past tense, and other variations of the word you specify, as long as they share the same root word. For example, searching for *bookmark* finds *bookmarks* and *bookmark's*.

However, Word Stemming is not really very smart about the language you are using. For example, Word Stemming doesn't allow the search word *use* to find instances of the word *using*, even though they are grammatical relatives. To find both *use* and *using*, you must search with a wildcard: *us**. Word Stemming also excludes matching words ending in *-er*, even when they do have the same stem. Word

Stemming only works with single words specified in the Find Results Containing Text box of the Search dialog box; it does not work with text in Document Info fields.

Using Thesaurus

The Thesaurus option finds words that have similar meanings to the one word you specify. The search engine has the Thesaurus built into it, much like a contemporary word processor. If you've ever used a thesaurus, you know that many words in the thesaurus will have divergent meanings. The result in a search is that the Thesaurus option may return matches against words that are unrelated to the meaning you want. If you don't want to look through a lot of unwanted matches, try using the Word Assistant to see what words the Thesaurus option will try to match against in your document. You can manually trim the list by forming a Boolean OR expression out of a select few synonyms of the word you are searching for, as listed by Word Assistant, rather than using the full power of the Thesaurus to search your document.

Using Sounds Like

The Sounds Like option is useful when you are unsure of the spelling of a word you want to search for. However, this option, even more than the Thesaurus, can lead to many spurious or uninteresting matches. You can trim the search by using Word Assistant to see which words will be matched using the Sounds Like option before you start your search.

Using Acrobat Catalog

Acrobat Catalog is the tool you use to enable your users to conduct a full-text search of your documents. Catalog builds a list of all the words used in the documents you index, along with the PDF files and page numbers where those words were found. You can deliver these indexes with your documents to allow any Exchange or Exchange LE user to search them. A static index can be distributed on a CD-ROM as part of a product, or you can maintain a continuously updated dynamic index of all the PDF documents in directories you select on your network. Catalog and Search can be one of the tools you use to keep up to date with all the activity in your workgroup.

Acrobat Catalog 2.0 is available only in a Windows executable version, but the newly released version 2.1 comes in both a Windows and a Macintosh version. The Macintosh version has some differences from the existing Windows version: Some menu items have been moved, and some new dialog boxes have been added for configuration. We cover both the Windows 2.0 version and the Macintosh 2.1 version in this chapter. We have not seen the Windows 2.1 version, but it should not bring any surprises. There is not yet a UNIX version of the program. However, Catalog can index PDF files created on any machine.

Creating an Index

To begin using Catalog, you must first create an index parameter file (a .PDX file). In Windows, select the Index | New menu item (on a Macintosh, its the File | New menu item) to bring up the dialog box shown in Figure 5.8 (for Windows; the Mac is similar). The Index Title field names the document collection that you are indexing; this name appears in Acrobat Search's Index Selection dialog box when the user selects an index for searching. The Index Description allows you to specify what options you used to create the index, as well as elaborate on the documents specified in the index. It's a good idea to tell the user what stopwords you are using, if any, and whether the index supports Word Stemming and Sounds Like. If your stopword list is long, you can either paste it into the description from the clipboard, or supply it as an extra PDF file and refer to the file here.

Figure 5.8
The New Index Definition dialog box

Use the Save As button to save the index on disk. Note that saving the index does not make it ready to use in a search; to do that, you have to use the Build button to build the indexes. If you use the Build button to construct an index before you have saved it, the Save As dialog box will be brought up for you. The path and file name you choose is important for several reasons:

- The files you plan to index must be on the same drive or volume where the index is stored.

- The index file name becomes the name of the subdirectory where the search database is stored.

- The directory you put the index file in will become the parent directory of the search database.

Catalog version 2.0 will not properly save index files in directories that do not have standard 8.3 (MS-DOS) directory names. The names should only use standard letters and numbers; Macintosh users in particular must avoid using directory and file names with high-ANSI characters in them (accented characters and other similar characters with codes greater than 127). In version 2.1, this requirement has been relaxed for the Macintosh version of Catalog, but it is an issue for mixed computing environments. Windows users may not be able to retrieve documents specified with Macintosh file names.

Choose a location for your index with enough disk space to hold the files and the index—and on a network drive if you expect to share the index over the network. You can estimate disk space requirements for the index from the size of your PDF files and some knowledge of their contents. If the PDF files are pure text, plan on the index requiring half the amount of disk space your PDF files use. This is for an index that uses common stopwords and excludes numbers. If your files have a lot of pictures in them, they will use less space; dense text will use more space. Add an additional 10 percent of the total PDF file size for each of the following:

- Not using any stopwords
- Including numbers
- Enabling options for Word Stemming, Sounds Like, or Case Sensitive searches

Make sure there is additional room for your index to grow in size if you plan to revise your documents or add new documents.

Specifying Documents to Index

You do not have to name specific documents for Catalog to process—instead you name directories where Catalog should look for files. Catalog will process all the PDF files it finds in the directories you include. To add a directory, select the Add button in the Include Directories section of the Index Definition dialog box (see Figure 5.8). Not only the directory you select, but all of its subdirectories as well, will be searched for PDF files to index. Use the Exclude Directories section to exclude specific subdirectories of the directories you add to the index.

Remember that all the files you index must be on the same drive as the index itself. (One exception: Macintosh version 2.1 of Catalog offers the option of using different drives; see Catalog Preferences below.) Catalog stores paths for accessing these files relative to the location of the index, rather than absolute paths beginning with a disk or volume name. This makes the index easy to move along with the PDF files themselves; just make sure you do not change the locations of any of the PDF files relative to the index file without running Catalog again. For a small set of documents (less than 25), putting them all in one directory with the index is the practical thing to do. For larger document collections using subdirectories, the index should be located at the top level of the subdirectory tree.

Catalog can be sensitive to the names of PDF files and directories you ask it to index. When using the Windows version of Catalog, names should always follow the MS-DOS file naming conventions even if they come from a Macintosh. The Macintosh version can handle Macintosh path names, but indexes containing these paths are not always portable to Windows users. Networks in particular do not handle file names in a consistent, portable manner. Catalog indexes will work reliably in mixed environments only if you use the lowest common denominator MS-DOS conventions for your PDF file names and the directories (folders) that hold them.

A bug in Catalog version 2.0 will not allow you to index two directories if one directory's name is a proper prefix of the other. For example, if you specified K:\DIR1 as a directory to index, you cannot also specify K:\DIR11; Catalog will erroneously tell you that DIR11 is already included in the index. The only work-around is to name your directories differently.

Guidelines for Choosing Index Options

Press the Options button on the Index Definition dialog box to bring up the Options dialog box. At the top of the dialog box is a section labeled *Words to not include in index*. The list box in this section contains the list of stopwords defined for the index. To add a stopword, type the word into the Word text box and press the Add button. Remove a stopword by selecting it and pressing the Remove button.

When should you use stopwords? If disk space is not an issue for you, do not use them. Including all words makes constructing search expressions more natural for the casual user, who may not even be aware of the idea of stopwords, much less which stopwords you are using. On the other hand, if you are trying to minimize the size of your index, you can name virtually all of the "helper" words as stopwords. Usually the important search words relate to the subjects in your document and are either nouns or verbs. For best results, use your computer to obtain a list of all the words used in your document, ordered by frequency. All of the non-essential words at the top of this list should be included as stopwords.

The same principle applies to including numbers in your index. If disk space is not a problem, users will find it much more natural to use numbers in their search expressions, so include them in your index. Also, numbers may not be a particularly significant part of your document, so you might want to include them for the convenience of the user even if you suffer from size constraints. On the other hand, you may be publishing a set of spreadsheets where numbers are a significant factor in the file size, but searching for particular numbers will not make a lot of sense. Exclude numbers by checking the *Do not include numbers* check box.

In the next section, labeled *Word Options*, you can select support for Word Stemming, Sounds Like, and Case Sensitive searches. Again, go ahead and enable these if you don't have to worry about file size. If you do worry, the only truly unique option here is Sounds Like. Word Stemming can be replaced by using wildcards in your search expressions (in fact wildcards are more flexible). Case sensitivity is rarely going to be an important factor in refining a search. On the other hand, the Sounds Like option has no other search counterpart, and it helps users who cannot spell properly find what they are looking for in your documents.

At the bottom of the Options dialog are two check boxes. Optimize for CD-ROM makes small reductions in the size of the index files by assuming that they will not be updated (since a CD-ROM is still a read-only device for most of us, the option will usually be used with this device, but it can also be used for an index located on a regular hard disk, as long as it is never updated). The second check box is for backward compatibility with Acrobat version 1.0 PDF files. Check this box if you are using PDF files created with Acrobat version 1.0 Distiller or PDF Writer.

Building and Rebuilding an Index

After entering all of the options described in the last section, you are ready to build an index. Just click the Build button in the New Index Definition dialog box to start the build. Catalog will display its running status in its main window. If you need to stop the build for some reason, click the Stop button in the center of the window. When the build is complete, Catalog will print "Index Build Successful" as the last line of the Messages field.

When you add new PDF files to your document collection, or change files using Exchange, you will need to index the new or modified files to incorporate them into a search. If you don't need to change the index options, just move the PDF files into your target

Using Acrobat Catalog 157

directories, and use the Index | Build command to select the index and build it. The index will be updated for every file that is new or has changed, based on the file's modification date in its directory. You can also schedule regular builds of your indexes with the Index | Schedule menu (see below).

If you want to change your index parameters, select Index | Open (or File | Open for Macintosh users) to select the index file. The same dialog box you used to create the index is displayed. You can change any of the options you want, or add or delete new directories for indexing. If you change an option, you must delete the old index and rebuild it; Catalog cannot incrementally change the index options. Catalog will give you a warning message that the index must be purged and rebuilt when you save the index file.

Macintosh Catalog users also have a new feature they can use to index a folder of PDF files. You can drag a folder from the desktop and drop it onto Catalog, and Catalog will index the files it finds in the folder and its subfolders, using the default index options to create the index. You set the defaults for both index options and drop folders in the Edit | Preferences menu (see below).

Purging an Index

Purging an index means deleting the contents of the index in preparation for rebuilding it. There are two circumstances when you would want to purge an index. First, when you change some index parameters, Catalog will inform you that you need to purge and rebuild the index for the parameters to take effect. Second, if you have been adding new documents and rebuilding your index without purging, then purging and rebuilding is a way to restore your index to top efficiency. Purging clears away all of the incremental updates to your index and starts the index from scratch.

There are two ways to accomplish purging. The first and quickest way is simply to delete the files yourself—but you can only use this method if you are not sharing the index with someone else (or your own copy of Exchange). You can use a delete command that operates over subdirectories, and delete the entire subdirectory tree that Catalog created for your index (but don't delete the .PDX file where your index parameters are stored). Remember that the index subdirectory has the same name as the index file, but with no extension.

The second way is to use Catalog to purge the index. Select the Index | Purge menu command from the Catalog menu bar; you will see a standard file selection box. Select the index you want to purge. Catalog takes about 15 minutes to complete purging the index (the waiting time can be changed—see "Preferences"). Most of this is time spent waiting for other possible users to complete any searches they may be doing. To prevent errors, the index files are not deleted until Catalog is reasonably sure that the indexes are not being used. When it is done purging, select Index | Build to rebuild the index.

Sometimes a purge operation will fail with an error message. This can happen when an Exchange user's machine crashes or is turned off without exiting Exchange properly (and releasing the index). You have to find the offending machine and reboot it to release the files.

Automating Index Builds

Catalog can automatically perform index builds for you on a set of index files. Several indexes can be batched together in a job and executed immediately, after a certain time interval you specify, or continuously. This is a very convenient feature for rebuilding indexes automatically at night or on the weekends. All you have to do manually is purge your indexes every so often to maintain their efficiency and let the automatic rebuild keep them up to date.

Select the menu item Index | Schedule to bring up the dialog box shown in Figure 5.9 (Windows version). At the top of the dialog box is a list of indexes that will be built on the schedule. Use the Add button to select index files to add to the list. Use the Remove button

Using Acrobat Catalog   159

to delete highlighted list members. At the bottom of the dialog box are the scheduling options:

- *Continuously.* Constantly looks for new files within the directories in your index.

- *Once.* Indexes all of the named files one time.

- *Every.* Establishes a regular schedule for indexing. Select a time unit (Minutes, Hours, or Days) and enter the number of time periods between builds in the text entry box. Use the Starting At field to establish a starting time for the first build; if you do not use this option, the first build starts immediately.

Figure 5.9
The Schedule Builds dialog box

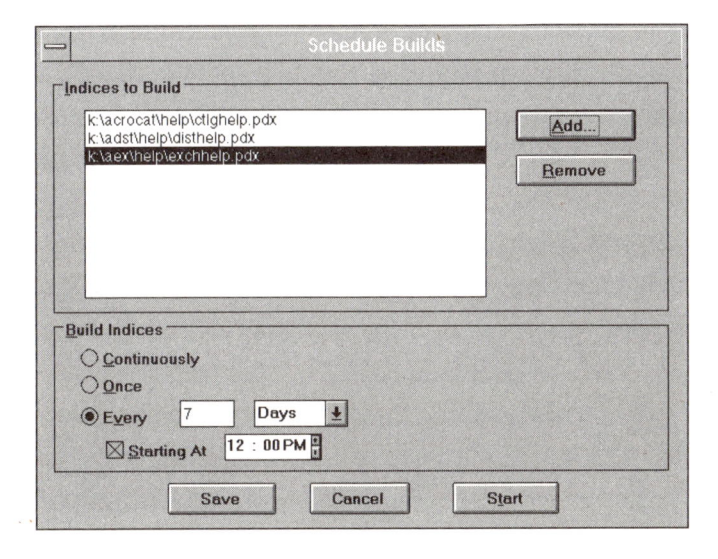

Click Start to start the build schedule. Unless you have specified the Every option with a starting time, the first index build starts immediately. Click Save to save the schedule without starting it. Catalog will not index other files while a schedule is active; if you try to use the New, Open, Build, or Purge menu items, Catalog will ask you to stop the schedule first.

NOTE: *You must leave Catalog running on a computer 24 hours a day after you start the schedule for scheduled builds to be performed. Catalog will not start itself at the right time in the schedule—it must remain running. Catalog reminds you of this if you try to quit the program while a schedule is active. If Catalog is terminated by some other means (e.g. power failure), you must restart the schedule by hand; it will not restart itself automatically.*

Errors in the Build

Sometimes you may get errors in your index build. Catalog may finish with the message "Index Build Failed." If this happens, don't panic; check the log file that Catalog creates. Catalog maintains a running log file in its home directory called ACROCAT.LOG. You should find the status of the last indexing operation at the end of the log file.

A common error message is "Insufficient memory to perform operation." Catalog wants a lot of memory to build the index file—at least 8MB of RAM, more if your document collection is large. If you are running other programs on your machine, Catalog may not be able to allocate enough memory to do its work. Kill other programs running on your machine so that Catalog is the only program running, then try the build again.

With network file collections, you may have problems with file ownership and attributes that prevent Catalog from accessing the files. Make sure that the machine Catalog is running on has access to all the files; are they protected, either by ownership or file attributes, from being read by Catalog, or are they being edited by someone else? Catalog also has to have write access to its home directory to write the log file, and to the index subdirectories to write the index. If you are using Acrobat version 1.x PDF files, Catalog wants to write to these files as well.

The Windows version of Catalog requires that you run the MS-DOS SHARE.EXE program to allow it to coordinate file sharing with other computers on the network. If you get the message "Failed after 1 attempts to lock file," this means you don't have SHARE properly installed. Normally you should add this file to your AUTOEXEC.BAT file so that it is loaded whenever your computer starts up.

Guidelines for Preparing Documents for Indexing

Technically, there is only one requirement your PDF files must meet in order to be used with Catalog: they must not be protected by a password. Catalog will not index files that have been secured with a password, so if you contemplate using this security feature, you must use Catalog first, then establish the password for the file.

The usefulness of your index can be enhanced if you take a few steps to prepare your files. First, consider the size of your PDF files. If you are indexing a huge PDF file, you and your users will be better off if you break the file up into smaller pieces. For example, in a book, it is better to make each chapter a separate PDF file. This helps the user narrow his search for information—he can see the search results returned for several chapters, and maybe some of them can be eliminated from consideration just by looking at their titles in the Search Results dialog box.

Another reason to keep your file size small is that the file size Catalog can index is limited by the amount of RAM memory available when Catalog is running. If your file is really big and Catalog encounters this limitation, Catalog will automatically break it up into pieces itself. See the section below on Catalog Preferences for a discussion.

The other thing you can do to enhance your index is to make consistent use of the Document Info fields. Encourage your authors to fill in these fields. If you are preparing a set of PDF files for publication (on a CD-ROM, for example), spend some extra time making the Document Info fields informative and consistent. By default, PDF

Writer and Distiller put the file name into the Title field—but this is not really very useful information. Spend a little time with Exchange and your document set to enter real titles for each PDF file. While you're at it, check the Author, Subject, and Keywords fields too. Consider using custom Document Info fields to enhance search capabilities if you have more information you could include (see below).

Choose values for fields like Subject and Keywords to use consistently throughout your document collection. Without consistency in these fields, searching with them becomes a waste of time. Used properly, they can help your clients eliminate whole documents full of unwanted matches from their search results, a big time saver when searching a large document collection.

Using Custom Document Information Fields

You do not have to settle for the Document Information (Doc Info) fields provided by Acrobat. You can create and name your own fields to contain almost any information you like (examples: ProjectName, ISBN, DocumentID, or CopyrightOwner). You can teach Catalog the names of the custom fields you create, and Catalog will index them along with the rest of your document. These fields can be accessed through Acrobat Search and used in a query just like the regular Doc Info fields.

If you intend to use custom fields, you must create them in your PDF files before starting to build your index. However, Exchange by itself does not display custom Document Info fields, nor does it let you enter your own. There are several alternatives for creating them: You can use the pdfmark operator with Distiller (described in Chapter 10), or you can use a plug-in module or a separate program designed for the purpose, or you can use Exchange's interapplication communication facilities. Adobe provides a plug-in with the free SDK that allows you to add Doc Info fields from a list specified in a file; see Chapter 7 for a discussion. There is also a shareware program for Windows called PIE (for *PDF Info Editor*) that allows you to interactively edit the contents of any Doc Info field, or create new ones on demand; it is available for download from Adobe forums on CompuServe. You can also add and modify Doc Info fields with AppleScript on the Macintosh, or OLE Automation under Windows (see Chapter 8).

Once you have created custom Doc Info fields in your PDF files, you need to tell Catalog about them. On the Windows platform, you do this by editing the ACROCAT.INI file (found in the \WINDOWS directory). Find the section labeled [Fields] (which may be empty or not exist; if it doesn't exist, create it). After this line, add lines in the following format:

```
Field0=CustomFieldName,DataType
```

Each line you enter will start with the word *Field* suffixed with a number. Start with zero and use numbers sequentially until you have entered all of your custom fields. Catalog finds these entries in the file by searching for Field0, then Field1, and so on, and if it does not find an entry for a field with the next consecutive number, it stops looking for custom fields.

The CustomFieldName should be replaced with the name of your custom Document Info field. The name of your field should be a single word (that is, no spaces). The DataType should be one of the following values:

- *Int.* For integer values (numbers from 0 to 65535).

- *Date.* For date values. The value must correspond to a date format as specified in the *PDF Reference Manual.*

- *Str.* For string or text values. This will handle any string of characters up to 256 characters long. All the predefined Document Info fields (such as Author) are of this type.

After you edit the ACROCAT.INI file, you must restart Catalog so that it will read the file. Then you can index the document collection and your custom Doc Info fields will be added to the index. If you have already previously indexed this collection, purge the index and rebuild it rather than incrementally updating it.

On the Macintosh (with version 2.1), life is a bit easier. The Edit | Preferences menu item brings up the Catalog Preferences dialog box, shown in Figure 5.10, which contains a new selection called Custom Fields. Click on the left side to select Custom Fields and the right side of the dialog box will display the editing controls for defining your custom fields. You will find a list of field names already defined (if any), and a text field called Field Name. Enter the names of your custom fields in this box (one at a time). For each field, select a data type from the pop-up list labeled Field Types. You have the same choices as above: Integer, Date, or String. You must make sure the data type you specify here matches the actual type entered in the file; String is a good choice if you are not sure (all the default Doc Info fields are strings). Press the Add button to add the field name and type to the Custom Fields list. After entering your fields, purge and rebuild the index.

Catalog Preferences

Catalog has a number of preference items, some of which affect how indexes are structured. On the Windows version (in Acrobat 2.0), where these preferences are available, they are entered in the ACROCAT.INI file in your \WINDOWS directory. In the Macintosh version (Acrobat 2.1), there are dialog boxes to allow you to modify these values directly; they are available from the Edit | Preferences menu. We'll review each of these dialog boxes and the fields they contain in this section, along with the names used in the Windows version so you can edit your own ACROCAT.INI file (except for the custom Document Info fields, which we covered above).

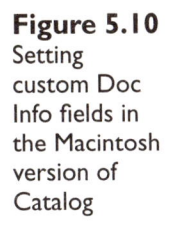

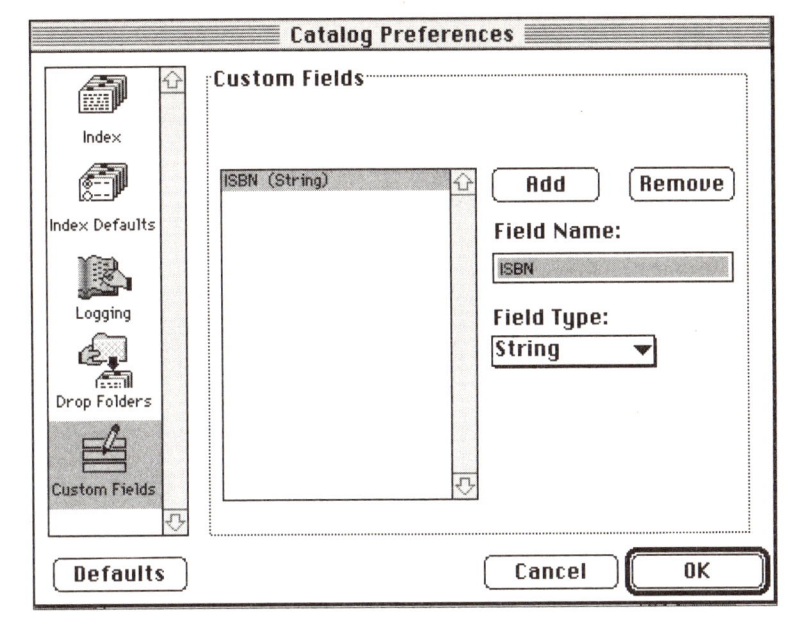

Figure 5.10
Setting custom Doc Info fields in the Macintosh version of Catalog

Index Preferences

The Index Preferences control parameters for creating an index and making it available for searching; these are probably the most important (and most technical) preference items. Figure 5.11 shows the Macintosh Index Preferences dialog box.

Time Before Purge   The first entry, Time Before Purge, sets the amount of time Catalog will wait for Exchange clients to release a search index before Catalog will purge it. The default value of 905 seconds (15 minutes) reflects Adobe's experience with its clients on a variety of networks, and is a safe value. You can reduce this value, but it makes more sense to purge your indexes when no one else is using them, in which case you can simply delete the index folder or directory (see "Purging an Index"). The Windows .INI file name for this value is PurgeTime, located in the [options] section of the file.

Figure 5.11
The Catalog Preferences - Index dialog box for Macintosh

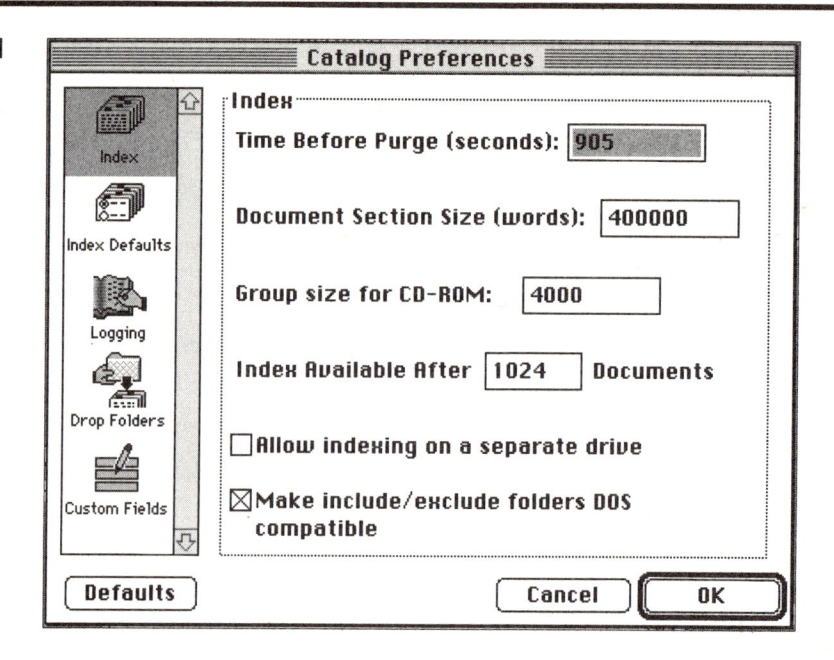

[Catalog Preferences dialog box showing:
- Time Before Purge (seconds): 905
- Document Section Size (words): 400000
- Group size for CD-ROM: 4000
- Index Available After 1024 Documents
- ☐ Allow indexing on a separate drive
- ☒ Make include/exclude folders DOS compatible]

Document Section Size   The second field, Document Section Size (words), is affected by how much memory you have in your computer for Catalog to use. The entry actually governs how Catalog handles documents that are too large to index in their entirety. Of course, your best bet is to break your files into small pieces yourself so you do not run into Catalog limitations (your users will be grateful); however, if you think you have no choice in the matter, then this option may affect you. Catalog will split your file (if necessary) into separate pieces for indexing purposes, and the size it chooses is the number of words specified by the Document Section Size value. A file with more than this number of words will have two (or more) indexes created for it; these will appear as separate entries in your Search Results list when you search the file. This may be somewhat confusing to your users, which is why it is best to find a natural boundary and split the file yourself rather than relying on the arbitrary division performed by Capture.

On the other hand, you may have more RAM available on the machine you use to run Catalog, allowing you to index larger documents. As a rule of thumb, you need free RAM equal to ten times the number of words you want to index. The default value for the Macintosh version of Catalog is 400,000 words, which requires 4MB of RAM. You can adjust this value for the amount of free RAM available on the machine running Catalog. (If you are running other memory-hog programs like Distiller on the same machine, you may need to quit those programs to make more free memory available.)

The Windows version of Catalog (version 2.0) has the same problem but it provides a slightly different mechanism for determining the value of the section size. The program maintains a value for a large, medium, or small section, and you set the values for these different sizes and then choose which one to use. The ACROCAT.INI file contains four fields in the [options] section (you may add them if they are not present):

- DocumentWordSectionsLarge=*number*

- DocumentWordSectionsMedium=*number*

- DocumentWordSectionsSmall=*number*

- DocumentWordSectionsSelection=*number*

The first three entries specify three different index sizes in words. The last entry specifies which index model to use (Large = 2, Medium = 1, and Small = 0). You may find it more convenient to stick with one model and set its size to reflect the amount of RAM you have available (using the same ten times the number of words formula), rather than choosing different selections for different files.

Group Sizes   Catalog is capable of handling large numbers of documents in an online database. Catalog batches files into groups and updates an index after processing the number of files in the group before going on. The group size controls the trade-off between how long you must wait for a batch of files and how long it takes to compile the entire index (also how much space the index takes up). Catalog provides two different group sizes, for two different needs: Group size for CD-ROM and Index Available After ___ Documents. These entries in the Macintosh dialog box have corresponding Windows .INI file values: GroupSizeforCDROM and IndexAvailableGroupSize, both in the [options] section of the ACROCAT.INI file.

The idea is that offline document databases, like those developed for CD-ROMs, do not require that the index be available before Catalog has completed the entire document collection, so the group size is set large (4,000 files by default). This makes the build run faster and results in a more compact index for the entire collection. On the other hand, for large online document collections (especially those that are continuously updated), it may be very inconvenient to wait for Catalog to finish before making the index available. The Index Available field controls the group size for online databases (an online database is assumed when you have not specified the Optimize for CD-ROM setting in the index options). This number is set by default to 1,024 files, meaning that every time Catalog finishes updating this number of files, it stops building new indexes long enough to make the index for the group available.

There are two circumstances where you might want to change these values. If you have an online database that you are updating continuously, then you may want to adjust the Index Available option to specify a smaller number of files, thus increasing the availability of your index. On the other hand, if you are using Catalog only during off hours, then you may want to increase the Index Available number, since it makes Catalog more efficient. The CD-ROM option is probably best left alone.

Disk and File Options   By default, Catalog requires an index to live on the same disk drive (or volume) as the files it indexes. This is necessary for index portability. In version 2.0 of Catalog, this was the only option. However, in version 2.1 on the Macintosh, you can cause Catalog to accept files stored on other disks by checking the Allow indexing on a separate drive check box. Indexes created with this option do not use relative path names to find files, which makes it difficult to move either the files or the index to a new location.

If you think you have a permanent setup for your document collection, you may want to use this option because it lets you index a larger collection of files spread out over more disks. Do not use this option with any index that you plan to move or redistribute with your files, as it probably will not work when installed in a different place.

An alternative to spreading your files over several disks is to put them on a network server where logical volumes can span disk drives (that is, you can increase the size of your disk volume by adding a new physical disk to the server, and adding its space to the existing volume). Novell Netware offers this feature, and others may as well.

The Macintosh version also offers another unique option: Make include/exclude folders DOS compatible. Whenever the files you index are in separate folders (directories), Catalog must store folder names to find the files. If the files are stored on a Macintosh file system, it is very likely the names will not be MS-DOS compatible, since MS-DOS requires a directory name to be only eight uppercase alphanumeric characters long (with an optional period and three character extension). Catalog can store the original Macintosh names, but MS-DOS users will not be able to find the files with Search if only the Macintosh names are indexed. This option allows you to include in the index the directory names MS-DOS users would need to find the files properly. Unless you are creating indexes for an exclusively Macintosh clientele, you should leave this option checked.

Index Defaults

The Index Defaults section of the Preferences dialog box (for Macintosh) simply provides default values for the options available when you create an index (see Figure 5.12). You can set these options to reflect your standard procedures. See the section above called "Guidelines for Choosing Index Options" for a discussion of appropriate values for these options. The default options are also used for folders dropped on the Catalog window (Macintosh version 2.1 only).

Figure 5.12
The Catalog Preferences - Index Defaults dialog box for Macintosh

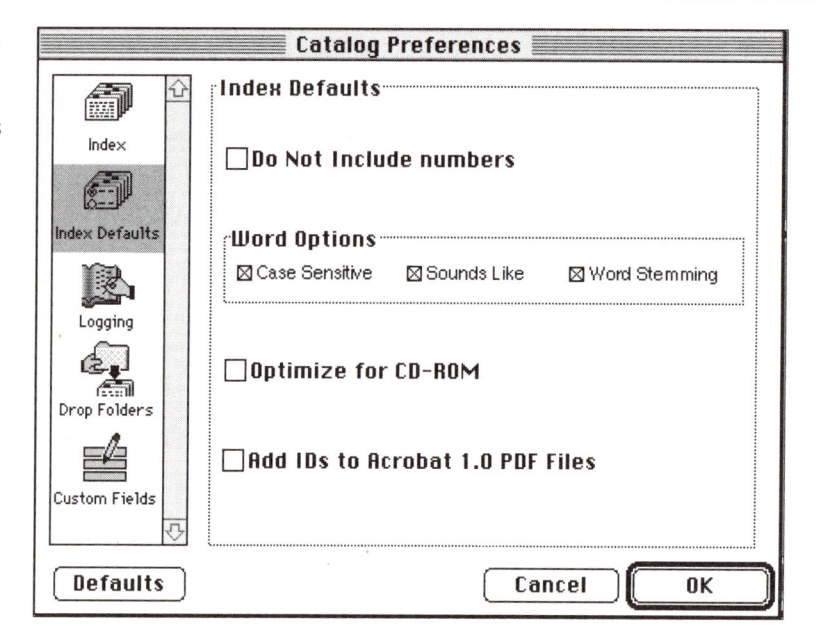

Logging

Catalog maintains a log file where it writes all the processing messages you see scrolling past you during an index build. In version 2.0 for Windows, this logging happened automatically to the file ACRO-CAT.LOG, which was kept in the Catalog home directory (usually

\ACROCAT). The Macintosh version of Catalog 2.1 offers more options, as shown in Figure 5.13. You can disable logging entirely, or control the kinds of messages that appear in the log file. Search engine messages are produced by the Verity search engine that underlies Catalog, while compatibility warnings concern files whose names or paths are not MS-DOS compatible.

Figure 5.13
The Catalog Preferences - Logging dialog box

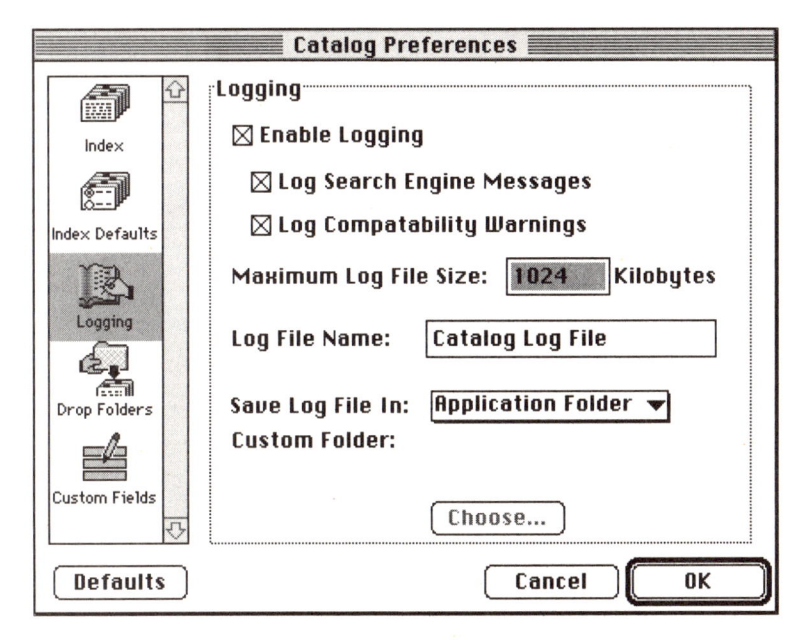

The Maximum Log File Size option controls how large the log file becomes before Catalog wraps the file to the beginning. The default is 1MB (or 1,024KB). You may want to reduce this size if you monitor the log file on a regular basis. This is the one option in this dialog box which has a Windows correlate: the ACROCAT.INI file contains a variable named MaxLogFileSize in the [options] section. In this instance, you specify a number in bytes, not kilobytes.

Chapter 5: Indexing and Searching PDF Documents

The remaining preference options control the name of the log file and where it is located. If you want to view the log file from Windows, you may want to give it an MS-DOS compatible file name instead of the default *Catalog Log File*. The Application Folder option for the Save Log File in field refers to Catalog's home folder, the other option is a custom folder you specify. Select the Choose button to specify the folder.

Drop Folders

A new feature in the Macintosh version of Catalog is the ability to drop a folder onto Catalog from the desktop and have Catalog index all of the PDF files in the folder (and its subfolders). In the Index Defaults section above, you set the indexing options Catalog will use for dropped folders. In this section you set other options (see Figure 5.14):

- *Default Index Name.* The name Catalog will use for the index it creates (if one is not present).

Figure 5.14
The Catalog Preferences - Drop Folders dialog box (Macintosh version)

- *Save Index.* Choose whether to save the index within the folder you have dropped or elsewhere.

- *Delete existing indexes.* If the folder already contains an index, Catalog will update the index unless this option is checked. With this option checked, Catalog deletes the old index and rebuilds it.

Summary

In this chapter we've gone full circle with the full-text search capabilites of Acrobat, from how to conduct a search to how to prepare and index documents for searching. We've described the differences between the Windows and Macintosh versions of Catalog, and how to create portable indexes. In the next chapter, we take a look at the latest Acrobat component, Capture, which allows you to scan a document and turn it into a PDF file you can index and search.

CHAPTER

6

Acrobat Capture

Capture Overview
Setting Up Capture
Using Capture
Using Reviewer

Capture Overview

Up until now, all of the Acrobat tools we have examined have been focused on creating PDF files from existing electronic documents. In this chapter we examine the newest member of the Acrobat toolkit, a program that lets you convert paper documents to electronic documents with built-in Optical Character Recognition technology. With Acrobat Capture and a scanner you can convert existing paper documents into a variety of electronic document formats, including PDF documents that preserve the look and feel of the original, or files in popular word processor formats.

Capture Overview

Acrobat Capture provides for all phases of document recognition, from scanning the image, to interactively correcting the text conversion errors, to producing the output file using two programs: Capture and Reviewer. Capture controls the process of scanning and converting image files to an output file format, while Reviewer lets you examine the results of text conversion and make the changes you need to correct any errors.

The Capture main window displays most of the whole process pictorially (see Figure 6.1). In the upper-left corner is a list of scanners (or really scanner device drivers, since you can have more than one configuration for a scanner). The scanner list is connected to two lists of directories: the input folders and the output folders. In each of these three lists, the currently selected item is highlighted with a white box. Each of the folders provides a directory listing displaying the contents of the currently selected folder to the right of the list.

The Scan button starts the scanner device driver to create a scanner source image file in an input folder; the currently selected scanner and input folder are used. The Process button takes an image file

Figure 6.1
The main Capture window

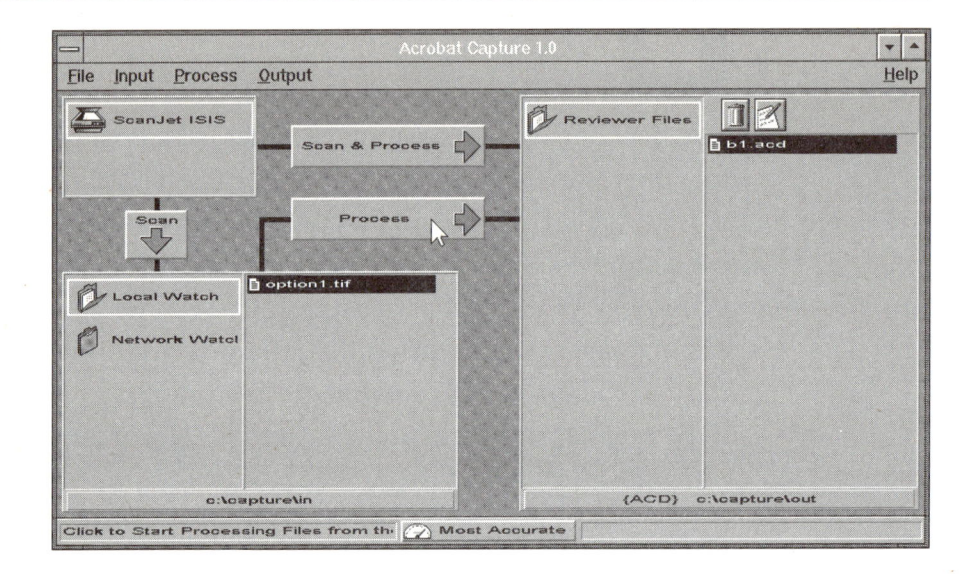

from the current input folder, performs text conversion, and writes it into a file in the current output folder. The Scan and Process button uses the currently selected scanner to generate an image, then it processes the image into a file in the current output folder.

The output folder directory list has two buttons at the top of the directory listing: a trash can button that deletes the selected file, and a pencil button that begins editing the selected file. Capture uses Windows's file associations to find the editor for the file you select (if you do not have an editor for the file type, you get an error message from Windows). The Reviewer uses a special file format with the extension .ACD, and of course Exchange or Reader handles PDF files.

Reviewer works by displaying the results of Capture's processing and the original bitmap image simultaneously in a window. Reviewer gives you options for highlighting words that are likely to be in error, and allows you to step from one of these suspect words to the next quickly. You can make corrections to the page, then produce the output file you really want (PDF or word processor) using Reviewer's Save As menu item.

Requirements

Capture requires a lot of system resources to work effectively. You need at least 16MB of real physical RAM, and a Windows 3.1 permanent swap file of 20MB for 8½-by-11-inch page scans, more if the pages are larger. Adobe suggests 20MB plus twice the size of your image file. Capture also requires some additional free space on your hard disk for its temporary use (at least twice the size of your image file)—this location is configured in the Capture Preferences dialog box (see below).

Capture comes with its own version of PDF Writer, which you should install even if you already have PDF Writer 2.0, because the Capture version is newer. You should not have this problem with PDF Writer 2.1. Capture installs version 3.0.1 of Adobe Type Manager if it is not installed already. You also need to run the MS-DOS SHARE.EXE program before you start Windows 3.1, or call for the VSHARE.386 Windows driver in your SYSTEM.INI file.

Reviewer also requires a lot of memory to run; if you are running other big programs alongside these two, do not be surprised if you get an occasional out of memory error from Windows when you try to launch a new program. In Windows 3.1, increase your swap file size using the Control Panel (even beyond Windows recommended maximum size—ignore the message from Windows saying that it will not use the extra memory). Due to shortcomings in the design of the original PC, you can also run out of memory below 1MB. Reviewer in particular claims a lot of lower memory. You should suspect this problem if you get insufficient memory error messages but a check of free memory shows that you seem to have plenty of it (most larger apps display free memory resources in their Help | About dialog boxes). In this case, it is helpful to obtain a program to control access to this memory (such as FIX1MB.EXE, available from the Microsoft Software Library on CompuServe and elsewhere). If you meet the minimum system resource requirements listed above, and you do not try to do other things simultaneously with this computer, you should not have memory problems.

Accessing the Scanner

Capture comes with a set of ISIS (Image and Scanner Interface Standard) scanner drivers for popular high-end scanners. These drivers support automatic document feeders and double-sided input pages where available. Adobe recommends using an ISIS driver if one is available for your scanner. Adobe provides drivers for the following scanners on the Capture 1.0 installation disks:

- Canon IX-4015, IX-3010 with ASPI
- Canon IX-4015, IX-3010 with SI4
- Epson GT-4000 to GT-8000 and ES-300C to ES-800C
- Fujitsu M3096Gm / M3097Gm
- Fujitsu SP10 / SP Jr
- Hewlett Packard AccuPage Technology 2.0
- HP ScanJet, ScanJet Plus, IIC, IIP, or IIcx
- KOFAX Kipp 2.0 (BIC) Driver (Simplex Only)
- Microtek ScanMaker II or IISP with Microtek PCZ card
- Microtek ScanMaker IIHR or III with ASPI
- Microtek ScanMaker IIHR or III with Microtex PCZ SCSI
- Microtek ScanMaker IIHR or III with Microtex PNR SCSI
- Microtek Scanner with Microtex PCX or PXY card

Capture Overview 179

- Ricoh IS-410 and IBM 2456
- Ricoh IS-50 and IS-60
- UMAX Scanner with ADF

Adobe is planning to make additional drivers available. Check with the Adobe online sources listed in Chapter 1. Capture can also use the TWAIN scanner drivers provided by many scanner manufacturers. TWAIN drivers offer previews of the scan (a feature not provided by ISIS drivers), but Adobe recommends using the ISIS drivers when you have a choice.

If your scanner is not supported by ISIS or TWAIN, then you can use software that comes with your scanner to produce files in a compatible format for Capture to process. Compatible formats are:

- TIFF (using Group 3, Group 4, or LZW compression)
- PCX
- BMP

Output Files

Capture converts the scanned image into an output file in one or more file formats. Capture can preserve the paper document exactly as scanned by using Acrobat PDF as the output format. Options allow you to save three different kinds of PDF file:

- *Normal.* Anything that can be converted to text is stored and displayed as text, with nontext regions saved as bitmap graphics.
- *Image Only.* The original image is saved without any text conversion.
- *Image + Text.* The entire original image is saved for displaying, but text conversion is performed and the text can be searched.

Capture can also create files in formats recognized by popular word processing applications, including:

- ASCII plain text.
- Ami Pro versions 1.x, 2.0, and 3.0
- Microsoft Word for Windows versions 2.0 through 6.0
- Microsoft Word for Macintosh version 5.0
- Rich Text Format (ANSI character set)
- WordPerfect for Windows versions 5.x, 6.0, and 6.1

Capture preserves text formatting within the document for all but plain text files (which contain no formatting). Capture also saves graphics within the word processor format files, and tries to preserve layout, but may not be able to if the layout is complex.

Capture also writes files in the ACD, or Capture Reviewer format. From Reviewer you can write to any of the other supported file formats. You will want to use Reviewer to optimize the text conversion process, adjust the boundaries of text and graphic regions, and display suspect words, allowing you to correct them before producing your final output.

Text Conversion

As Capture identifies words during the text conversion process, it gives each word a score that relates to the degree of confidence Capture has in its result. Using Reviewer you can view all words whose score falls below a level you set (the *word confidence threshold*). These low-scoring words are called *suspect words*. Reviewer lets you skip from one suspect word to the next, viewing both the original image and the converted text, and making corrections to the converted text as required. When you are finished you can write the corrected file to disk in any of the supported file formats.

One of the ways Capture verifies the correctness of a word is to look it up in the dictionary. Capture comes with a standard dictionary of English words and a custom dictionary you can add your own words to. Capture even provides a way for you to import custom dictionaries you may have already created for your word processor. Words that are not found in the dictionary can be flagged as suspect words for your review.

Capture gives you a choice between how accurately it identifies words and how much processing time it spends doing it. The options are shown in Figure 6.2, the Setup Processing Options dialog box. Our experiments show the Most Accurate setting takes anywhere from 30 to 40 percent longer than the Fastest setting. The Most Accurate setting produced from 8 to 16 percent fewer suspect words and improved character recognition, reducing the total number of errors. We prefer the Most Accurate setting for general purpose use.

Figure 6.2
The Setup Processing Options dialog box

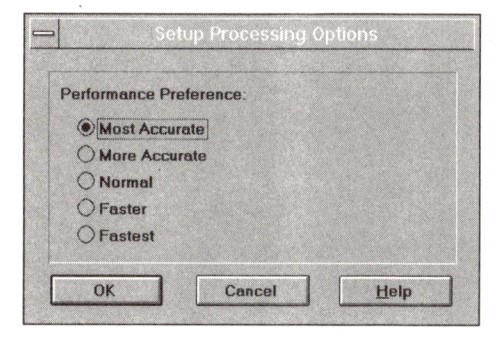

Setting Up Capture

Before you can use Capture, you must provide some setup information to the program. At the very least Capture requires definition of an output folder, because options associated with the output folder tell Capture how to proceed with text conversion. Capture creates several input and output folders when it installs, which you can alter and use. You do not have to run Capture with a scanner attached. In fact, like Distiller, you can set up Capture in a server mode where it continuously monitors a directory on your network file server and converts files found there to the currently selected output file format. Unlike Distiller, however, Capture can only monitor one directory at a time.

Capture Preferences

Capture's user preferences are set by selecting the File | Preferences menu item; this displays the dialog box shown in Figure 6.3. The confirmation check boxes allow you to require confirmation whenever Capture is about to delete a file, replace an existing file, or cancel its processing.

Figure 6.3
The Capture Preferences dialog box

The PDF Output Options relate to Capture's use of PDF Writer to write its output. This option allows you to use the Capture defaults for PDF (text and image compression options, resolution for bitmap images, and font embedding) or use your standard PDF Writer defaults. Using Capture's defaults allows you to keep different settings for users of Capture and for other users of PDF Writer.

When Show Graphical Process Feedback is set, Capture updates the display while it is processing a file. This is usually a good idea, but if you run Capture unattended you may want to disable it to save a few CPU cycles. Show Splash Screen on Startup displays the Capture logo screen as the program starts (or not).

Capture maintains log files for each job it processes. You can control automatic deletion of these log files after the number of days you specify here. Finally, you can specify the location for Capture's temporary work files. Choose a place with free space equal to at least twice the size of your input files, and ideally on a local disk (not a network disk) for speed. This space is in addition to the large virtual memory space Capture requires.

Scanner Setup

To add a new scanner to your scanner list, select the Input | Add Scanning Device menu item. To modify an existing scanner list entry, you may use your mouse to double-click it or right-click it, or select the Input | Setup Scanning Device menu item. All of these methods display the Setup Scanning Device dialog box shown in Figure 6.4.

Figure 6.4
The Setup Scanning Device dialog box

Enter whatever name you want in the Description text box; this name will appear in the scanner list. The Select Scanning Device lists all of the installed scanner device drivers on your system. ISIS drivers have an asterisk as their first character. If you do not find your scanner listed, see below to install drivers.

ISIS Drivers

You can install ISIS drivers from the Capture SETUP.EXE program located on installation disk 1. Just check the box for ISIS Drivers and leave the others unchecked.

TWAIN Drivers

The Capture installation process installs support for TWAIN drivers present at that time. If you add another driver, use the Input | Refresh Device List menu item to instruct Capture to look once more for new drivers.

Input Folders

Capture's input folders hold scanned images waiting to be processed. An input folder is the destination for an image file in a Scan step and the source of the file in a Process step. You can also use input folders as watched directories, providing Capture services to a network, or as a place to marshal all of the scans for the pages of the book you are converting. Create a new input folder using the Input | Add Input Folder menu item. This does not actually create the directory itself; you must do that first. Edit the configuration of an existing folder by either double-clicking or right-clicking it with your mouse, or selecting Input | Setup Input Folder after selecting the folder you want to edit. All of these commands bring up the Input Folder Setup dialog box (shown in Figure 6.5).

The Description field provides the input folder name that appears in the Capture window. The Location field specifies the actual

Setting Up Capture

Figure 6.5
The Input Folder Setup dialog box

directory used by the folder. The three check boxes select options that apply to all of the files in this folder:

- *Watch Folder for New Files.* Like Distiller, Capture can be set up to continuously monitor a folder and automatically process files placed there by checking this option. When this option is active, the input folder will be depicted by an icon with a pair of eyes looking at the folder name in the main window. Capture will start watching for new files when you press the Process button and the selected input folder has this option enabled.

- *Move Image to Output Area When Processed.* If you do not move them, they stay in the input folder. This option must be used when you tell Capture to watch a folder (Capture enables it automatically).

- *Collate Pages by Common Prefix.* Select this option if you are scanning a multiple-page document. When Capture scans a multiple-page document, each original page image is stored in a separate disk file. The file name used for each page file is a combination of a base name you supply (the prefix) and the page number added by Capture's scanning module. This option tells Capture to recognize those files as pages in a multiple-page document, and it combines them into a single output file. If this option is not enabled, the files will be processed as individual one-page documents.

Removing an Input Folder

You can remove a folder from Capture by selecting the folder, then selecting Input | Remove Input Folder. Capture displays the dialog box shown in Figure 6.6. Answer No and the input folder is removed from Capture. Answer Yes and the input folder is both removed and the contents of the directory are deleted. Cancel aborts the whole operation without deleting anything.

Figure 6.6 Removing a folder from Capture

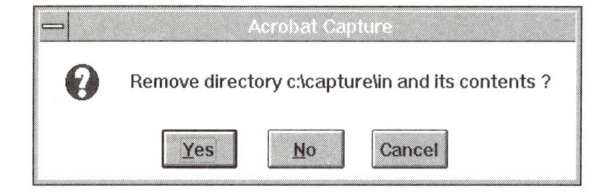

Note: If the actual directory has already been deleted, and you answer Yes to delete the directory again, the command will fail and the input folder will not be deleted. Just answer No to delete only the folder, not the directory.

Guidelines for Setting Up Input Folders

When you want to collate pages to form a document, you have two choices for doing it: You can use the Scan and Process procedure to go directly to the output folder, or you can complete all of your scans into an input folder, then process the folder. The latter usually makes more sense, because you can scan pages without waiting for Capture to perform text conversion on the page it just scanned. With scheduled processing, described below, you can set up Capture to process overnight the files you scan during the day.

Scans can be rather large, so you will need a disk big enough to collect all of the scans you need at one time. To make use of Capture's ability to collate individual scan pages together into a single document, you need space in your input folder for all the pages you want to collate. A basic grayscale scanner image file is at least 100KB using compression, and is probably closer to 300KB, so plan accordingly.

Unlike Distiller, Capture will only handle a single watched folder at a time.

Output Folders

Capture uses output folders to organize the output it produces. Each output folder has a name and a set of options that govern what type of output gets produced for that folder. To create an output folder, select the Output | Add Output Folder item (this does not create the actual disk directory—you will have to do that separately with Windows File Manager). To modify an existing folder, either double-click the folder, right-click it, or left-click it (selecting it) and use the Output | Setup Output Folder menu item. You use the same dialog box for both creating and modifying the output folder (shown in Figure 6.7).

Figure 6.7
The Output Folder Setup dialog box

Enter the name of your folder in the Description field, and a path to the actual directory you will use for this folder in the Location field. In the Document Creation Options section, select the file formats you want Capture to write into this output folder. Capture will write a file for each file format you select every time it processes a file using this output folder.

Removing an Output Folder

You can remove an output folder from Capture by selecting the folder, then selecting Output | Remove Output Folder. This dialog works identically to the Remove Input Folder dialog described above: Answering either Yes or No deletes the folder, but answering Yes also deletes the directory and its contents from the disk. Also, the same caveat about the directory already deleted applies to output folders as well.

Guidelines for Setting Up Output Folders

You can specify the same output directory location for more than one output folder if you want all of your output to go to one place. You can also specify more than one output file format for the same output folder (use Ctrl+left click to select or deselect entries after you make your first selection).

If you are lucky, the quality of your source material scanned by your scanner will produce virtually error-free conversions. In this case, you can just set up an output folder specifying that Capture write directly to your final preferred file format and process your scans.

More likely, you will need to check your output with Reviewer, at least until you are comfortable with the conversion. In that case, write your Capture files in Reviewer format only; you can produce the other file formats from within Reviewer after you have corrected the errors. This will eliminate time spent on unnecessary file conversions. To cover these two cases, create two output folders, each creating files of the appropriate type; then you can easily select one of them in the main Capture window when you begin processing.

Dictionaries

Capture uses two dictionaries to assist in the text conversion process: a built-in English dictionary and a custom dictionary. If Capture can find a word in one of these dictionaries, it raises that word's conversion score; if not found, the word's score goes down. You can improve Capture's ability to identify text quickly and accurately by adding words that Capture does not know to the custom dictionary.

You can add words to the custom dictionary from Capture by using the menu item File | Edit Custom Dictionary. This brings up the dialog box shown in Figure 6.8. When you enter the first letter of a word in the blank text box at the top, the Contents box shows you all of the words in the custom dictionary that start with that letter. Enter your full word and click the Add button to make the new entry. Select a word from the Contents list and click the Remove button to delete it. You can also add words from within Reviewer (discussed in the Reviewer section below).

Figure 6.8
The Edit Custom Dictionary dialog box

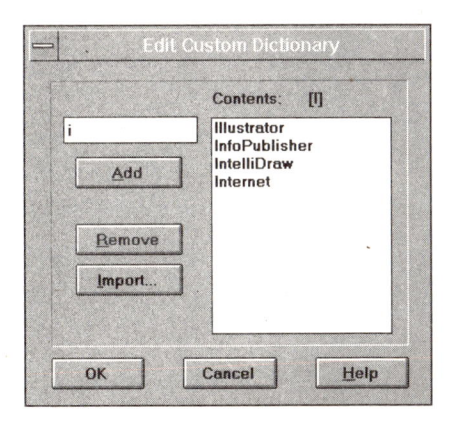

Importing Words from Other Sources

Press the Import button in the Edit Custom Dictionary dialog box to import the contents of another file. This file should be a simple list of words with one word per line. If your word processor uses a different format, see if you can export the custom dictionary from that application. Ignore the instructions in the Capture and Reviewer help files concerning file name extensions; use a .DIC extension for your file. The Import dialog box displays files with the .DIC extension by default.

Using More than One Dictionary

It is easy to swap out the custom dictionary file Capture uses with a different file—if you know which file to swap. The correct file name is CUSTDICT.SPL (the Reviewer help file in some places incorrectly calls it CUSTDICT.TXT). You can copy this file to another file name to save it, and then recopy it back to CUSTDICT.SPL when you want to use it again. A situation when you might want to use this procedure: When you have very large custom dictionaries and you are running out of memory. Reducing the size of your custom dictionary will free more memory for other parts of the application.

Using Capture

Once set up, Capture is exceptionally easy to use: all you do is click the input and output folders you want to work with, then click the processing button for the operation you want to perform. Capture displays a processing dialog box, shown in Figure 6.9, which tells you what step Capture is taking right now. A Stop button at the bottom of the dialog box lets you abort the current job. If you press this button, be patient; Capture is very compute-intensive, and it does not pay close attention to the user interface while it is processing a scan. If you have started a multiple-file process, there does not seem

Figure 6.9
Capture's Processing dialog box

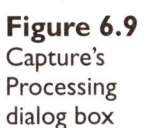

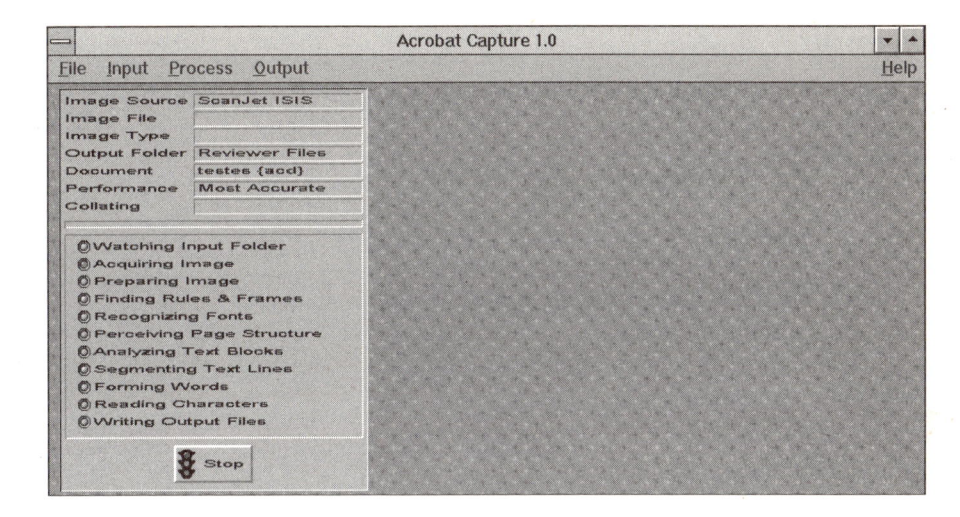

to be a way to abort the entire job; when you press Stop for one file, Capture aborts that file but then starts the next one.

Scanning a Single Page

Scanning is initiated by pressing either the Scan or Scan and Process buttons. These buttons work with the currently selected scanner and input or output folder, respectively. Figure 6.10 shows the dialog box displayed by the Scan button. In the Base Name field, enter the file name you want to use (no extension).

Select the One Page check box in the middle of the dialog box. Finally, at the bottom select the File Format for the scanner output; usually you should select *Tiff Compressed [Most Compatible]*. After you click OK in this dialog box, Capture starts up the scanner driver and it lets you select scanning options (see below) and actually make the scan.

If you select Scan and Process instead, you get the slightly simpler dialog box shown in Figure 6.11. You do not have to select a file format because that is determined by the output folder you have

Figure 6.10
The Scan Images to Input Folder dialog box

selected. All you need to enter is a file name to use and whether this is a single page scan or multiple pages. As soon as the image is acquired, Capture begins processing it.

The scanning process itself is controlled by a device driver: either an ISIS driver or a TWAIN driver, depending on the scanner configuration. The dialog boxes that control scanning are different for each scanner, so we do not try to cover them here. There are, however, several controls that all scanners have in common, including most importantly the resolution of the scan, followed by the brightness control and the contrast control (all are discussed below).

Figure 6.11
The Scan and Process Images dialog box

Scanning Multiple-Page Documents

Usually you will want to scan all the pages of your document first, then process them in a batch (this way you do not have to wait on Capture to process each page). The Scan operation does this using a file naming convention in order to keep track of the individual scanned images in a multiple-page document. In this convention you supply a base name for the page files, and Capture adds the page number as a suffix (followed by the file extension). The total length of the base name and the page number must be no more than eight characters to meet MS-DOS file name requirements, so make sure you leave enough room for all the page numbers you will require (three digits covers 999 pages).

If you are using an automatic document feeder, refer ahead to that section. For manual scanning, usually you will select the Single-Sided Stack option in either the Scan Images dialog box (Figure 6.10) or the Scan and Process dialog box (Figure 6.11). Enter a base name only for Scan operations; Scan and Process operations go straight to the output file so enter the name you want for that file (again, no extension). With the Single-Sided Stack option selected, Capture expects you to perform the scans in page number order from the first page to the last. It names the image files accordingly without intervention from you (e.g., BASE0001.TIF, BASE0002.TIF). It prompts you for the next page after completing the first; you either tell it to scan the next page or to stop scanning.

If you need to stop scanning in the middle of your document, you can restart again by entering the page number you need in the Start Numbering At entry box in the Scan Images dialog box. The file name of the next scan will contain that page number along with the base name you specify.

TIP: *Do not scan a multiple-image file into a watched directory. Capture will not know to wait until you are finished scanning all* *of the pages before it begins processing image files. Instead, scan all of the images into an input folder and set up Capture to process the folder later.*

Choosing the Correct Scanning Resolution

The correct resolution can make all the difference in the world to the success of Capture's text conversion process. If you err on the side of too little resolution, then Capture will make many mistakes as it attempts to translate shapes on the paper into letters. Figure 6.12 gives an example from a document scanned at 300 dpi. The text we are converting is from a bid request from the State of California; it uses an 8-point typewriter font. This figure shows a portion of the document displayed in Reviewer. The original scan is displayed at the top of the window, and Capture's result is at the bottom.

As you can see, the *a*'s and *e*'s in the original scan are just black blobs without much to distinguish them from each other. Consequently, Capture easily mistakes the two letters. This is a characteristic of scanning with insufficient resolution. Figure 6.13 shows the result when the same document is scanned at 400 dpi; though the image is not much better, now Capture can distinguish the *a*'s and *e*'s.

Figure 6.12
Scanning with too little resolution causes errors.

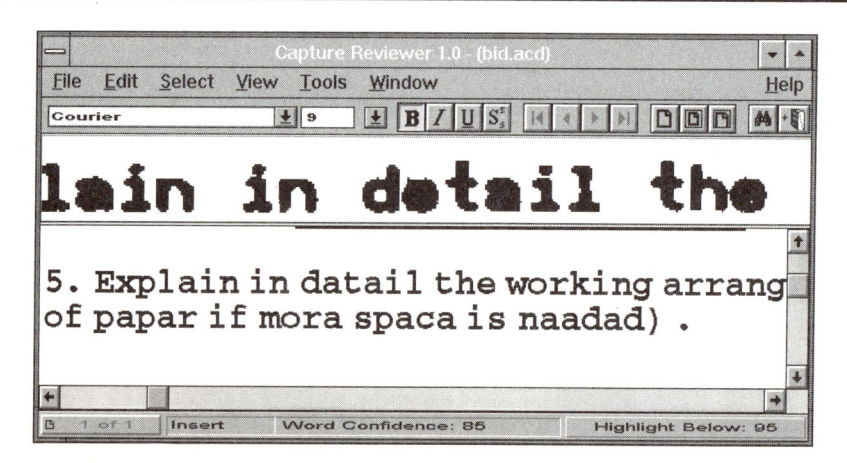

Figure 6.13
Scanning with sufficient resolution

While it is still uncertain enough to flag a lot of suspect words, Capture rarely makes a mistake in converting this image to text.

This illustrates the general principle for choosing the correct resolution: Use a large enough number so that the details you are trying to see are clearly present in the scanned image. There is an upper limit imposed by Capture: It will not accept scans at greater than 600 dpi. The true optical resolution of most flatbed scanners today is 600 dpi, so this is not an unreasonable limit. A scanner that offers to give you a scan at a higher resolution than its optical resolution is really only interpolating new data points between the ones provided by the optics. The interpolated pixels are assigned an average of their surrounding pixel values. This process improves the quality of scanned photographic images, but only makes text conversion more difficult, so do not use it with Capture.

Sometimes you can benefit from using a lower resolution. If you are scanning a large type document that has a lot of spurious marks on it, lowering the resolution of the scan will get rid of at least some of the spurious marks. Experimentation is the rule with problem documents (ones that generate many errors).

Selecting Other Scanning Options

If you have the choice of grayscale or black and white, choose the latter unless you also have photographs on the page. Capture can find text easier using a black-and-white scan, but a photo will be rather ugly when rendered in black and white. However, if your page contains colored text on a different colored background (other than black on white), you will need to use a grayscale scan.

If you do a lot of mixed image and text scans, you should consider a smart scanner that can tell the difference between text and graphics and scan them differently. Hewlett Packard's AccuPage technology provides this feature.

Set the scanner's brightness control so that the scanned image is neither too light nor too dark. This desirable state is achieved when the text in the image is solidly visible but not too thick so that characters start to run together.

Another way to enhance recognition is to reduce the contrast in the scan. Contrast settings are biased towards the high side because they improve scans of images, but high contrast makes text recognition more difficult. Lower the contrast so that the image gets lighter than normal.

Avoid enabling or using the following scanner features for pages you plan to convert with Capture, as they make the recognition task more difficult:

- Diffuse
- Dither
- Halftone

Scanning Tips

Keep your image flat on the scanner bed (use force if necessary). Books and magazines with bindings that do not let the page stay flat will provide inconsistent quality across the page.

Plan to make a few test scans, viewing the results in Reviewer, so that you can make adjustments to the scanner's brightness control and resolution (if necessary). If you are using TWAIN drivers, you may be able to preview different settings, rather than going through Capture and Reviewer. You can also preview a scan with an image file editor (like Adobe PhotoShop), which may be faster than running Capture.

Scanning Landscape Images

Capture will recognize text in landscape mode if the image is facing the way Capture wants to see it. However, the right way depends on your scanner; you have to determine this by experimentation. If the landscape page is not converted to text by Capture, but appears only as an image, then the page should be turned upside down and scanned again.

Using Automatic Document Feeders

An automatic document feeder (ADF) picks up and moves paper through the scanner from a stack of waiting pages, scanning each page. Capture's ISIS scanner device drivers can drive the ADF when you select either the Single-Sided Stack or Double-Sided Stack options (see Figure 6.10) and it finds an ADF attached to your scanner to control. When you select a Scan operation using the ADF, a new image file is created for each page, and Capture names the image as discussed above for multiple-page files. In a Scan and Process operation, the whole stack of pages are processed directly into the output file. In either case, Capture prompts you only when the ADF runs out of pages to scan, so that you can add more pages or terminate the scanning.

When you perform a Scan operation, you have the choice of Single-Sided Stack or Double-Sided Stack. If your pages have printing on only one side, use the Single-Sided Stack option. If they have printing on both sides, then typically your ADF will scan all the pages on one side, then you will turn the stack over manually and tell it to scan the other side. Use the Double-Sided Stack option if this is how your ADF works. What actually happens in this case is that the odd-numbered pages are scanned first, followed by the even-numbered pages in reverse order. Capture arranges the file names properly to keep the image files in page number order.

TIP: *If you are scanning double-sided pages with the Double-Sided Stack option, when you are finished scanning the first side of all of the pages, do not just turn the pages over and start scanning the other side. First you have to tell Capture that you are finished with the first side so that it will start numbering the even-numbered pages correctly. Tell Capture you are finished scanning by clicking the Finished button when it prompts you for more pages; it will then ask you to turn the pages over and begin scanning the other side.*

If your ADF can turn the page over and scan the back side in a single operation, use the Single-Sided Option, since the pages will be scanned in page number order. Note that you cannot use the Scan and Process operation to handle double-sided stacks. This is because Scan and Process does not store images on disk; therefore they cannot be processed out of order.

Processing Scans

If you have already collected scanned images into a directory (from either a Scan step or from using other software), you use the Process button to initiate text conversion on the files. Select the input folder you want to process files from, and an output folder as a destination for the conversions. When you select an input folder, files in the folder will be listed in the list box to the right of the input folder list. All of the files will be selected by default. If you press Process now, all of the files in the input folder will be processed sequentially. If you only want to process certain files, select them first by clicking them with the mouse (after the first file you must Ctrl-click the additional files you want). There appears to be a bug in the file listing display such that if there are too many files to display, Capture displays nothing. In this case, either move some of the files elsewhere, or process the entire folder.

Scheduling Processing for Off-Periods

It may be convenient for you to scan a set of images and process them later, perhaps overnight when systems are less busy. You can set up Capture to process an input folder at a preset time using the Process | Process Input Folder Later menu item. Selecting this item brings up the dialog box shown in Figure 6.14. The current time and the time to start processing are shown beneath the clock face. To change the time for processing, drag the arrow on the clock face around the clock to the time you want. To change from a.m. to p.m., drag the arrow for a complete revolution of the clock face. To cancel this mode, click on the Stop button in the bottom of the window.

Figure 6.14
The Capture window when Process Input Folder Later is in effect.

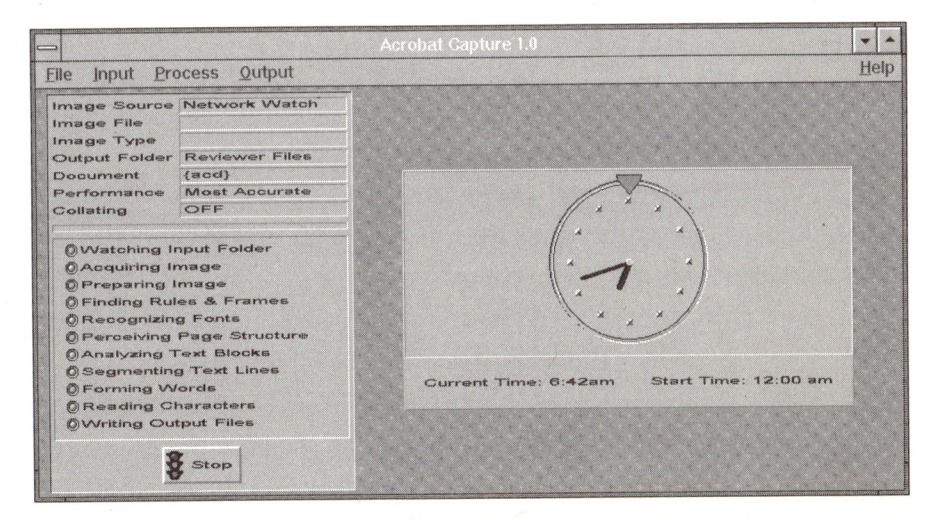

Using Continuous Monitoring

If the input folder you select has the watch folder option enabled, then when you press the Process button, Capture begins continuous monitoring of the directory, processing files when they appear. Capture displays the now-familiar processing status box with the Watching Input Folder entry highlighted. Press the Stop button to stop continuous monitoring.

Capture Log Files

Capture keeps a log file listing job start and stop times and job status. If errors occur during the processing of a file, usually there will be messages in the log file. Capture creates a new log file every day, using the date in numeric form as the name of the file (with the extension .LOG). The files are kept in the Capture .\LOG subdirectory. To view the current day's log file, you must first stop Capture by quitting the program.

Using Reviewer

Reviewer is your tool for correcting errors in text conversion. It shows you the original scanned image side by side with the converted text. Reviewer can flag several categories of suspect words, and it lets you use the Tab key to quickly skip to view only these flagged words (of course, you can also review the entire document). Reviewer also lets you see and change the font and font size of the converted text, as well as the ordering of blocks of text on the page.

Reviewer works only with .ACD files produced by Capture itself. It uses the .ACD file along with the original image file (or sometimes it creates a .ACI file which holds a de-skewed version of the image) to display the results of Capture's text conversion. Both the .ACD and .ACI files use the name of the source file as their name. If you copy these files to a new location, make sure you copy all of them together so that Reviewer can find the image files.

Reviewer Window Organization

Figure 6.15 shows the Reviewer window. The toolbar displays the font and font size of the current word or text selection and whether the text is bold-faced, italicized, or underlined. You can select text and use these controls to change the format values. These are followed by familiar buttons for page navigation, display view size, and finding text. The last button is used to add a word to the Custom Dictionary.

Figure 6.15
The Capture Reviewer main window and its controls

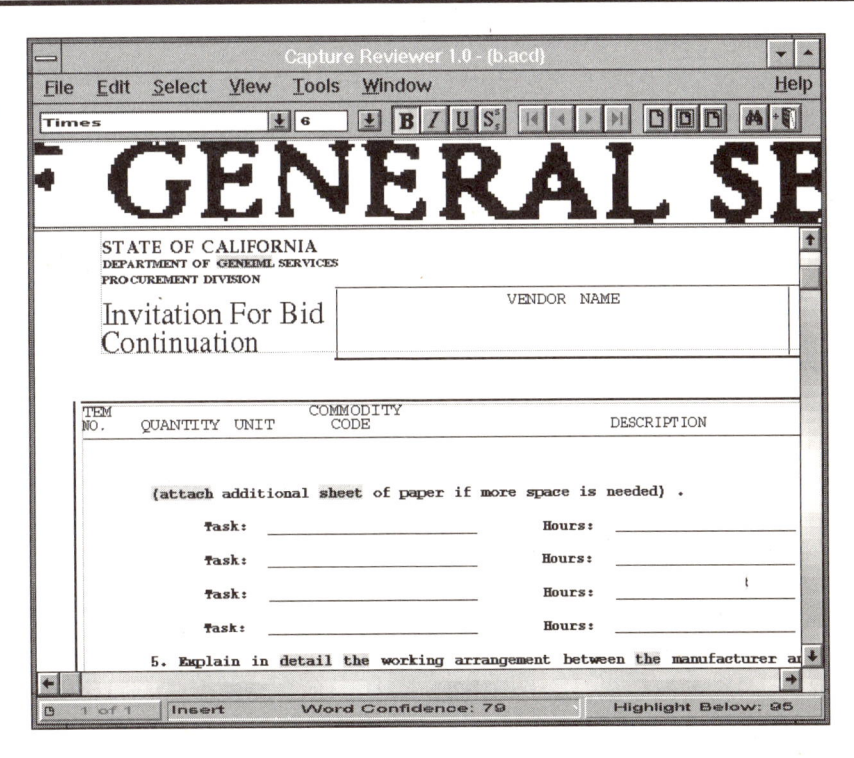

The status bar at the bottom of the window displays the current page number in the lower-left corner. Reviewer displays whether it is in insert or overstrike mode for characters you enter, and the word confidence value for the current word. On the right side the word confidence threshold value you have set is displayed; this is a button you can click on to change the suspect-word settings.

Your view of the file is split into two window panes. In the top pane, the original scanned image is displayed at high magnification, but only for areas of the image identified as text blocks. In graphic areas and undefined areas, the top pane is empty. The bottom pane contains the current view of the Reviewer file (the .ACD file). You adjust this view by selecting a viewing option.

Reviewer Preferences

Reviewer has a set of preference items accessed from the File | Preferences menu item (see Figure 6.16). The first item, PDF Output Options, allows you to choose whether Reviewer should use Capture's defaults for PDF Writer or use the existing PDF Writer settings for compression and font embedding options. You do not have the opportunity to change the Capture defaults, so you must choose PDF Writer settings if you want specific control over one of the output options (see the section "PDF Page Setup Options" in Chapter 3 for a discussion of these options).

Figure 6.16
The Reviewer—Preferences dialog box

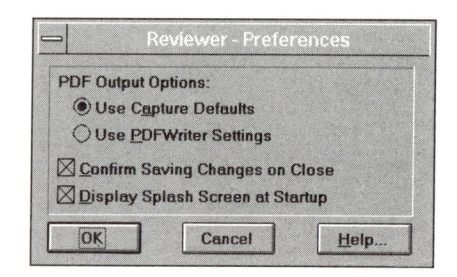

The other two entries in the dialog box are self-explanatory. If you do not select Confirm Saving Changes on Close, Reviewer will exit without saving files (unless you specifically save the file).

Document Views

Reviewer only lets you look at one document at a time (technically speaking, it is not a Windows MDI application). You must close the document you are currently reviewing before clicking on another one in the Capture window, or you will get an annoying error message from Capture.

Viewing Options

Reviewer first displays a file in the viewing mode established in the View Options dialog box (shown in Figure 6.17). You access this dialog box by selecting View | View Options menu item. The Default Magnification field sets the initial view of the document; it features the now familiar Fit Width and Fit Page modes, as well as a set of fixed magnifications. Text Height for AutoZoom sets the text height when AutoZoom is in effect (see below).

Figure 6.17
The View Options dialog box

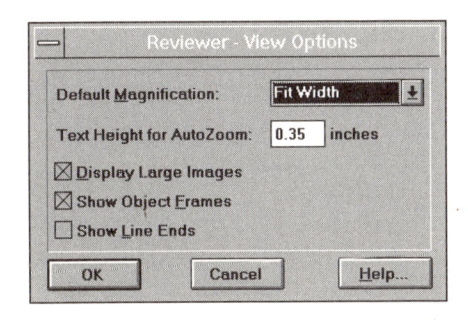

Large images take a comparatively longer time to display, so like the Reader, Reviewer gives you the option to save time by disabling the display of large image blocks in your file. Just check the box for

Display Large Images to restore the display. Object frames are the gray lines around text and graphic areas of your image. If the page has a complicated layout, you will need to see these frames (check the Show Object Frames box), otherwise you may not need them. Checking the Show Line Ends box causes Reviewer to display a right bracket at the end of each line (the point at which it will insert a new line character in text output).

Viewing Commands

Reviewer has a set of viewing commands largely borrowed directly from Exchange, so except for AutoZoom (covered in the next section), they should be familiar. Reviewer gives you Zoom In and Zoom Out commands instead of letting you set a magnification level. All the commands are listed below.

Command	Menu Command	Keyboard Accelerator	Toolbar Button
Display page actual size	View | Actual Size	Ctrl+H	[icon]
Display page scaled to fit in the window	View | Fit Page	Ctrl+J	[icon]
Display page scaled to fit visible width	View | Fit Width	Ctrl+K	[icon]
Increase magnification	View | Zoom In	Ctrl+I	None
Decrease magnification	View | Zoom Out	Ctrl+T	None
Go to first page	View | First Page	Ctrl+1	[icon]
Go to last page	View | Last Page	Ctrl+4	[icon]
Go to next page	View | Next Page	Ctrl+3	[icon]

Go to previous page	View | Previous Page	Ctrl+2	
Go to a particular page	View | Go To Page	Ctrl+5	

Correcting Text Conversion Errors

If you have text conversion errors, the first thing you should do is try to improve your scan of the document. Use Reviewer to look at the results of processing the scan with Capture—its ability to show you the original image alongside the converted text will help you to see what is causing the errors. Try increasing the resolution you are using (but not higher than 600 dpi) and adjusting the brightness to bring out the text clearly. Review the guidelines for scanning in the previous section.

Understanding Conversion Errors and Their Detection

It is important to understand that neither Capture nor Reviewer has the intelligence to know whether it has made an error in text conversion or not. That is why they are called *suspect words*—they are suspicious according to Capture's built-in rules, but Capture does not know whether they are truly in error or not.

The other side of this coin is that Capture may make mistakes that it does not suspect. For example, if the image is not clear Capture may mistake the word *a* for a list bullet symbol (•) and never suspect a problem (higher scanning resolution usually fixes this problem). Capture may also convert the image to a word that is a valid word but is not the correct conversion of the scanned text (for example, recognizing *famish* instead of *furnish*). Usually a page with few suspect words also has few actual errors, and vice versa, a page with many suspect words has a greater potential for undetected errors as well.

Another kind of error occurs when Capture thinks a region of the page is a graphic and you want it to be text. In this case, Reviewer will not have any text for you to correct. See the "Working with the Page Layout" section below for advice in this situation.

Using Suspect-Word Options

Suspect words are the keys to Reviewer's ability to show you potential conversion errors and allow you to correct them. You set the options for identifying suspect words with the Tools | Set Suspect-Word Options menu command (see Figure 6.18). There are four types of suspect words:

- Recognition suspects. When Capture's word confidence level is below a threshold value (95 percent by default). This number represents Capture's confidence in its conversion of the characters in the word. This is a must-use option for correcting errors.

- Spelling suspects. The word is not found in the dictionary. This may be because of a text conversion error by Capture, a typo in the original document, or the word is correct but not in the dictionary. This is a must-use option for correcting errors.

- Font suspects. Capture is uncertain of the font it chose for the word. This has not been very useful in scanning our documents. In some documents, Capture makes many actual font identification mistakes but does not flag them as font suspects.

Figure 6.18
The Setup Suspect-Word Options dialog box

- Alphanumeric terms. The word is a mixture of numeric and alphabetic characters.

You can also mark a word as suspect yourself by using the Edit | Mark Word as Suspect menu command. Pressing Ctrl+M will mark the current word. This is a useful way to flag mistakes that Capture did not catch itself if you are not going to correct the error immediately.

You can establish suspect-word options for either Reviewer ACD files or PDF files or both. When a box is checked in the Highlight (ACD) column, Reviewer will highlight suspect words in that category in the Reviewer window (recognition suspects in yellow and all other suspects in blue). Then you can use the AutoZoom feature to get a close-up view of the suspect word and the original image, making corrections easy. Note that whenever you change a word in Reviewer (adding, changing, or deleting characters) the word confidence level is moved up to 100 percent and the word is not highlighted anymore.

When a box is checked in the PDF column, Capture and Reviewer will copy the original bitmap image for display in the PDF file instead of the converted text. This is useful if you are not planning to correct your pages with Reviewer, and would rather look at the original scan data in your PDF file when there is some doubt about the text conversion.

Using AutoZoom Mode to View Suspect Words

AutoZoom is a viewing mode which displays the text cursor and the word it is in at a constant height in the viewer, adjusting the magnification as required. AutoZoom mode, used with the suspect-word commands listed below, makes correcting text conversion errors in your page very easy. You set the text height for AutoZoom mode in the View Options dialog box described above. This number is specified in inches; usually a fraction like .5. (an apparent bug: If the size is very large, like one inch, Reviewer sometimes will not bring the word into view in the window.)

To use AutoZoom mode to step through and correct (if necessary) all of the suspect words in your document, begin by selecting a suspect-word option to display using Tools | Setup Suspect-word Options (described above). In a full-page view of your file, you should see some words colored yellow or blue, depending on which suspect-word options you picked. Click with the mouse on the first highlighted word in the upper-left corner of the page (when the cursor is over a text region, it will change to an I-beam). Now select the View | AutoZoom menu item to enable AutoZoom. The two window panes do not synchronize and display the same portion of the page until you move the text cursor, so press the left arrow (or right arrow) once, which moves the text cursor and causes the two window panes to display the same portion of the page.

The AutoZoom commands are listed in the table below; keyboard accelerators are probably the best way to navigate while in this mode. AutoZoom mode stays in effect until you select another page view using the menus or toolbar.

Suspect-Word Command	Menu Command	Keyboard Accelerator	Toolbar Buttons
Start AutoZoom mode	View	AutoZoom Also on the right mouse button menu in a text block	Ctrl+U	None
Move to next suspect word	Tools	Next Suspect	Tab	None
Move to previous suspect word	Tools	Previous Suspect	Shift+Tab	None
Accept suspect word	Tools	Accept Suspect	Ctrl+Tab as correct	None
Tag word as suspect	Edit	Mark Word As Suspect Also on the right mouse button menu in a text block	Ctrl+M	None

Editing Text

Editing and correcting the text itself is just like using a word processor. The editing commands are shown in the following table. You are either in Insert mode or Overstrike mode (shown on the status bar at the bottom of the window). Switch back and forth using the Insert key. Use the Delete and Backspace keys to delete text to the right and left, respectively.

Text Editing Commands	Key
Toggle Insert/Overstrike mode	Insert
Delete character to the right, or current text selection	Delete
Delete character to the left, or current text selection	Backspace
Move text cursor to the left or right	Left arrow or Right arrow
Move up or down a line of text (moves to next or previous text block if no more lines in the current block)	Up arrow or Down arrow
Move text cursor to the beginning or end of the line	Home or End
Move text cursor up or down a full page in the file	Page Up or Page Down
Revert current line of text	Ctrl+L
Revert current block of text	Ctrl+B

The font name, font size, boldface, italic, and underline attributes are set in the toolbar according to where the text cursor is located. These attributes apply to the current word, unless you have some text selected.

You can select text in the usual way by dragging the mouse, or by holding the Shift key down while you move the text cursor using any of the cursor movement commands listed below. Double-clicking a word selects it, and triple-clicking selects the entire current line of text. You can quickly select all the text in a text block with the Select | Select All Text in Block menu command; likewise select all the text in the entire page with Select | Select All Text.

Reviewer does not provide the traditional word processor's Undo command for restoring edited text. Instead it remembers the original contents of each line of text you modify, and it allows you to revert the line (or the entire block of text the line is in, or the entire page) back to its original form when the file was last loaded or saved. After saving the file, you will not be able to revert any changes you have made.

Correcting Text Format Errors

Capture determines the font and font size for each word it converts by comparing the scanned image with its own font outlines. When the source text is average size (10 point or larger), this process gives good results, but small text can be confusing to Capture's text converter. It gives some pages a postmodern look by switching font size and even the font itself in midsentence (Figure 6.19 gives an example).

Figure 6.19
Font selection errors

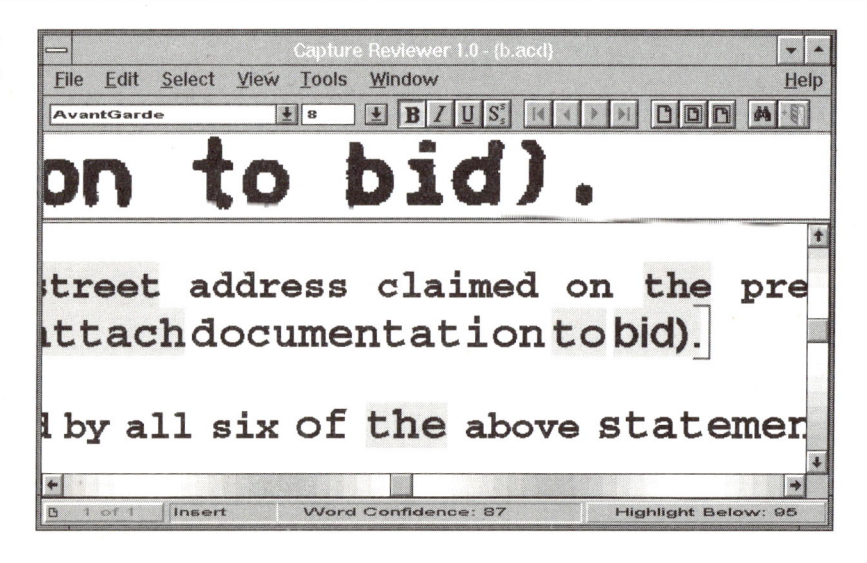

These errors are easy to fix if your text is actually supposed to be all one font. Simply select the entire block of text, then choose the font name and point size you want to apply to the text selection. The same process applies to the boldface, italics, and underlined text buttons on the toolbar.

Superscripts and Subscripts

When Capture encounters a subscript or superscript character, it may not correctly decipher the text or get it placed in the right spot on the line. Using the Superscript/Subscript button you can correct these errors by selecting the piece of text and rotating it through three different positions, all by pressing the button repeatedly. The first press reduces the font size of the selected text without changing the position of the text. The second button press moves the selected text to a subscript position on the current line, while the third press moves the text to a superscript position on the line. A fourth press restores the text to its original state.

Function	Toolbar Button
Shift text to super-/subscript position	

Adding Words to the Custom Dictionary

You can add words to the custom dictionary while using Reviewer to view the result of a text conversion. First select the Tools | Setup Suspect-Word Options menu item and make sure that *If word not found in dictionary* is checked. These words will be highlighted in blue, although if the word also rates a yellow highlight (because Capture's confidence in the word is low), the blue highlight will be masked by the yellow highlight. Turn off all of the other suspect-word options to get a clear view of the words not found in the dictionary. Review the highlighted words and add those that are spelled correctly to the dictionary using the Tools | Add Word to Custom Dictionary menu item. You can use the toolbar button to add the current word to the dictionary. Selecting this menu item brings up the Edit Custom Dictionary dialog box (see Figure 6.8), which shows you the word you are about to add. Click the Add button to do so. If the word is already present in the dictionary, the Add button will be disabled.

Function	Menu Command	Toolbar Button
Add word to custom dictionary	Tools | Add Word to Custom Dictionary	

Saving Reviewer Files

Use the File | Save As ACD menu item to save a Reviewer file for continued editing later. When you save a file, you can no longer revert the file back to its previous state; the newly saved file becomes the starting point for new modifications.

Reviewer can also write to all of the same file formats that Capture can, using the File | Save As menu item. Selecting this brings up the standard Save As dialog box; select the type of file you want to write from the list box in the bottom-left corner.

Working with the Page Layout

Capture analyzes the scanned image, looking for text regions to try and convert and graphics regions to pass through to the output. In Reviewer you can make some changes to the decisions Capture made in processing the file:

- Create new text or graphics regions
- Change the size of existing text or graphics regions
- Change text regions to graphics
- Delete text or graphics regions

You cannot change a graphics region to a text region, or cause Capture or Reviewer to try converting a text region a second time. In most documents this will not be a problem; however, if Capture has misidentified a text region of your document, you will need to create your own text object and enter the text yourself.

Page Layout Objects

Capture and Reviewer think of the page in terms of a set of objects that correspond to the regions mentioned above:

- Text blocks are regions of the document that contain lines of text. Only text blocks are processed for text conversion by Capture.

- Text lines are single lines of text within a text block. All of the actual text in the document is contained within text line objects, which are in turn contained within text blocks, even if the block has only one line in it.

- Graphics lines are straight horizontal or vertical lines drawn on the page.

- Black and gray rectangles are solid blocks of color found by Capture. You can create colored blocks as well as grayscale blocks of color.

- Source image rectangles are regions of the original bitmap image, passed through to the output without modification.

You can create any of the above objects to add to a page using Reviewer, and you can also modify the location and size of objects identified by Capture. To see the boundaries of the objects, you must have Show Object Frames enabled in the View Options dialog box. The boundaries are displayed as gray lines.

Each object has its own shortcut menu—right-click on the object when it is selected to display the menu. The menu contains a list of commands related to the object.

Selecting and Deselecting Objects You can select objects individually in order to modify, rearrange, resize, or delete the object. When an object is selected, its object frame is displayed in blue instead of gray; lines are displayed with a blue line running down the center of the black line on the page. You can just click on some objects to select them; others you must Ctrl-click:

- To select a source image rectangle, a color-filled rectangle, or a graphic line, click anywhere within the rectangle or on the line. Deselect these items by Ctrl-clicking them.

- To select a text block, Ctrl-click the the block's gray object frame. Deselect the block by Ctrl-clicking on the border again. Try to select the text block away from the borders of any text lines within the block to avoid selecting the text line instead. In a crowded text block you may need to temporarily make a text line smaller in order to move it out of the way so you can select the text block.

- To select a text line, Ctrl-click inside the area of the line. Deselect the text line by Ctrl-clicking the blue border of the text line.

Creating Objects   You can start creating a new object anywhere on the page where there is not an object already defined. In these undefined areas, the curser will display as a crosshair; click and drag with the left mouse button to describe a rectangle. The rectangle can be drawn so that it overlays previously defined objects. When you release the mouse button, the Select Object Type dialog box will be displayed (see Figure 6.20). Select the object type that you want to create.

Figure 6.20
The Select Object Type dialog box

To create a line, you must draw a long narrow rectangle, otherwise the Line option in the dialog box is disabled. Also, lines must be horizontal or vertical. The Single Text Line selection is disabled unless you are creating a new text line within an existing text object; this requires a slightly different procedure that is described below.

When you select a color-filled rectangle, Reviewer will fill the rectangle with black and then ask you to select a color from the standard Windows color selection dialog box. Select a different color and Reviewer will change the rectangle to use that color.

We discuss creating text objects below.

Deleting Objects   Select an object and press the Delete key to delete it. You can undo the last object deletion by choosing the Edit | Undelete Object menu item. Source image rectangles are unique among objects in that you can delete them without losing any data; you can create a new one and it will contain the same graphic material (this is because the source bitmap is always part of the file, and cannot be deleted). On the other hand, do not delete a text object and then create a new one expecting the text to reappear in the block. Also, since text lines exist within a text block, when you delete all of the text lines in a block you will still have the text block itself left to delete.

Overlaying Objects   You can control the layering of overlapping objects on the page to produce foreground and background effects. For example, you can create a colored rectangle and move it behind a text block or image block to add a highlight (or to restore one that did not scan very well). All objects except text blocks can be reordered; text blocks always float on top regardless.

Overlaying is controlled by selecting objects and moving them to the back of the display, behind other objects that may be present. Use the Move To Back command, located on the right mouse button menu for all objects that can accept it. To move an object to the back, select it, then select the Move To Back command from the right mouse button menu.

Text Blocks and Text Lines

Capture creates a text block for every distinct region containing text it finds on the page. Each text block contains one or more text lines that hold the actual converted text. Capture usually does a good job of correctly identifying these regions, but sometimes you will need to make changes yourself. You can create your own text blocks, create new text lines within existing text blocks, and manipulate the text regions to change the display of text.

There are two typical problems you may run across in more complicated page layouts:

- Capture did not recognize the region as text due to some extraneous noise in the scan. In this case, Capture creates a source image rectangle instead of a text block for the problem area. If you need the region to be in text form in the document rather than image form, you can create a text block to replace the source image rectangle. You will have to enter the text yourself; there is no way to tell Capture to reexamine an image once it has been processed.

- Capture is confused by something in the layout and produces some garbled characters. In this case you can correct the text in the normal way (using AutoZoom), but you may need to delete some extraneous elements or resize the text block to hold the new characters.

Creating Text Blocks   You begin creating a text block just like you would any other object by clicking and dragging with the crosshair cursor. When you release the mouse button, Reviewer displays the Select Object Type dialog box (see Figure 6.20). Select the Text Block entry and specify the number of lines you want inside the block. Reviewer fills the rectangle you've drawn with these text lines, sized to fill the rectangle. The height of the text lines will be equal to the height of the original text block divided by the number of lines you specify.

After creating the text block, Reviewer fills in each line you specified with the word *Text*. You replace this word with the text you desire by first deselecting the text block (Ctrl+left-click the border) and then selecting the text line with the I-beam cursor and typing as usual.

Creating Text Lines   You can only create a text line within an existing text block (in an empty portion of the block). First select the text block so that its border is a blue rectangle. Then use your mouse to drag a new rectangle within the borders of the text block. When you release the mouse button the Select Object Type dialog box will appear (see Figure 6.20); select the Single Text Line choice. Reviewer will convert the rectangle to a new line of text within the selected text block and place the word *Text* within it. To edit the new text, first deselect the text block by clicking outside of it's border, then click with the I-beam cursor to position the text insertion point for entering and deleting text.

Changing the Size and Format of Text Lines   The size of a text line is controlled differently for height and length. The height of the text line is specified by the font size selected for it. You can change the font size for a particular word by moving the cursor to that word and selecting a new value for font size from the toolbar; to change more than one word at a time, select the text by clicking and dragging with the I-beam cursor and then make the font size selection. If you cannot make a choice in the font size control, it is because you do not have text selected—instead you may have a text line object or text block selected. This can be somewhat confusing, but it is easy to fix—click on a blank portion of the page outside any of the gray object boxes to deselect all objects, then try again.

Reviewer offers you a range of font size selections centered around the current font size; if the size you want is larger or smaller than shown in the list, select one of the extreme values, then click on the control again, and a new set of choices will be offered. Alternatively, double-click in the font size control in the toolbar and enter the value you want directly.

The length of the text line also controls the intercharacter spacing of the text in the line—characters are stretched or squeezed as necessary to fill the entire length of the text line. To change the length of a text line, Ctrl-click on a text line to select it. The cursor will change to a double-headed arrow in the neighborhood of the border of the text line. Click and drag the border to the position you want. You can only drag the borders to the left or right, not up and down.

Changing the Size of the Text Block   You may need to change the size of a text block in order to increase the size of a text line, make room for another new line of text, or perhaps you want to make the text region smaller. In any case, Ctrl-click the border of the text block to select it; the cursor will change to a double-arrow near the selected border. Click and drag with the mouse to move the border.

You can stretch a text block to cover part or all of another object; both objects will continue to be displayed, with any text lines you create in the new region of the text block floating on top of other objects in the image. You cannot, however, make the text block smaller by dragging its border past the borders of any of its constituent text lines. You must delete the text line before you can drag the border of the text block past the text line; the text lines do not change size with text block.

Reordering Text Blocks   Capture establishes an ordering for text blocks by assigning each one a number. This order is used when writing the file to a plain ASCII file or to a word processor format—the text of block 1 is written out before the text of block 2, and so on. In a complicated page layout, Capture may not assign numbers to

Using Reviewer 219

the text blocks in the order you would like, but Reviewer gives you the ability to change the order of the text blocks. Note: Text block order is not an important issue if you are using Capture to generate PDF output. PDF preserves the ordering of text on the page directly.

The first step is to display the text block numbering so you can see what Reviewer will do with the text. You display the text block numbering by selecting the View | Show Text Block Order menu command. Reviewer displays the text block numbers in red, with red lines connecting the blocks in order. Figure 6.21 gives a simple example.

Figure 6.21 Reviewer shows the order of text blocks.

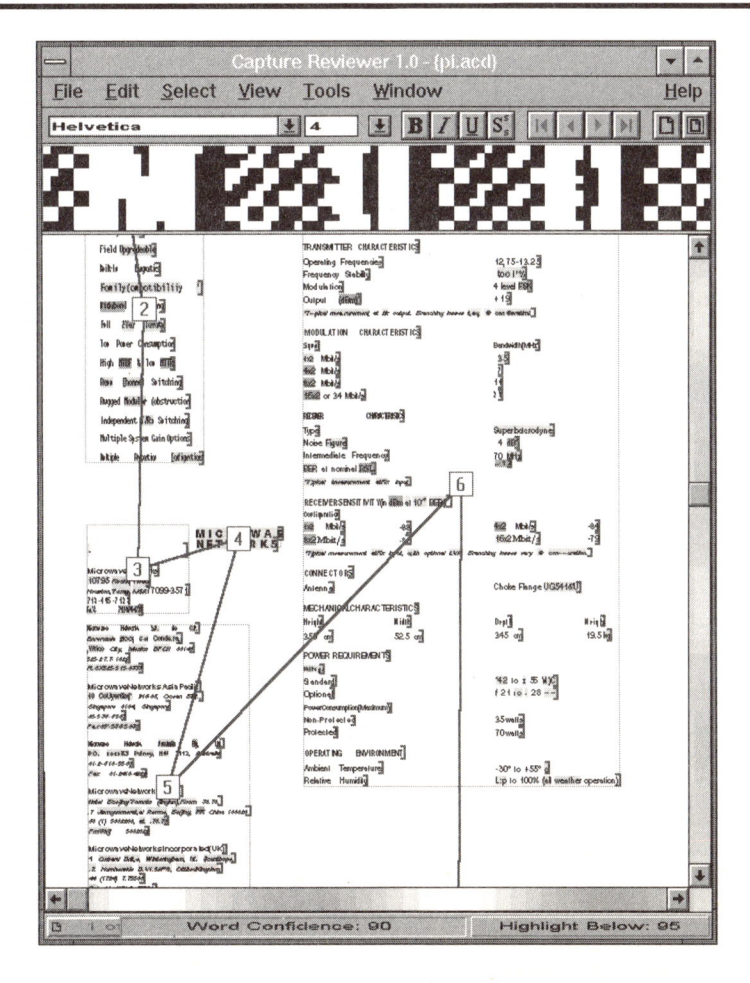

In this figure, the blocks numbered 3 and 5 contain text that should be contiguous, but Capture has ordered the blocks in columns, and it will write text from the title block (numbered 4) in the middle of the address list. We want to swap the position of blocks 3 and 4 so that the title text comes first. To do so, select either one of the blocks and use the Edit | Swap Text with Previous or Edit | Swap Text with Next menu commands to make the swap. Reviewer will renumber the blocks accordingly and display the new order in the Reviewer window. You can repeat this command to move the text block backward or forward several blocks if need be.

Repairing Text Conversion Problems— Some Examples

In this section we will look at several conversion problems and discuss some techniques for solving them. In the pictures that follow, we use the Show Object Frames and Show Line Ends viewing options to clarify where objects start and end on the page.

It is worth repeating that before considering how to fix your text conversion problems, you should first try to make the problem go away by improving your scan. Increasing the resolution used in capturing the image (up to 600 dpi) and adjusting contrast and brightness controls can help to clarify the original image. All of the initial problems we will look at in this section occurred with a complex document scanned at only 300 dpi. By increasing the scan resolution to 400 dpi, most of the problems with this image were at least greatly improved if not eliminated.

Choosing Image or Text Representations Figure 6.22 shows an example where someone circled the date on the original page, confusing Capture into thinking the text of the date and the line beneath it were actually graphics. It saw the first line (containing the words *DUE DATE*) as text but made errors in the conversion due to the handwriting. There are two ways to repair this problem, depending on what kind of result we want: We can either replace the

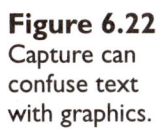

Figure 6.22
Capture can confuse text with graphics.

existing set of objects with a source image rectangle which shows the original handwriting clearly, or we can delete the source image and create a new text block, entering the correct text in the block. The advantage of the latter is that the text we enter will be available for searching, but it takes more steps to accomplish this. We will show you both methods below.

To convert the entire region to a source image rectangle:

1. Delete all of the objects except the image object in the center of the region. Select the line of garbled text („..*X?Z%Date*) by Ctrl-clicking it and delete it by pressing the Delete key. This still leaves a gray box on the screen representing the text block that contained the text line we deleted. Select this text block and delete it too. For simplicity we also delete the small source image rectangle at the bottom of the region that contains a fragment of the handwritten circle.

2. At this point we should have nothing left but the large source image rectangle containing the date and the title *VENDOR NAME AND ADDRESS*. Select this object by clicking on it. Drag its borders outward to cover the area previously occupied by the other

objects. After you drag a border outward, Reviewer fills in the original image in the new region. The result is shown in Figure 6.23.

Figure 6.23
Repairing the page using the source image

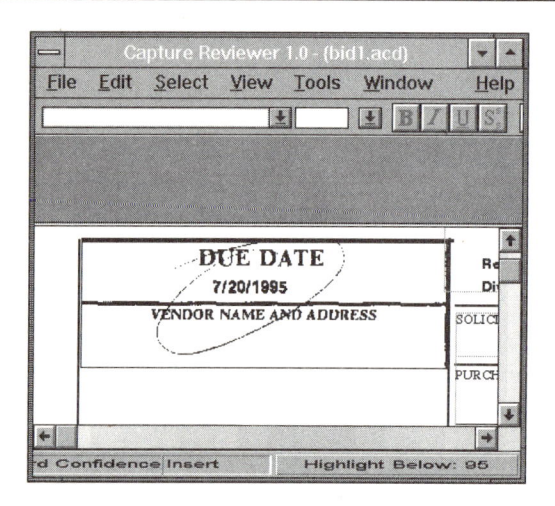

Another way to use the source image is to simply convert the text block containing the garbled Due Date text to a source image rectangle. Select the text block and then choose the Edit | Convert Text Block to Image menu command (this command is also available from the right mouse button menu). Now you will want to adjust the boundaries of all of the source image rectangles to restore the complete image to the page.

Alternatively, to convert the entire region to a text block:

1. Delete the two image objects, leaving only the line of garbled text at the top of the region.

2. Since the borders of this text line coincide with the borders of the text object that contains it, we will have to move the border of the text line over so we can select the text block. Do this by Ctrl-clicking on the text, then moving the cursor to the left or right border and dragging that border towards the center. The border of the underlying text block is revealed.

Using Reviewer 223

3. Ctrl-click the border of the text block to select it, and drag its borders to expand the text block to fill the space where the image blocks were.

4. With the text block still selected, create a text line to hold the date by dragging a rectangle with the mouse and selecting the Single Text Line entry in the Select Object Type dialog box. Reviewer will display the new text line with the word *Text* in it. We cannot edit this text until we deselect the text block, but we're not finished with the text block yet. First we'll create the other new text line we need to restore the VENDOR NAME AND ADDRESS title beneath the text line we just created (leaving a little space between the two to add the dividing line to the page).

5. To restore the line that separated the date from the title underneath, drag a long thin rectangle from the left side of the enclosing box to the right side, and select Line for the object type.

6. If the text block is still selected, deselect it now by clicking outside the text block. The image should now look something like Figure 6.24.

Figure 6.24
Repairing the image using new text lines

7. Correct each of the text lines in the expanded text block by clicking in each one and typing the text you want. You can also change the font name and font size at this time by making a new selection in the toolbar controls.

At a scan resolution of 400 dpi, Capture correctly deciphers the text in this image except where the handwritten line crosses through some characters. Figure 6.25 shows the result. In this case, Capture has translated the handwritten line into bogus text which is easy to delete. No complicated rearrangement of text blocks is necessary.

Figure 6.25
Higher scan resolution produces a better text conversion.

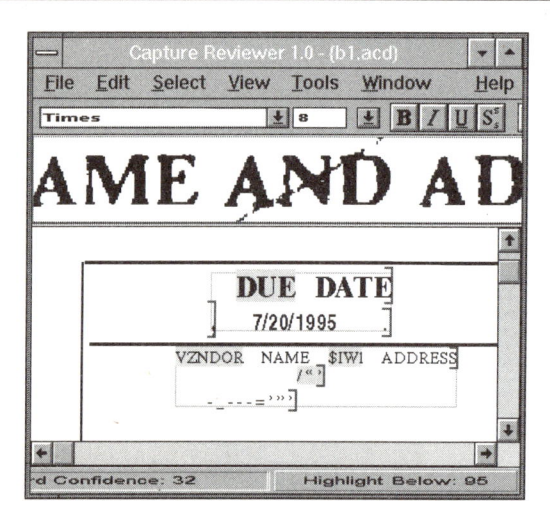

Errors around Object Borders   Figure 6.26 shows another part of this page, a region where lines drawn on the page are very close to the start of lines of text. At 300 dpi Capture apparently does not see all of the *F* in *Federal* or the *T* in *Telephone*, though it gets the rest of the text right.

It is easy enough to fix this text using AutoZoom. There is potentially more to the problem than just substituting text, however. Adding text to these short lines can cause noticeable compression of the

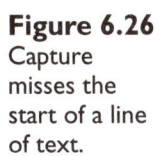

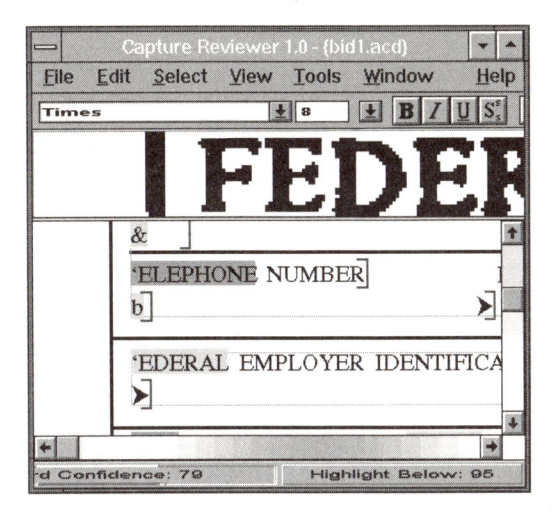

Figure 6.26
Capture misses the start of a line of text.

text. In the case of the text line containing *TELEPHONE NUMBER*, adding the *T* causes the two words to run together into one. To correct this problem, you have to resize the text line by selecting it and dragging its right-hand border out to the right (you cannot drag the left border because it is up against the edge of the text block border).

At a scan resolution of 400 dpi, this problem is not entirely solved, as you can see in Figure 6.27. While Capture correctly identifies the *F* in *Federal*, it still does not see the *T* in *Telephone* (and it mistranslates the arrow symbol as well).

Changing Text Block Ordering Figure 6.28 shows this same page in full-page view with the View | Show Text Block Order option enabled. Capture did a good job with this complex layout, generally assigning the text blocks to a reasonable order on the page. The text block numbering starts in the upper-left corner of the page, shifts to the center to pick up the page title, then proceeds down each of the columns of the upper half of the page.

It is when we get to block 22 that we have our first real problem. Text block 22 and block 23 are actually part of the same paragraph

Figure 6.27
Errors are still present at higher resolution.

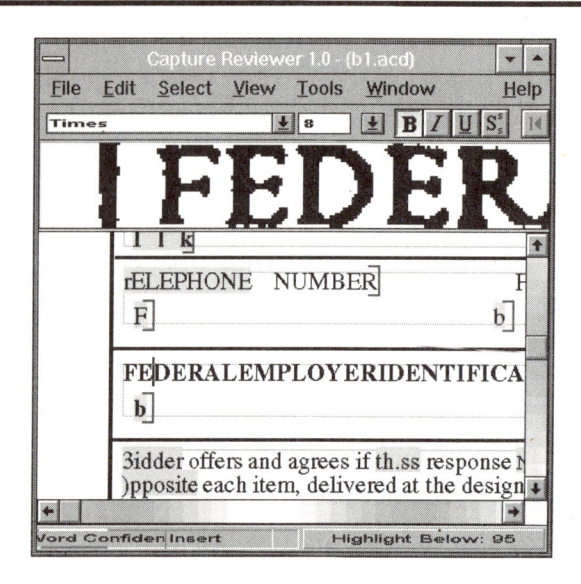

on the page; Capture has mistakenly split the paragraph into separate parallel text blocks. In a PDF file this will not be a problem, because the page will still look the same even if Capture did not get the block numbering right. (This is not strictly true. While the page will still appear correct to a viewer, the words where the text blocks are split will no longer be adjacent to each other in the text encoded within the PDF file. This means that a search phrase incorporating a quotation of this sentence fragment will not be found by the Search plug-in.) However, in a word processor output file, this text will be garbled. Block 22, representing the ends of the text lines in the real paragraph, will be output before the beginning of the paragraph in block 23.

Reviewer will not let you merge text block 22 with block 23 to produce the correct result. The best solution we found for this page was to rescan the image at a higher resolution. At 400 dpi, Capture correctly identified the text of the paragraph as a single block, thus eliminating the problem. However, if that does not work for you, the

Figure 6.28
A complex text block structure

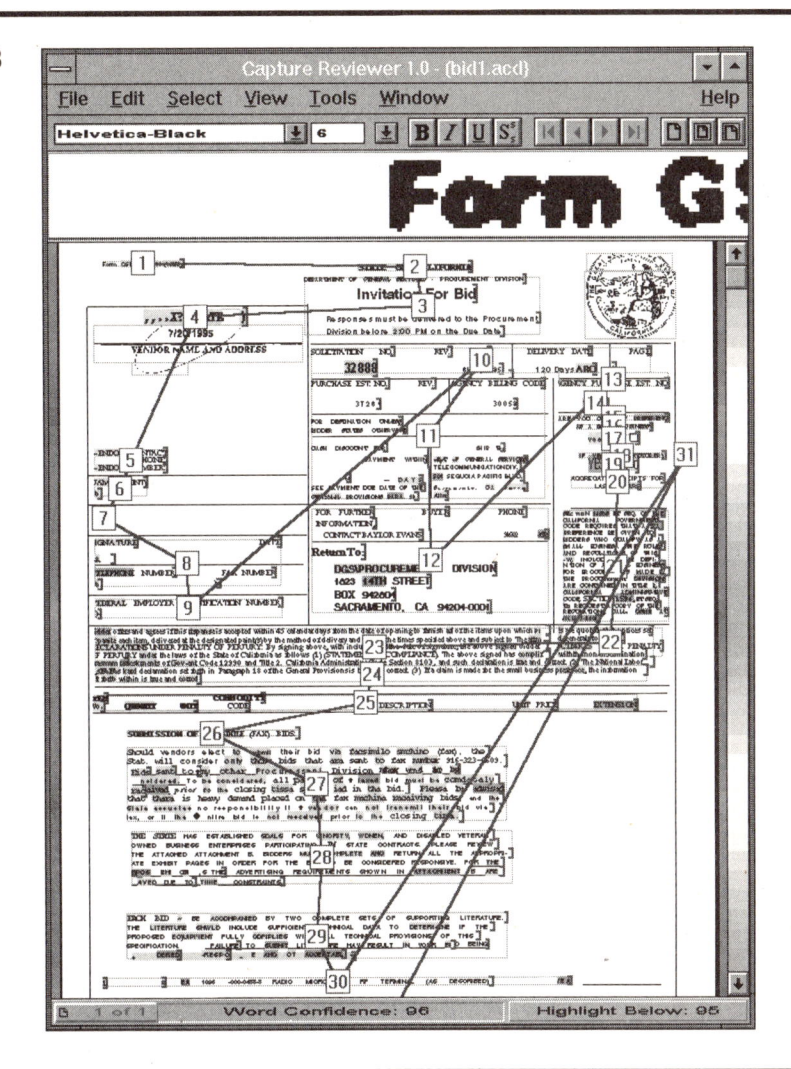

only solution for this problem is to cut and paste the text or correct the text in your final word processor document.

The other standout on this page is text block 31, which is actually just some extraneous marks on the page that Capture converted to text. This whole block should be deleted.

Summary

In this chapter we've covered the process of converting paper documents into PDF documents using Acrobat Capture's document recognition capabilities. In particular, you now should be able to:

- Setup Capture to work with your scanner
- Process scanned images to produce output files in Reviewer, PDF, and word processor formats
- Use Reviewer to correct errors in text conversion

In the next chapter, we will examine a key innovation that Adobe has used successfully in a number of their products: the plug-in interface. This interface, and the plug-in modules that work with it, allows new features to be added to the Acrobat toolset incrementally, without having to upgrade or replace the existing Acrobat tools themselves.

CHAPTER 7

Plug-ins

Installing and Removing Plug-ins

WebLink

Movie

Plug-ins from the Software Development Kit

Acrobat Exchange (and now the Reader, too, in version 2.1) provides a way to add new program modules to your existing installation through the use of plug-ins. Plug-ins are program modules written to a specification called the plug-in interface. Through the plug-in interface a plug-in module can have access to all parts of Exchange itself and the PDF files it is viewing. Plug-ins can provide interfaces to other programs or can add new data structures to a PDF file; WebLink, described in this chapter, does both. You can purchase a software development kit from Adobe if you are interested in this kind of software development; contact the Adobe Developers Association for more details.

Exchange 2.0 came with a single plug-in, Acrobat Search. In Acrobat 2.1, not only are there more plug-ins delivered with Exchange (WebLink and Movie) but the Reader has been enhanced to accept some specially designed plug-ins as well (including these two). The addition of the plug-in interface to Reader is a welcome development for Acrobat publishers; it insures that Reader will be able to keep up with new PDF features as they are made available.

In this chapter we will review two important new plug-ins that are available now for Acrobat Exchange 2.0 and will be shipping with version 2.1 of Exchange and Reader: WebLink and Movie. We will also examine the plug-ins available with the Acrobat Software Development Kits (SDKs), including the free SDKs described in Chapter 8.

Installing and Removing Plug-ins

To activate a plug-in, you must place it in the subdirectory of the Exchange (or Reader version 2.1) main directory reserved for active plug-ins (and restart Exchange or Reader if it is already running).

Plug-in files found here are automatically added to your system whenever Exchange starts up. The Macintosh name of this subdirectory is *Plug-Ins* while the Windows name is *PLUG_INS*.

To disable a plug-in, remove its file from the active plug-in directory by copying the file to the OPTIONAL subdirectory (Optional on Macs), provided by Adobe for this purpose, then delete it from the active plug-ins directory. Though other files may be used by the plug-in, it is sufficient to remove only the files with the .API extension (like WEBLINK.API). Alternatively, you can rename the plug-in file by giving it a new extension (anything other than .API will do).

WebLink

The WebLink plug-in (WEBLINK.API) provides World Wide Web (WWW) connectivity to any PDF document. WebLink works with Exchange version 2.*x* and with the new version 2.1 Reader to provide a new link action type, *World Wide Web Link*, which works in conjunction with a Web browser installed on your computer. A link with this action type contains the address of a document on the Web; this address is called a *Uniform Resource Locator* (URL). When activated, the URL is passed to your Web browser and the Web page is fetched from the network.

Configuring WebLink

To begin using WebLink, you must first select a Web browser for WebLink to work with and set other preferences. Select the Edit | Preferences | WWW Link menu item to bring up the dialog box shown in Figure 7.1. The View section of the dialog box contains parameters defining how the link is displayed:

- Link Information determines whether the Web URL for the link is displayed in the status bar at the bottom of the viewer window

Figure 7.1
The WWW Link Preferences dialog box

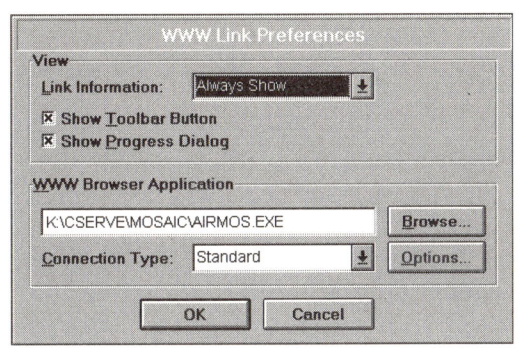

when the cursor is over the link. You have the option to always show the URL, never show it, or show it only when the Ctrl key is pressed while the cursor is over the link.

- Show Toolbar Button, if checked, puts a new button in the toolbar which starts your Web browser when pushed. If WebLink is not configured with a Web browser, this button will display an empty circle; if ready, it displays a globe.

- Show Progress Dialog activates the display of a dialog box showing how much of the linked file has been transferred.

In the next section of the dialog, WWW Browser Application, you must select the Web browser to use with your application. Press the Browse button to bring up a file selection dialog box; use it to find and select your Web browser program (changing directories if required). Usually the Connection Type will be Standard, in which case there are no options to select (currently nothing but Standard is defined by Adobe).

At the time this is being written (summer 1995), WebLink is known to be compatible with the latest browsers from NetScape and SpyGlass, but it is not compatible with all Web browsers. To test your setup, after completing this selection, press the new WWW button on the toolbar. The browser should begin executing after you press the button, but that alone is not enough. If there is a problem, WebLink will issue an error message saying the browser is not responding. Check with your browser vendor for an update or switch to a supported browser if you have this problem.

You may also need to configure your browser to start a viewer when it receives a PDF file. The details may vary with the particular browser you are using; in general, look for the configuration of "helper" applications, and make sure there is a valid entry for .PDF files.

Using WebLink in Your Documents

The basics of using WebLink are just like those of a regular link, as discussed in Chapter 3. When you select the *World Wide Web Link* action type, the Link Properties dialog box changes to look like Figure 7.2. Press the Edit URL button to enter the address of the document you want to link to. You can set a base URL for your PDF file (see below); if set, the URL you enter here is concatenated onto the end of the base URL string to form the entire address, saving you from entering the same root address over and over again.

Figure 7.2
The Create Link dialog box after selecting a WebLink action.

WebLink

Whai is an URL

Behind every hypertext link to a page on the World Wide Web is a Uniform Resource Locator, or URL. An URL gives the name of the page in a format such that anyone in the world can find it by using the Web. This book has a home page on the Web; the URL for our page is:

    http://www.zdnet.com/

The URL gives three items of information about the Web page:

- The transfer protocol to use. This is indicated by the first word before the colon in the URL. The standard protocol is HTTP, or Hypertext Transfer Protocol, which identifies a normal Web page. Part of the power of the Web is that it can also access other protocols, such as File Transfer Protocol (FTP) or gopher.

- The machine it is on. The part of the URL between the first pair of slashes and the second slash is the name of a computer on the Internet.

- The name of the disk file to retrieve and the directory it is found in. The rest of the string contains a file path on the machine named in the second part of the URL.

When you create a Web page for yourself, you will need a URL for your page. Each individual site will have its own requirements for where files can be located and what address you need to use. Contact the administrator of your Web server to get a URL for your own documents.

Selecting a Base URL

You can specify a prefix string that will be attached to the URLs in your document automatically by the viewer when they are selected. This saves you the trouble of specifying the full URL for each link you use, when all of your links point to pages at the same location. For example, you may have a set of documents online at a particular address, say *http://www.mysite.org/*. You can set this address as your base URL for each document in the collection; then you need only specify a file name within each Web link you create and they will all be relative to the base URL you specify. The two strings (the base URL and the URL specified in the link) are concatenated together, with the base URL first, to produce the final URL that is passed to the Web browser.

Base URLs are set on a per-document basis. To set the base URL for a document, select the File | Document Info | URL menu item while viewing the file to bring up the dialog box shown in Figure 7.3. Enter the base URL in the text field and press OK, or select Clear to erase the URL. If all of your files are in one directory, it is a good practice to put the portion of the URL that specifies the location up through the directory name in the base URL field. Include the terminating slash character; otherwise you must provide the slash in the individual links.

Figure 7.3
Setting the base URL for a document

TIP: *The base URL is used only when the WebLink URL field does not contain a valid URL prefix (like http://www.someplace.com/). You can use a base URL for links to other files in your own Web site and fully specified links to other Web sites in the same document with no problem.*

Opening a Web Page from the Acrobat Viewer

WebLink also adds a function to the Acrobat viewer which allows you to open a Web page directly from the viewer by entering its URL. Select the File | Open URL menu item and enter the URL for the page you want to see (see Figure 7.4). This name is passed to your Web browser and the page is fetched. The URL does not have to be for a PDF document; your Web browser will activate the correct application for the page you specify.

Figure 7.4
The Open URL dialog box

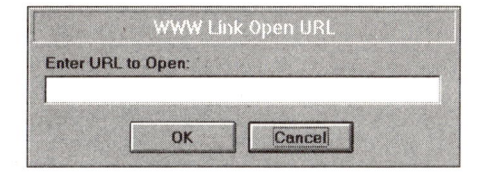

Guidelines for Using WebLink

It is important to keep in mind what kind of links you can use with a given document. If you are designing documents to be used primarily with a Web browser, these documents usually cannot rely on links to other documents because those documents may not be present on the system. The only types of links that you can rely on in such a situation are links within the document (GoTo actions) and WWW links to other documents on the Web. We discuss this issue further in Chapter 9.

The Web thrives on speedy interactive access to information. The speed of access is directly affected by the size of the PDF file you use, so keep your files small. Try to design your document set to deliver information in small "chunks" to keep the files small, using links between them to keep the information tied together.

Movie

The Movie plug-in provides another new Action Type for a link: a link to an Apple QuickTime Movie file. QuickTime Movies are the de facto standard for delivering video on both Macintosh and Windows machines. The plug-in adds a new Movie Player tool to the Tools menu and the toolbar (the button has a face that looks like a strip of film). The Movie plug-in works with both Exchange and the version 2.1 Reader.

Currently Macintosh computers with System 7 include QuickTime as part of the system. Windows users will need to install QuickTime for Windows in order to use Movie. QuickTime for Windows is distributed along with the Movie plug-in; it is alos available from on-line sources.

Movie Authoring

Acrobat does not provide the tools you need to create QuickTime Movies. For that, you need a vidco capture board and video editing tools (like Adobe's Premiere). If you have a Movie file that you want to access from a PDF file, you can use the Movie plug-in to create a link to that file. At this time (summer 1995), the Movie plug-in does not allow you to attach or embed the Movie file into the PDF file. The Movie file must be a separate file on the user's system. This means that you cannot deliver a Movie file with a PDF document via the Web (at least not with WebLink), but we look for this to change, perhaps in a future release.

Choosing a Movie File

To create a Movie link, select the Tools | Movie Player menu item or press the Movie Player button. The cursor will change to a crosshair. You can select a position for the link either by just clicking on the PDF page or by drawing a box for the Movie to play in. If you just click, the Movie will create a window using its default size (this is best for the performance of the Movie on a slower machine). The standard Open File dialog box is displayed; use this dialog to select a Movie file. After the file is selected, the Movie Properties dialog box is displayed.

Movie files are accessed via a path name saved in the link. The path name used is a relative path if the file is on the same disk drive as the PDF file. This is the preferred way to specify a file, since absolute paths are not very portable. It is best to arrange your files in their final locations for distribution before creating any Movie links. If a Movie file specified in a link cannot be found on the end-user's system, the Movie plug-in allows the user to browse for another Movie file to use in its place.

Movie Properties

Figure 7.5 shows the Movie Player Properties dialog box. Use this dialog box to set options for displaying the Movie file. The box in the top-left corner shows you the path name used for the Movie file and the title of the movie.

Figure 7.5
The Movie Player Properties dialog box

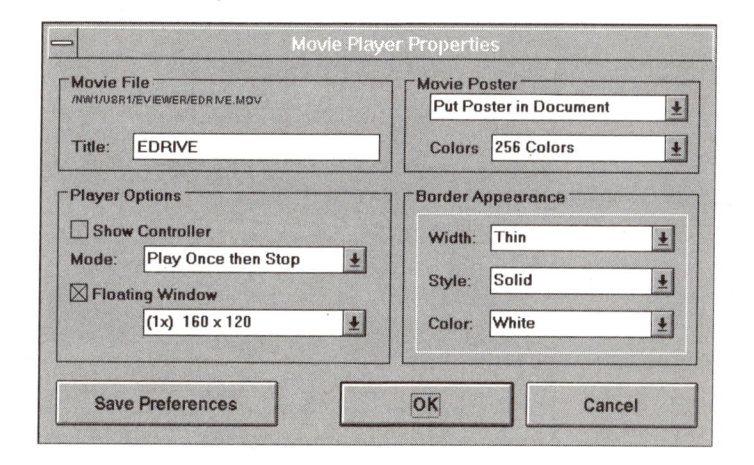

At the bottom of the dialog box are the usual OK and Cancel buttons, and a Save Preferences button. This button saves the current values of the Movie Properties to use as the default values for future movies.

Player Options

The Player Options affect how the movie is played when the user clicks the link. The Show Controller check box allows you to specify that the QuickTime Movie Player control panel should be displayed while the movie plays. A Movie annotation with the controller active is shown in Figure 7.6. The controller allows the user to stop and restart the video, rewind or fast-forward it, and change the playback volume. If Show Controller is not checked, the video will just play

Figure 7.6
Movie window with the QuickTime controller displayed.

when the user clicks on it without allowing any user control of the movie except through the keyboard commands listed below.

The Mode for playing the movie is selected from a drop-down list box; the choices are:

- Play Once then Stop—plays the video once then returns to the document.

- Play Once, stay Open—plays the video once and leaves the last frame displayed. The controller, if enabled, also remains available.

- Repeat Play—plays the video repeatedly from the beginning.

- Back and Forth—plays the video forward, then backward, continuously.

The next check box is labeled Floating Window. Check this box if you want the video to play in its own window floating on top of your PDF document; otherwise the movie will play in place in the document. The advantage of using a floating window for the player is that the window can be adjusted for an ideal viewing size for the movie, while the annotation in the document can be sized independently to fit the document.

If Floating Window is checked, the drop-down list lets you select the size of the floating window. The choices are given in multiples of the standard movie size. The size of the window can affect performance on slower machines, so its best not to choose one that is too large. The largest sizes are also too large for low-end screens; the 2x or 3x choices makes a good compromise.

Movie Poster

The Movie Poster section of the Properties dialog box allows you to specify whether to display a poster from the movie, and if so, how many colors to use. Each QuickTime Movie has a still frame which is used as a poster for the movie; when the movie is created, the poster frame is chosen.

You have three options for displaying the poster frame in your PDF document:

- Don't Show Poster—selecting this option leaves the box you drew for the movie annotation empty and transparent on the PDF page, like a regular link.

- Put Poster in Document—this option takes the poster frame from the movie and copies it into the document, displaying it in the box you have drawn. Even if the Movie file is not present, the movie poster will display.

- Retrieve Poster from Movie—with this option, the poster is not saved in the PDF file, but when the PDF page is displayed, the viewer retrieves the poster from the Movie file.

The Colors drop-down list box becomes active when you select Put Poster in Document. It has two choices: 256 colors or Millions of colors. The poster is saved in the PDF file with the number of colors you specify. The 256 color option will produce the smallest file.

Border Appearance

The Border Appearance section lets you select the appearance of the border around the box you have drawn for the Movie link. Within this section, a sample of the currently selected border is displayed around the three drop-down list boxes. You can choose the border's Width, Style, and Color from the selections listed.

Playing a Movie

When the cursor is over a Movie link, it changes to the same graphic used on the Movie link toolbar: a strip of film. Click on the link and the movie will play. While the movie is playing, certain keyboard commands are available; these are listed in Table 7.1. You can also left-click with your mouse on the movie while it is playing to pause it; restart the movie by double-clicking on it.

Table 7.1 Keystroke Controls Available for QuickTime Movies

Key	Function
ESC	Stop the movie and exit the player
Return Space	Toggles between Pause and Play
Up Arrow	Increase volume
Down Arrow	Decrease volume
Home	Go to start of movie
End	Go to end of movie
Right Arrow	Step forward one frame
Left Arrow	Step backward one frame
Ctrl + Right Arrow	Play forward
Ctrl + Left Arrow	Play backward

Plug-ins from the Software Development Kit

Even if you are not interested in developing software for Acrobat, you may want to pick up one of the Acrobat Software Development Kits after you read this section. Adobe provides a set of plug-ins that add some useful enhancements to Exchange; these plug-ins are available in all versions of the different SDKs (see Chapter 8 for details, including how to download the free SDK for Macintosh and Windows). Within the SDK there is a subdirectory called PLUG_INS (on Windows; the Mac version uses the more elegant name Plug-Ins) that contains the set of sample plug-ins.

Some of these plug-ins exist simply to illustrate a point to software developers, and are not interesting to us, but many of them perform useful functions. However, the problem is that none of the plug-ins are documented in the SDK (unless you get the full-blown Plug-in Development SDK). We remedy that situation here for the plug-ins we think are interesting.

Follow the instructions in Chapter 8 to retrieve the free SDK files from Adobe (they are compressed file archives) and decompress them on your system. After decompressing, you will find the Windows plug-ins in the directory *\acrosdk\source\win\plug_ins*, while the Macintosh versions are in the folder *:Acrobat SDK:Source:Mac:Plug-Ins:*. The files in this directory are listed in Table 7.2. To use a plug-in, just copy it to your Exchange PLUG_INS directory (or Plug-Ins folder for Macintosh) and restart Exchange. These plug-ins work with Exchange 2.0 and 2.1, but they are not capable of working with the version 2.1 Reader at the time this is being written (look for possible enhancements in new versions of the SDK).

Table 7.2   Software Development Kit Plug-in Summary—Windows Version

Name	Function
ACTHREAD.API	Adds new link action: start viewing an article
ADDBOOK.API	Automatically adds bookmarks for a Table of Contents and a Table of Figures to a PDF file
ADDINFO.API	Adds Document Info fields to PDF files from dictionaries stored in a separate disk file
ADDPS.API	Lets the user specify a PostScript file to send to a printer before each page of a PDF file is printed
BALLOON.API	Creates a new link action type that pops up a window with text you specify—like a pop-up definition
BOOKMARK.API	Adds or removes Acrobat page numbers from bookmarks
CLIP.API	Macintosh-only; adds paper-clip annotations to pages
COMP.API	SDK example plug-in
CSTMIZE.API	Allows users to add, change, or delete menu items and toolbar buttons
DEBUGWIN.API	SDK debugging tool
FIX.API	SDK example plug-in
FULLPATH.API	Displays full path of a PDF file in the viewer's window title bar
HELLO.API	SDK example plug-in
IMAGESEL.API	SDK example plug-in
KILLLINK.API	Removes all bookmarks and annotations from a PDF file
MARKUP.API	Allows you to make and save marks on the document page itself as a kind of annotation
MERGENOT.API	Show or hide notes
MODPDF.API	SDK example plug-in
NAMEDQRY.API	Allow Named Queries for Search
NOTIFY.API	SDK example plug-in
OPENALL.API	Lets you drop a file onto Exchange, have it converted to PDF, and opened for display
RPLCDEMO.API	SDK example plug-in
SELINFO.API	SDK example plug-in

Table 7.2 Software Development Kit Plug-in Summary—Windows Version (continued)

Name	Function
SNAPZOOM.API	Adds a tool that doubles the current magnification while the cursor is held down
SPREAD.API	Copies a table to the clipboard in the SYLK format supported by spreadsheet programs
STAMPER.API	Adds an OK stamp annotation
STARTER.API	A Macintosh-only SDK example plug-in
STATS.API	Adds display of document statistics including word count and annotation count
STORE.API	Adds Store File and Extract File menu items that allow you to embed another file within a PDF file (such as a source file)
STORYTLL.API	Reads articles out loud
TEMPLATE.API	SDK example plug-in
TEXTFLTR.API	SDK example plug-in
WORDFIND.API	Scans a PDF file and creates two text files listing all the words in the PDF file and their word offsets

One difficulty with these plug-ins is that they are not guaranteed to be installed on every user's system. If you wish to rely on some of the features provided here (such as ACTHREAD), you will want to talk to the Adobe Developers Association about redistributing the plug-ins with your files. Adobe does not provide technical support for these plug-ins except to licensees of the Plug-in Development SDK, through the Adobe Developers Association.

AcThread

ACTHREAD.API provides a new link action type: When you create a link or bookmark, you can specify *Go to Article* to start reading an article in the PDF file rather than just getting a page view. When you select this action type for your link, the bottom button in the Create

Link (or Link Properties) dialog box changes to Select Article. Press the button to see a list of articles in the document. You must create the articles before using this link to access them.

AddBook

ADDBOOK.API will automatically create bookmarks and links in a PDF file for a Table of Contents and a Table of Figures. The plug-in looks for specially named articles to define where these tables are, and relies on a particular format to the tables themselves to work properly. The plug-in adds a new menu item, Plug-Ins | Add Bookmarks, that gets the process started.

When you select this menu item, the plug-in looks for an article in your file named *Contents*. The article must consist of your Table of Contents, in the format described below. If the Table of Contents is split across several pages, create a separate bead in the article for each page. The plug-in creates both a bookmark and a link for each Table of Contents entry. After processing the Table of Contents, the plug-in looks for another article named *Tables* that contains the list of tables available in the document. The same process is applied to this article to produce links from the list of tables to the actual tables in the document itself.

To use this plug-in, your Table of Contents must consist of lines of text with a page number at the end. The pages must be numbered the way Exchange numbers them, with *1* being the first page in the file. If the text of the Table of Contents entry contains a number other than the page number at the end, the number must be in a bold typeface; a number in a regular typeface is assumed to be the page number. Indentation in the Table of Contents entries is detected and used to create subordinate bookmarks. The list of tables must contain lines of the form *Table X Title text <PgNum>*; these are converted into links to the page number *<PgNum>*. In both cases the page view created for each link and bookmark destination is a view of the entire page. After both articles are processed, they are deleted from the PDF file (though the text of the articles themselves is not deleted).

This plug-in is really designed to illustrate the possibilities of developing plug-ins for automation, rather than being a powerful automation tool itself. However, if you can live within its format requirements, it can save you some tedious work.

AddInfo

The ADDINFO.API plug-in adds a new menu item, Plug-Ins | AddInfo, and a toolbar button; selecting either prompts the user for a text file. AddInfo uses instructions it finds in the file to add information to a set of PDF files. The text file must contain some PostScript dictionaries in a particular format. The dictionaries specify which PDF files to process and what fields to add to the files. You can easily create these files yourself if you want to process a set of files.

The PostScript dictionary format is simple: it consists of a name followed by a list of key-value pairs. The list is enclosed in double-angle brackets, and the dictionary is terminated by an *x*. The names all begin with a slash, and the values must all be strings enclosed in parenthesis (numeric values will crash the viewer). Here is an example:

```
/Name << /Key1 (value1) /Key2 (value2) >> x
```

At the start of your text file is an optional dictionary of global items called */globals*. Any key-value pairs listed here are added to the Info dictionary of each PDF file processed. The global dictionary is followed by a separate dictionary for each PDF file you want to process, which contains key-value pairs for insertion only into that file's Info dictionary. Here is a listing of a file for use with AddInfo; it defines fields as they might be used for a portion of this book.

```
/globals <<
    /Title (Acrobat 2.1: Your Personal Consultant)
    /Author (Roy Christmann)
    /ISBN (1-56276-336-1)
    >> x

/ch01.pdf <<
    /SubTitle (Chapter 1: Introduction)
    /Keywords (Acrobat introduction)
    >> x

/ch02.pdf <<
    /SubTitle (Chapter 2: Acrobat Reader)
    /Keywords (Acrobat Reader)
    >> x
```

AddPS

ADDPS.API is a plug-in that allows you to insert the contents of a PostScript file in front of each page of your PDF file as Exchange prints the file. AddPS only works with a PostScript printer; the plug-in does not attempt to add the file to print streams going to other printers. You can put PostScript commands in this file to write or draw on the page before Exchange draws the PDF page. This allows you, for example, to print a watermark or other graphic, or print a word (such as *Draft* or *Confidential*) across the page as a background object to the PDF page.

It is up to you to make the file you send work with your printer (which can be tricky—do not try this unless you are experienced with PostScript). To use AddPS, select the new menu item Plug-Ins | AddPS. The program will ask you to select the file you want to send with each page. Select a file and press the OK button to send that file; press the Cancel button to stop sending files. Unfortunately, there is no visual indication that AddPS is active for a print job; you will have to check its menu item to see if it is enabled before printing a file.

Balloon

BALLOON.API adds the capability to show balloon help similar to that provided by Microsoft Help (not like Balloon Help on the Macintosh). When the user clicks on a link which has the new Action type DisplayBalloonHelp, a box pops up displaying the text you specify. You can use this type of link to provide definitions for words or other brief explanations. Figure 7.7 shows a sample message box.

Figure 7.7
A Balloon Help message

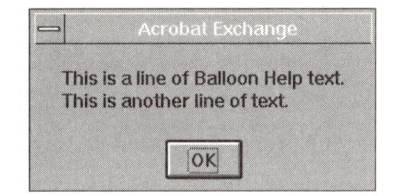

With BALLOON.API properly installed, the new Action type *DisplayBalloonHelp* is added to your Link Properties dialog box; select it as the type of action and the configuration button beneath the Type selection changes to Enter text. Select this to enter the text to be displayed when the link is activated. Enter the text you want. When displayed, the line breaks you enter will be preserved if possible; the message will be sized to fit the screen if necessary.

Bookmark

BOOKMARK.API (called BookMarkMunge.api on the Macintosh version) adds several new menu items to the Edit | Bookmarks pop-up menu. Open All causes the entire bookmark hierarchy to be displayed, while Close All closes all of the subordinate bookmarks, leaving only the topmost level visible. Add/Remove Page #'s modifies the text of the bookmarks themselves to add or remove the PDF file page numbers from the bookmark title text.

Cstmize

CSTMIZE.API is a Windows plug-in that lets you delete or rename menu items and delete toolbar buttons from the Exchange user interface. The buttons and menu items are not really deleted; the plug-in stores the names of buttons and menu items you specify in a file, and uses that file to modify Exchange after it has started up.

The plug-in adds two new menu items: Edit | Preferences | Menus and Edit | Preferences | Toolbar. Each of these brings up a dialog box that allows you to select menu items or toolbar buttons and delete them. Figure 7.8 shows the Customize dialog box for menu items. Select a menu item from the left box and either move it over to the list of deleted menu items on the left, or change its name by pressing the Change Name button. You cannot change or delete the main menu items like File or Edit, only their submenus. The Customize dialog for toolbars is similar, except that the dialog box displays the internal names for toolbar buttons, which can be a little confusing. The buttons are listed as they appear from left to right. Breaks between groups of buttons are also listed in the dialog box as separators (for example, Acrosrch:Separator).

If you need to restore your menus or toolbar and you do not have access to the Preferences menu items provided by CSTMIZE (because you have deleted them), you have two ways to restore Exchange to working order. Either move the CSTMIZE.API module from the PLUG_INS directory to the OPTIONAL directory, or on Windows, delete the CSTMIZE.INI file from your Windows main directory.

FullPath

FULLPATH.API is a simple plug-in that displays the full path of the PDF file in the window title bar (instead of just the file name). This is handy when you are viewing two files of the same name from different directories. There is nothing more to using this plug-in than

Figure 7.8
The Customize dialog box

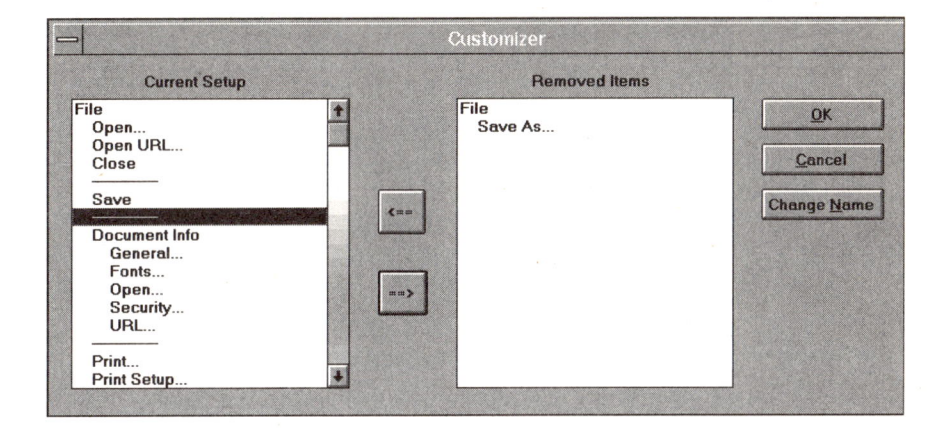

putting it in your PLUG_INS directory; however, using it does have one drawback. A side effect of using FullPath: while FullPath is active, files are not added to the list of recent files at the bottom of the Files menu.

KillLink

KILLLINK.API adds a new menu item, Plug-Ins | Remove All Extras; selecting this menu item deletes all links, bookmarks, and notes in a PDF file. This is a quick way to wipe a file clean of all annotations; but beware, there is no safety net with this function. It does not ask you if you are sure you want to do this, and there is no undo capability.

Markup

MARKUP.API provides a new tool, the Mark Up tool, which allows you to add a freehand drawing as an annotation to your document. The plug-in adds a new toolbar button (a picture of a hand holding a pencil), and a new menu item, Tools | Mark Up. Selecting either the button or the menu item changes the cursor to a crosshair. Now when you press the left mouse button, you can draw a freehand line.

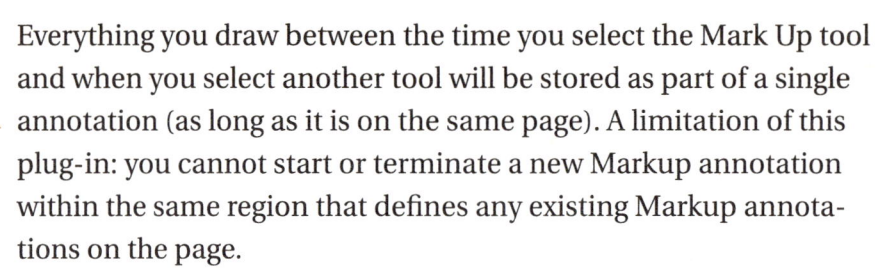

Everything you draw between the time you select the Mark Up tool and when you select another tool will be stored as part of a single annotation (as long as it is on the same page). A limitation of this plug-in: you cannot start or terminate a new Markup annotation within the same region that defines any existing Markup annotations on the page.

Markup is more of a demonstration plug-in than a finished product. There is no ability to change the color or line width of the pen you draw with. If you are interested in this capability, take a look at the commercially available plug-in Re:mark™ by Software Partners, Inc, (415) 428-0160.

MergeNote

MERGENOT.API provides the ability to hide or show all the notes in a document at once. The plug-in adds a new menu item, Edit | Notes | Hide All, which when selected hides all of the notes in the PDF file and changes its title to Show All. When selected again, it displays the notes again, and resets its name to Hide All.

Named Queries

NAMEDQRY.API gives you the capability to save an Acrobat Search query under a name you assign, and call the query back up again later and use it in a new search. It adds the menu item Tools | Search | Named Queries to the Exchange menus; selecting this menu item brings up the Named Queries dialog box shown in Figure 7.9. This dialog box contains a list of names for the queries you have saved. Use the Add, Change, and Delete buttons to manage the list of queries, and the Search button to invoke the query currently selected in the list box.

Figure 7.9
The Named Queries dialog box

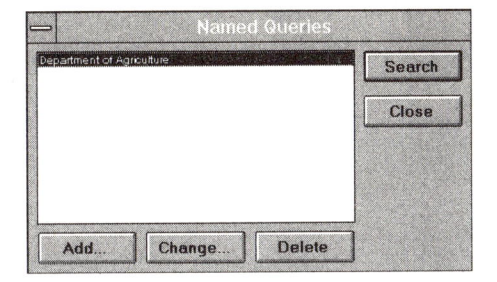

When you press the Add button, the dialog box shown in Figure 7.10 appears. Enter the new name and the contents of your query just as you would for a standard search; press the OK button when you're finished. The Change button uses a similar dialog, except that you may not change the name of the search.

Figure 7.10
The Add Query dialog box

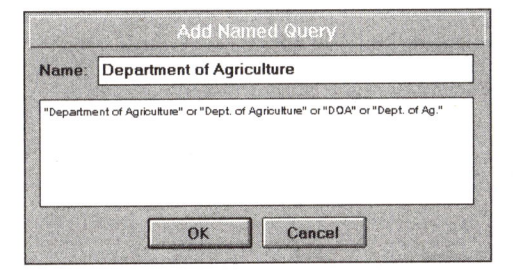

OpenAll

OPENALL.API is a Windows plug-in that gives Exchange the ability to accept dropped files other than PDF files and convert them to PDF; it also allows the File | Open command to be used on a non-PDF file and have Exchange convert it. It does not work with all application source files; but it does work successfully with Windows Notepad and Microsoft Word.

SnapZoom

SNAPZOOM.API adds a handy new tool to the toolbar. When selected, it allows you to zoom in on the document where your cursor is positioned by pressing the left mouse button. When you release the mouse button, the display returns to its previous magnification. SnapZoom doubles the current magnification (if possible—it is constrained by Exchange's limit of 800 percent). If you hold down the Ctrl/⌘ key while clicking, SnapZoom will halve the current magnification (so it works like the regular zoom tools).

Spread

SPREAD.API is a Windows plug-in that provides a way to copy PDF data to the clipboard in SYLK format. This format is used by spreadsheets to exchange data in tabular form. Spread adds the menu item Edit | Copy Table to Clipboard. When some text is selected, choosing this menu item copies the selected text to the clipboard in SYLK format. Go to your spreadsheet program and paste the clipboard into a spreadsheet. Your results will vary, depending on how well defined the table is in the PDF file.

Stamper

STAMPER.API provides a new type of annotation: an OK stamp. Stamper adds a new toolbar button and menu item Tools | Stamper. When selected, the cursor changes to the outline of a stamping machine. Single-click the left mouse button to stamp the document at that location.

Stats

STATS.API displays various data fields from your PDF files, and calculates one new and sometimes vital statistic. It adds a new menu item, File | Document Statistics, which displays the dialog box shown in Figure 7.11. Most of this display is redundant, but one new item of information is the word count, displayed at the bottom of the dialog box.

Figure 7.11
The Document Statistics dialog box

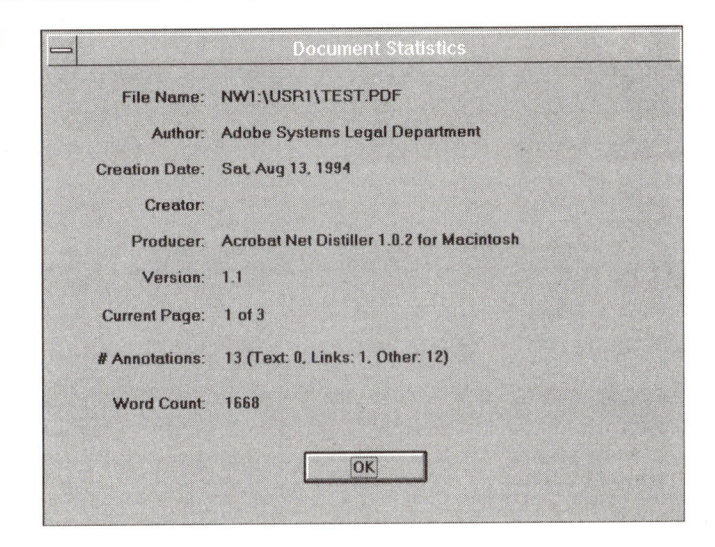

```
Document Statistics
File Name:        NW1:\USR1\TEST.PDF
Author:           Adobe Systems Legal Department
Creation Date:    Sat, Aug 13, 1994
Creator:
Producer:         Acrobat Net Distiller 1.0.2 for Macintosh
Version:          1.1
Current Page:     1 of 3
# Annotations:    13 (Text: 0, Links: 1, Other: 12)
Word Count:       1668

                    [ OK ]
```

Store

STORE.API is a Windows plug-in that allows you to store another file within a PDF file and extract it again later. The file is invisible to those without the plug-in installed. One possible use of this capability is to keep the source for a PDF document (such as a word processing file) with the document. Store adds two menu items: File | Store File and File | Extract File. Selecting Store File brings up the dialog box shown in Figure 7.12. Select the file you want to add. The file is not compressed or encrypted, but you can embed compressed or encrypted files if you like.

Figure 7.12
The Store File dialog box

Selecting Extract File brings up the dialog box shown in Figure 7.13. Select a file to extract from the list box, and provide a name for the new file. Press the OK button and the file is extracted. The embedded file is not removed from the PDF file; there does not seem to be a way to remove a file once you have embedded it with Store File.

Figure 7.13
The Extract File dialog box

StoryTell

STORYTLL.API is a Windows-only plug-in that will read articles in your PDF file aloud if you have an audio-equipped computer.

However, this plug-in requires a file, FB_SPCH.DLL, which cannot be redistributed without a license, so the file is not in the SDK. Consequently, we did not test this plug-in, but if you are interested, contact First Byte at (310) 793-0610 for more information.

WordFind

WORDFIND.API is useful as a debugging tool if you are trying to manipulate the contents of a PDF file using OLE or Apple Events. WordFind processes a PDF file and generates two new files:

- name>.WRD contains a list of all of the words used in the PDF file.
- name>.MAP contains a list of word offsets into the PDF file for those words.

WordFind adds two new menu items: Plug-ins | Create Map to create the files and Plug-ins | Find Word by Offset to demonstrate using a word offset address to grab a word from the file. While not particularly useful to non-developers, this gives you a listing of the words and their offsets if you are trying to access them via IAC.

Summary

In this chapter we have introduced Adobe's plug-in interface and some of the software available for it, including WebLink and Movie. Adobe has used the plug-in concept successfully in their other products, such as PhotoShop, so we expect more plug-ins to become available for Acrobat as well. In the next chapter, we talk about how to use the Acrobat tools alongside other tools to create larger data-processing systems using interapplication communications.

CHAPTER 8

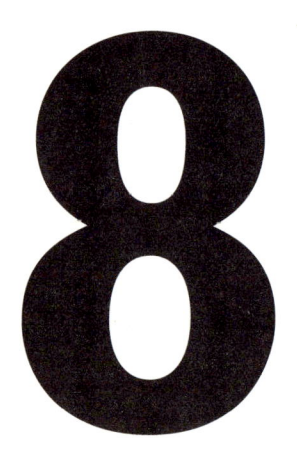

Integrating Applications with Acrobat

Introduction to Interapplication Communication

The Acrobat Software Development Kits

Integrating with Acrobat Reader

Integrating with Acrobat Exchange and Exchange LE

Integrating with the Acrobat Search Plug-in

Integrating with Acrobat PDF Writer

Integrating with Acrobat Distiller

Integrating with Acrobat Catalog

The Acrobat tools have extensive capabilities for communicating and integrating with other applications running on your Windows or Macintosh system. These can be applications you are already using or ones you write specifically for the purpose of automating some task you must perform. Adobe calls these capabilities *interapplication communication* or IAC. The Acrobat IAC facilities allow you to set up automatic processes that create, manage, or display PDF files as some part of a larger task.

This chapter introduces the interapplication communication and control capabilities of the various Acrobat tools. We give some examples of how to program these capabilities, but we assume you already have some experience with IAC concepts and programming techniques on your particular platform. If you don't have this level of experience, don't be intimidated by the technical nature of this discussion. Use the tables in this chapter to determine which IAC mechanisms you will need to use to accomplish your goals, then study only those techniques in some of the references we mention at the back of the book.

Introduction to Interapplication Communication

Interapplication communication (IAC) occurs when one running program on your machine talks to another running program through some communication channel provided by your system. The programs may exchange data, or one program may issue commands to the other program. You, the developer, design this interaction to integrate the two (or more) applications to produce the result you desire.

Collectively, Acrobat supports the common IAC mechanisms used on both Macintosh and Windows platforms; however, individual tools do not support all the options. In the following sections, we will briefly discuss each of the IAC mechanisms available to the developer on these two platforms.

Windows IAC

Microsoft Windows (version 3.1 and Windows 95) provides several different IAC mechanisms. Windows versions of the Acrobat tools use all of them in various combinations to provide a robust IAC implementation. Unfortunately, if you are developing an application that requires you to use more than one Acrobat tool, this means you'll probably have to learn more than one of them. The three primary mechanisms are introduced below. Later, the section on each Acrobat application program describes the individual choices.

On the Macintosh platform, a single programming tool, AppleScript, provides access to almost all of the IAC capabilities of the Acrobat tools. Windows doesn't have a similar tool for IAC programming; the closest thing to AppleScript available for Windows is Microsoft's Visual Basic. Visual Basic defines high-level objects to handle most of the task of programming the two most important IAC mechanisms: Dynamic Data Exchange and OLE automation.

Message Passing

Windows is a message-passing system, and any introductory book on Windows programming will describe the huge variety of Windows's messages. Acrobat uses message-passing for IAC, although not extensively. Several of the Acrobat tools will send messages in response to events such as starting or terminating a job, and they offer limited status query capabilities as well. We discuss the messages that each program can send and receive in the appropriate sections below. Message-passing is generally available only to C and C++ programmers; Visual Basic users do not have access to the Windows message-passing interface.

Dynamic Data Exchange

Dynamic Data Exchange (DDE) is an IAC method based on a special message-passing protocol defined by Microsoft. DDE access is supported by the macro languages of many software products, including spreadsheets and word processors, making it an easy to use option for automating some tasks using the Acrobat tools. Developers also have easy access to DDE from C, C++, and Visual Basic, as well as other popular languages.

Within the Acrobat tools, the level of support for DDE is mixed. The Reader provides a minimal DDE interface; Exchange provides more capabilities but only at the document level (inserting and deleting pages, for example). Catalog provides a small set of DDE commands, and the Search plug-in can perform searches via DDE. Adobe recommends favoring OLE automation (described in the section below) instead of DDE for controlling the viewers (and in fact OLE offers more capabilities). However, currently only the viewers support OLE; Catalog, Distiller, and Search do not have OLE interfaces.

DDE is a client-server protocol where the server answers to a particular sequence of names supplied by the client in order to establish the communication (called a *conversation*). Usually there are three names the client must supply: the *application name*, the *topic*, and the *item* name within the topic (in some cases, you only need the first two names). Each Acrobat program that supports DDE has its own set of names you must supply; we describe the proper names for each Acrobat program under its own section below. The free Acrobat software development kit described below provides a sample Visual Basic program that searches a set of files using a DDE interface to the Search plug-in.

Object Linking and Embedding

Object Linking and Embedding (OLE) is Microsoft's object-oriented technology for combining data from different applications into a single document. Like DDE, OLE is a client-server protocol, but DDE is geared more toward communicating simple data values and commands, while OLE works with the entire data file of the server application. For Acrobat, this means you can link or embed a PDF file with any OLE client application, and when you activate the PDF portion of your compound document an Acrobat viewer is run to display or edit the file.

OLE is complicated by the transition currently under way between OLE version 1 and version 2. OLE 1 provides the basic ability to create a compound document; OLE 2 adds an object-oriented command structure called OLE automation. OLE automation allows the OLE server program to be controlled by the client, just as if you were operating the program yourself. Exchange and Exchange LE provide extensive OLE 2 automation capabilities for PDF files, but they are the only Acrobat tools that do so. The free Acrobat SDK described in the next section provides several OLE example programs that demonstrate how to use this complex interface.

In the real world as it is in mid-1995, OLE 1 is supported by virtually every major Windows application (including all of the Acrobat viewers). OLE 2 is slowly gaining acceptance among developers (slowly no doubt because of the vastly increased complexity of OLE 2). However, Windows 95 programs must support OLE 2 to be certified by Microsoft, so within the next year OLE 2 should eclipse OLE 1 as the dominant technology for compound documents. Microsoft recently released OLE 2 for the Macintosh as well, and Adobe is working on supporting OLE 2 in its Macintosh products in a future release of Acrobat.

Macintosh IAC

Apple introduced a new IAC mechanism called AppleEvents with the release of the System 7 operating system. AppleEvents are (loosely speaking) the Macintosh equivalent to Microsoft's OLE automation technology for controlling other programs. Apple is also promoting a different technology called OpenDoc to create compound documents, but it is not yet available. With the advent of System 7.5, Apple now provides a scripting language called AppleScript that lets you easily create with a text editor sequences of AppleEvents to control your applications. With AppleScript the Acrobat tools are all accessed through a single easy-to-use IAC mechanism; in contrast, Windows users will have to learn at least two mechanisms to accomplish all of the same tasks. The simplicity and power of AppleScript make the Macintosh the ideal platform to use for automation.

AppleScript provides two ways to create a script: by recording and by editing. Recording a script means that you use the Script Editor to remember everything that you do with the mouse and keyboard, saving the result as an AppleScript. Unfortunately, not all applications support AppleScript recording, including the Acrobat tools. To use AppleScript with the Acrobat tools, you will have to write your script manually with the Script Editor. We show you the commands to use later in this chapter.

You can also use AppleEvents in programs that you write in other languages. Acrobat uses the Required and Core suites of AppleEvents and defines some additional events of its own. Adobe provides header files in the free SDK for Macintosh (described below) that specify the AppleEvent constants used for each of the new events defined by the Acrobat tools.

AppleScript Essentials

You use the Script Editor application to edit and test AppleScripts. The main window of the Script Editor is shown in Figure 8.1.

AppleScript provides for a common set of commands used by all applications, supplemented by special commands that perform functions for specific applications. Since an AppleScript command is not necessarily specific to a particular application, AppleScript provides the tell statement to direct the AppleEvents in your script

Figure 8.1
The Macintosh Script Editor main program window

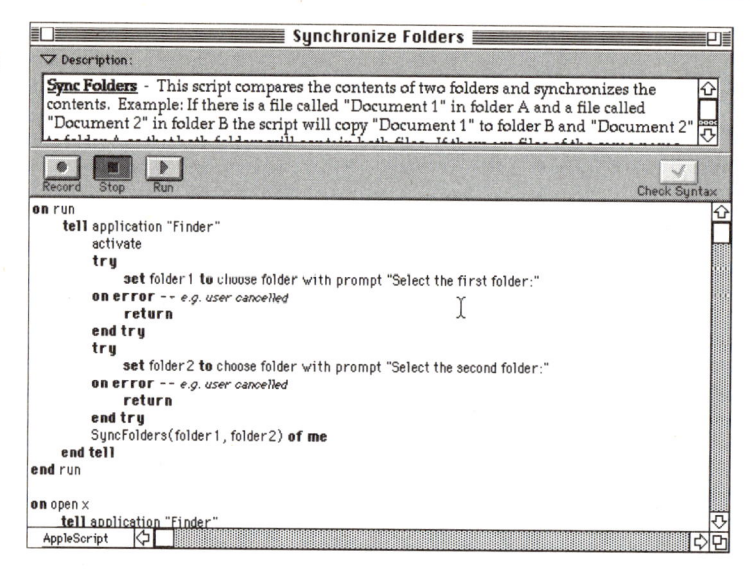

to the right application. Use a tell statement like the one shown below, specifying the name of the application you want to use between double quotes.

```
tell application "Acrobat Exchange"
  --AppleScript commands listed here are sent to Exchange
end tell
```

Comments in the script begin with two dashes as shown. Once you've entered a script, use the Check Syntax button to verify that you have written a valid AppleScript. If during the syntax check the Script Editor identifies an error, it highlights the text it believes is responsible for the problem. However, sometimes the problem may be caused by an error on a previous line, so if you cannot find an error in the highlighted text, look back at previous lines in the script to be sure they don't have an error.

When the syntax of your script is correct, the Script Editor also compiles it as part of the syntax check. Then it is ready to be tested. Click the Run button in the active script window, or choose the

The Acrobat Software Development Kits

Controls | Run menu command. To stop a script that is running, press the Stop button.

When your script is first run, the Script Editor substitutes the formal name of the application it found in place of the name you specified:

```
tell application "Acrobat™ Exchange 2.0"
  --AppleScript commands listed here are sent to Exchange
end tell
```

You can save your AppleScript in one of three ways:

- *Text file*—A standard TEXT file. This format allows you to edit your script in other applications, and it is the only format you can use to save a script that contains syntax errors.

- *Compiled Script*—A script that has been compiled by the Script Editor. It has no syntax errors and is ready to run, but it can still be edited.

- *Application*—The script is saved as its own application program. An application script cannot be edited with Script Editor. This is an ideal format for completed scripts because the script cannot be modified by an end user—but remember to save a copy of the original script in one of the other two forms so you can edit it.

Use the Script Editor to examine the sample AppleScript files located in the free Macintosh SDK described in the next section.

The Acrobat Software Development Kits

Adobe provides several software development kits (SDKs) you can use to access Acrobat features from other applications and develop new Acrobat plug-ins. At the high end, Adobe sells the Plug-in SDK (on CD-ROM), which includes everything needed to develop both IAC with Acrobat tools and plug-in software for Exchange. It also includes versions of Reader, Exchange, Distiller, Catalog, the PDF

Text Extraction Toolkit for Sun workstations, and all the available technical notes. Adobe considers the plug-in interface to be proprietary technology and they require developers to sign a nondisclosure agreement before purchasing this SDK. Contact the Adobe Developers Association for more details.

Adobe also sells a version of their SDK (also on CD-ROM) that only supports IAC development (not plug-in development) for considerably less money and with no disclosure restrictions. This version also includes the Acrobat programs plus all the technical documentation not pertaining to the plug-in interface. It is also available from the Adobe Developers Association.

Most of the contents of the IAC version of the SDK are also available for free directly from Adobe's FTP server on the Internet (only the Acrobat programs themselves are missing). There is one file for Macintosh, one for Windows, and one for UNIX (which we do not cover). These are not small files: The Macintosh version is about 16 megabytes, while the Windows version weighs in at a little less than 12 megabytes. But they are a great value, well worth the download time if you are considering IAC development with Acrobat. They contain header and library files to use when developing your code, sample programs complete with source code, and PDF versions of all the pertinent technical notes. The Windows version supports programs written in generic C, C++ with Microsoft Foundation Classes, and Microsoft Visual Basic. The Macintosh version supports programs written in Think C and AppleScript. In the next section we'll examine each of these products in more detail. Note: Adobe had not updated their SDKs to reflect the new 2.1 version of Acrobat as we went to press, so the contents of the SDKs may change in the near future when they are updated.

The Free Acrobat Windows SDK

The free Windows SDK is available from the Internet via FTP from ftp.adobe.com as the file:

    \pub\adobe\Acrobat\SDK\acrosdk.zip.

In addition to the header files, libraries, and sample code described below, this file contains technical documentation in PDF format (including full-text indexes created with Catalog) and a set of sample plug-ins, some of which are described in Chapter 7. The file itself is a small subdirectory tree compressed using the PKZIP compression utility (PKZIP and its partner PKUNZIP are widely available online). Uncompress the file using the following command at a DOS prompt from within your root directory:

    PKUNZIP -d acrosdk.zip

This will create the subdirectory \ACROSDK\ and put all of the SDK files within it. Table 8.1 describes the directory structure it creates (if you do not get this directory structure, you forgot the -d option in the command above).

Table 8.1 The Windows SDK Directory Structure

Directory	Contents
OTHERDOC\	Miscellaneous documents: samples, technical support and testing information, and the Acrobat logo licensing agreement. These files have a full-text search index in OTHERDOC.PDX.
TECHDOC\	All of the technical notes discussing IAC, PDF format updates, and pdfmark. These files have a full-text search index in TECHDOC.PDX.
SOURCE\WIN\SDK\	The header files and libraries you need for using Acrobat IAC in your own programs.
SOURCE\WIN\PLUG_INS\	Sample plug-ins you can use (see Chapter 7).
SOURCE\WIN\SAMPLES\	Sample IAC program source code in C, C++, and Visual Basic.
SOURCE\WIN\APPS\	Sample IAC program executable files.

Header Files and Libraries

The SDK provides a set of files you can use as a developer to access Acrobat services via IAC. They are located in the \ACROSDK\SOURCE\WIN\SDK\ directory. Key files include:

- *ACROAUTO.H*—Defines C language entry points for accessing Exchange OLE automation facilities.

- *DISTCTRL.H*—Definitions for accessing Distiller IAC facilities.

- *IAC.H*—C language typedefs defining values used with Exchange OLE automation.

- *PDFWCTRL.H*—Definitions for accessing PDFWriter IAC facilities.

- *SRCHDDE.H*—Definitions for accessing the Search plug-in through DDE.

- *ACROAUTO.LIB*—A link library implementing the entry points defined in ACROAUTO.H.

- *ACROBAT.TLB*—A Microsoft Visual C++ Type Library file that defines an OLE automation control interface to Exchange using C++ classes.

- *ACROBAT.ODL*—A Microsoft Visual C++ Object Definition Library file that defines the OLE 2 interface to Exchange.

The directory also contains files needed for Exchange version 2.0 to complete OLE 2 installation under Windows. The standard Exchange 2.0 installation program fails to install these files during its own installation, with the result that OLE automation doesn't work properly if no other OLE 2 application has been installed on the user's system. These files allow you to correct this situation. See the file README.TXT for instructions.

Sample Applications

The SDK also provides several demonstration applications you can study to learn to use Exchange with OLE 2 and DDE. No sample programs are provided in the SDK demonstrating the message-passing interfaces with the Acrobat tools; instead we provide an example to show you how to use this mechanism.

Acroauto   The \ACROSDK\SOURCE\WIN\SDK\SAMPLES\ACROAUTO\ directory contains the source code for the ACROAUTO.DLL library and several small test applications. ACROAUTO.DLL is a dynamic link library (DLL) you use with your applications to access the OLE 2 capabilities of Exchange. The header file ACROAUTO.H described above defines the routines found in this library for C programmers. To use this DLL, you should add it to the directory where Exchange is installed (or some other directory on the path).

Underneath the ACROAUTO directory are three subdirectories:

- *TEST* contains a test program for ACROAUTO.DLL written in Microsoft Visual C++ and using Microsoft Foundation Classes. This program provides the menu item Automation | Test which moves the Exchange window on the screen using OLE automation.

- *CTEST* is an OLE automation demonstration program that uses ACROAUTO.DLL but is written in C rather than C++. The program creates a new Exchange window, then deletes it and exits. The only thing that happens visually is that Exchange is launched if it is not running already.

- *LAUNCH* is another OLE automation demonstration program written in C. It opens a standard Open File dialog box, allowing the user to select a PDF file, then it launches Exchange with the file the user selected.

Microsoft Foundation Classes Sample Programs   The Acrobat SDK provides several sample programs that use the Microsoft Foundation Classes to access Exchange. The programs make use of an OLE 2 feature that allows Exchange to draw the PDF file into the sample application's window, instead of Exchange's window. The following two projects are located beneath \ACROSDK\SOURCE\WIN\SDK\SAMPLES\MFC\:

- *CVIEWER* puts up a simplified version of the Exchange user interface and uses Exchange to draw PDF files into its own window. It uses the PDDoc OLE object (described below).

- *CVIEWER2* is also a PDF file viewer, but it uses the AVDoc OLE object instead of PDDoc. AVDoc provides a more complete interface for a PDF document (see descriptions below).

Visual Basic Sample Programs   Visual Basic 3.0 (VB) offers an ideal environment for IAC programming because of the high-level support it provides for OLE and DDE. The free SDK provides several VB sample programs in subdirectories of the directory \ACROSDK\SOURCE\WIN\SDK\SAMPLES\VB\:

- *CONTRACT* demonstrates how to use DDE commands to ask Acrobat Search to perform a full-text search over a collection of documents. The directory contains source for the program SQUERY.EXE, which puts up its own dialog box to collect the parameters for the search, then uses DDE to issue the commands to Search and display the results.

- *VBTEST* lets you create OLE automation objects in separate windows and control all of their features through its own custom dialog boxes. You can use this program to observe what Exchange does through each of its OLE automation interfaces.

- *VBVIEW* is a complete PDF file viewer that demonstrates how to get Exchange to draw into a Visual Basic window. Like CVIEWER, it is implemented using the PDDoc OLE object.
- *VBVIEW2* is also a PDF file viewer, using the AVDoc OLE object for its implementation.

Even if you don't have VB, if you have Microsoft's Visual C++ compiler, the application DISPTEST.EXE (located in the \MSVC\BIN\ subdirectory) is actually a limited version of Visual Basic that allows you to test OLE automation interfaces. Unfortunately the Visual Basic files in the free SDK are not directly compatible with DISPTEST, but you can still use it to experiment with your own interfaces, before committing yourself to a C or C++ implementation.

The Free Macintosh SDK

The free Macintosh SDK is available from the Internet via FTP from ftp.adobe.com as the file:

```
\pub\adobe\Acrobat\SDK\acrosdk.sit
```

This file includes both the Macintosh SDK and most of the Windows SDK files, which makes it a bit bigger than the Windows version: about 16 megabytes. This file is compressed with the Macintosh standard StuffIt program. It creates a directory tree underneath the directory Acrobat SDK. Table 8.2 gives a summary of the contents.

Header Files and Libraries

The Macintosh SDK supports C programming with files found in the :Acrobat SDK:SOURCE:MAC:SDK directory.

- *UserInteraction.c* and *UserInteraction.h* are the two files that describe how to access PDF Writer using C from another program. PDF Writer does not have an AppleScript interface.

Table 8.2   **The Macintosh SDK Directory Structure**

Directory	Contents
:OTHERDOC:	Miscellaneous documents: samples, technical support and testing information, and the Acrobat logo licensing agreement. These files have a full-text search index in OTHERDOC.PDX.
:TECHDOC:	All of the technical notes discussing IAC, PDF format updates, and pdfmark. These files have a full-text search index in TECHDOC.PDX.
:SOURCE:WIN:	Most of the Windows SDK as described above.
:SOURCE:MAC:SDK	The C source and header files you need to use Macintosh IAC with your applications.
:SOURCE:MAC:Plug-Ins:	Sample Mac versions of plug-ins you can use with Exchange (see Chapter 7).
:SOURCE:MAC:Samples:	Sample IAC program source code using C and AppleScript.
:SOURCE:MAC:Apps:	Sample IAC program executable files.
:SOURCE:MAC:UTILITIES:	Utilities to change the type of a file to PDF or TEXT.

- *aetypes.h* provides the definitions of all the AppleEvents that are specific to Acrobat. (Acrobat also uses the standard suites of AppleEvents, which are defined as part of your C compiler on the Mac.)

- *iac.h* is a header file containing definitions of miscellaneous data types required by other IAC functions.

- *searchae.h* is a header file defining AppleEvents and data structures used to access Acrobat Search with AppleEvents.

Sample Applications

The Macintosh sample applications are made much simpler by the fact that there is only a single IAC mechanism to deal with. There are three directories of sample programs:

- *SCRIPTS* provides three AppleScript scripts designed to show how to use AppleScript to control Exchange.

- *AEVIEW* contains the source for a Think C program that uses AppleEvents to cause Exchange to draw within another application's window.

- *OPENALL-Distiller* provides an AppleScript that demonstrates how to tell Distiller to process specific PostScript files into PDF.

Integrating with Acrobat Reader

The IAC capabilities of the Reader are defined in Technical Note #5155, "Acrobat Viewer Interapplication Communication Support" (available in the TECHDOCS directory of the free SDK). However, you don't need that document to understand the Reader, because its capabilities are so limited.

The Windows Reader DDE Interface

The Reader provides limited support to other programs as a DDE server. The Reader responds to the DDE application name of "acroview", and the topic name of "control". No item name is required. It supports three commands that allow you to:

- Open and display a PDF file
- Print a PDF file to the system printer
- Exit the Reader

The formats for these commands are shown in Table 8.3 below. Italicized words in the table are parameters you must supply values for when you create the command string. See the Exchange DDE section for more information applicable to using DDE with the Reader.

Table 8.3   **Windows Reader DDE Commands**

Command	Format
Open the document for viewing or editing.	[FileOpen(*filename*)]
Print the document on the system printer. No print dialogs are displayed.	[FilePrint(*filename*)]
Close the viewer.	[AppExit( )]

Note: When specifying a file name in a DDE command, specify the entire path for the file as well as the name. The DDE commands are shown enclosed within square brackets; these brackets (as well as the empty parentheses with AppExit) must be supplied as part of the command string.

Macintosh Reader AppleEvent Support

The Macintosh version of the Reader supports only the Required suite of AppleEvents, shown in Table 8.4 in their AppleScript versions. When used with AppleScript, each of these commands must occur within an appropriate tell...end tell statement.

Table 8.4   **Macintosh Reader AppleEvent Support**

Command	AppleScript Format
Launch the viewer	run
Open a file	open *filename*
Print a file	print *filename*
Quit the viewer	quit

Integrating with Acrobat Exchange and Exchange LE

The IAC capabilities of Exchange and Exchange LE are defined in Technical Note #5155, "Acrobat Viewer Interapplication Communication Support." This document is part of the free SDK, and is also available separately from Adobe's FTP site. It is an essential document to keep by your side if you are considering using IAC programming with Exchange.

There is one simple difference between Exchange and Exchange LE: The LE version cannot save a file to disk. Consequently, all commands that modify a PDF file are disabled in Exchange LE. In the tables below, commands which change a PDF file or write the file back to disk storage are not available for use in Exchange LE. In the text that follows, when we refer to Exchange, we include Exchange LE unless otherwise noted.

Windows DDE Services

Exchange provides a set of DDE commands that include the three commands described above for the Reader; they also include a set of commands oriented toward page manipulation that are described in the table below. To access more of Exchange's capabilities than what is provided with these commands, you will have to use OLE automation instead of DDE.

Like the Reader, Exchange responds to the application name "acroview" and the topic name "control". No item name is required. Some notes on using DDE with Exchange:

- These DDE commands only operate on files you open via DDE with the DocOpen command described below; they will not work on files the user has opened manually. Use this command before using any of the other commands on the file.

- When you specify a PDF file, use the full path name in the DDE command. Once you have opened a file and made it the topmost document, you can leave the file name blank in future commands relating to that file (unless you reference another document in the meantime). When no file name is specified, Exchange will apply your command to the topmost open document window (the most recent document you worked on). Instead of a file name, leave a space (and the comma if there is more than one parameter).

- You can send more than one command at once by concatenating their command strings together. They will appear as a single operation to the user. Make sure you include the square brackets for each command.

- Page numbers used with DDE commands start with zero, not one. A limitation of DDE is that there is no command to return the number of pages in the document. You can get this number using OLE automation or by counting them yourself (issuing DDE Request transactions to turn pages until you get a false return value, indicating that you are at the end of the document). Alternatively, use the following values:

Page Number Command	Value
Before the first page	–1
The last page	–2
All pages	–3

- Use double quotes if you must send a string with an embedded space in it. Otherwise, no quoting is necessary.

- Each of the commands in Table 8.5 can return a Boolean result (true or false) indicating whether the command was successful or not.

Integrating with Acrobat Exchange and Exchange LE   277

These commands can be sent using two different DDE transaction types. Use an Execute transaction if you don't care about receiving the result code produced by the command (WM_DDE_EXECUTE in C, or LinkExecute in Visual Basic). Use a Request transaction if you do want the result (WM_DDE_REQUEST in C, or LinkRequest in Visual Basic).

Table 8.5   **Exchange Windows DDE Support**

DDE Commands	Format
Hide the viewer window.	[AppHide()] Use this command to prevent user interaction with the viewer while you are using DDE.
Show the viewer window.	[AppShow()] Use this command to restore the viewer after hiding it.
Hide the toolbar.	[HideToolbar()]
Open the document for viewing or editing.	[DocOpen(*PdfFileName*)] *PdfFileName* is the full path (drive, directory, name, and extension) to the PDF file.
Close the document without saving it.	[DocClose(*PdfFileName*)]
Save the document to its current disk file.	[DocSave(*PdfFileName*)]
Save the document under a new name.	[DocSaveAs(*PdfFileName, NewPdfFileName*)] *NewPdfFileName* becomes the new name for the document window too.
Print the document or part of a document.	[DocPrint(*PdfFileName, StartPage, EndPage*)] *StartPage* and *EndPage* are PDF page numbers, which start at zero (not one).
Insert pages into a document.	[DocInsertPages(*DestPdfFileName, InsertAfterPage, SourcePdfFileName*)] *InsertAfterPage* is a page number starting at zero.
Replace pages in a document.	[DocReplacePages(*DestPdfFileName, StartDestPage, SourcePdfFileName, StartSourcePage, EndSourcePage*)] The number of pages replaced is defined by the difference between *StartSourcePage* and *EndSourcePage*; all page numbers start at zero.
Delete pages in a document.	[DocDeletePages(*PdfFileName, StartPage, EndPage*)]

Table 8.5 Exchange Windows DDE Support (continued)

DDE Commands	Format
Set the view magnification level.	[DocZoomTo(*PdfFileName, ZoomType, Scale*)] *ZoomType* is one of the string literals: AVZoomNoVary—a fixed zoom. AVZoomFitPage—fits page in the window. AVZoomFitWidth—fits page's width in the window. AVZoomFitVisibleWidth—fits visible width in window. *Scale* is the magnification level in percent (that is, 100 is normal size).
Go to a particular page in a document.	[DocGoTo(*PdfFileName, Page*)] *Page* is a PDF page number starting at zero (not one) for the first page of the document.
Move back one page.	[DocPageUp(*PdfFileName*)] Same as the Page Up keyboard command.
Move forward one page.	[DocPageDown(*PdfFileName*)] Same as the Page Down keyboard command.
Set document viewing mode.	[DocSetViewMode(*PdfFileName, ViewType*)] *ViewType* is one of the string literals: "PDUseBookmarks", "PDUseNone", "PDUseThumbs".
Scroll the current page.	[DocScroll(*PdfFileName, X,Y*)] *X* is the x-coordinate on the page to place in the upper-left corner of the window. *Y* is the y-coordinate on the page to place in the upper-left corner of the window.
Scroll page to the right.	[DocPageRight(*PdfFileName*)] Same as Shift-Right Arrow keyboard command.
Scroll page to the left.	[DocPageLeft(*PdfFileName*)] Same as Shift-Left Arrow keyboard command.
Find a string in the file.	[DocFind(*PdfFileName, SearchString, CaseSensitive, WholeWords, ResetPage*)] *SearchString* is the string to find (in double quotes if it contains spaces). If *CaseSensitive* is true, character case in the search string must be matched exactly. If *WholeWords* is true, the search string must match against a single whole word, not a portion of a word or more than one word. If *ResetPage* is true, the search starts at the beginning of the document; otherwise it starts on the current page.

Windows OLE 2 Automation

OLE automation allows an OLE server application like Exchange to provide a set of services centered around objects defined in the server application. In the case of Exchange, these objects represent Exchange, its windows, the PDF files, and their component parts. Client applications that you write manipulate these objects through the OLE automation interface.

Adobe recommends OLE automation as the IAC solution of choice when possible. At the moment it is only possible with Exchange (and Exchange LE) and only on Windows; however, Adobe intends to extend its OLE coverage both to other programs and to the Macintosh platform now that OLE 2 is available for it.

Exchange's OLE automation interface provides an object-oriented representation of Exchange itself, PDF files, and their components. The objects defined by Exchange are described in Table 8.6. Figure 8.2 shows the hierarchical structure of the primary objects defined within Exchange. You can access these objects from programs written in C, C++, and Visual Basic (and other languages that support OLE automation).

Table 8.6 **Exchange OLE 2 Objects**

Object Name	Object Definition
App	Exchange itself: the program, its window, menu, and toolbar, and the set of AVDoc windows it has open
AVDoc	A PDF file displayed in an Exchange window. The window includes Exchange window controls, and links and bookmarks in the file are operative.
AVPageView	A view of a page in an AVDoc
PDDoc	A PDF file. Use this to manipulate the file contents (pages, annotations, and text selections), or to access individual pages of the file.
PDPage	A single page in a PDDoc. Can be used to display the PDF page without annotations or bookmarks.
PDAnnot	An annotation in a PDDoc (a link or a note)
PDBookmark	A bookmark in a PDDoc

Table 8.6   **Exchange OLE 2 Objects (continued)**

Object Name	Object Definition
PDTextSelection	A text selection
Point	A point in the plane
Rect	A rectangle
Time	A time value
HiLiteList	A list of words and characters to highlight

Figure 8.2
Structural view of the primary Exchange OLE objects

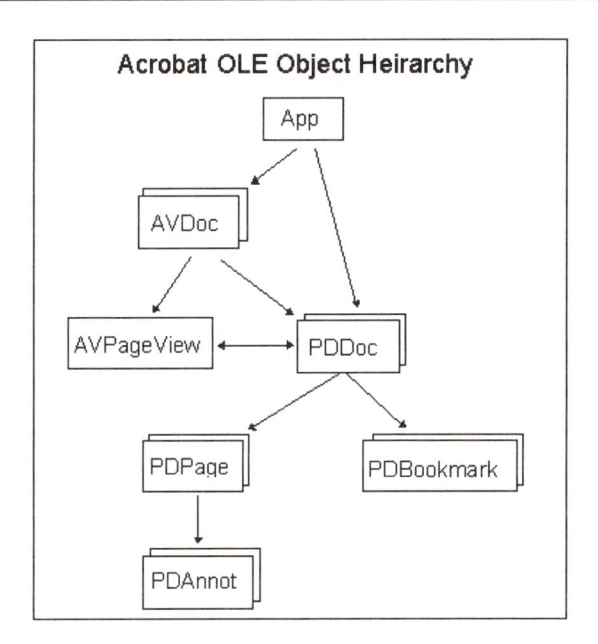

```
Acrobat OLE Object Heirarchy

              App
             / | \
            /  |  \
         AVDoc |   \
         /  \  |    \
        /    \ |     \
   AVPageView ← → PDDoc
                  /    \
                 /      \
              PDPage   PDBookmark
                |
              PDAnnot
```

As a programmer, you create instances of these automation objects and then manipulate them using the methods defined for the object. Adobe provides support for three languages: C, C++, and Visual Basic. Each supported language has its own means of representing the objects:

- C++ users can declare, instantiate, and manipulate versions of the automation objects directly. Microsoft Visual C++ users can use SDK\ACROBAT.TLB, a type library file, to define the C++

classes supported by Exchange. Add this file to your project. You can also refer to the SAMPLES\MFC\VIEWER project subdirectory to find ACROBAT.H and ACROBAT.CPP if you cannot use the type library file.

- C users declare data structures for each automation object and pass them to subroutines to access the object's methods. Use the subroutine definitions found in SDK\ACROAUTO.H and the values defined in SDK\IAC.H. Before calling any routines in the subroutine library, follow the instructions in ACROAUTO.H about initializing the library. Link your program with SDK\ACROAUTO.LIB to include the subroutines in your program.

- Visual Basic 3.0 programmers can use its built-in support for OLE automation. First dimension a Visual Basic data type called an Object, then use the CreateObject method to initialize the Object to work with a particular Exchange OLE automation object. You tell CreateObject the name of the Exchange object you want (the names are listed in Table 8.6). Attach the prefix "Acroexch." to the name from Table 8.6, as shown below. You must declare a Visual Basic Object for each OLE automation object you need. Here's a simple example that creates an instance of an App object:

```
Dim AcroApp as Object
Set AcroApp = CreateObject("Acroexch.App")
'Now use AcroApp to access the App object's methods
AcroApp.Maximize(1) 'maximize the Exchange window
```

In the sections that follow, we provide tables that list all of the methods available for the most important OLE automation objects that Exchange provides. These tables use the Visual Basic names and data types for these methods. C and C++ programmers use similar names; the definitive source for the correct names to use are the header files named in the list above. In the tables that follow, Visual

Basic data types are indicated by a suffix character appended to each variable name. The suffix characters and their meanings are:

Character	Meaning
%	Integer (16 bits)
&	Long (32-bit integer)
$	String (zero-terminated ASCII)

Sometimes Boolean values are called for in the OLE interface, either in parameters to the methods listed below or as return values. Visual Basic implements Boolean values as integers, where a non-zero value is true, and a zero is false; C and C++ programmers should be familiar with this as well. In other cases, a handle to an Exchange object is required as a parameter or return value. We do not show a data type character for these values; generally, you must dimension variables as VB Objects for each one of these you require. Finally, sometimes constant values are required. The definitive source for constant values is SDK\IAC.H, which contains enumerated constants declared in the C language. To translate these to actual numbers for Visual Basic, remember that unless specified otherwise, the value of an enumerated list item in C starts with zero and adds one for each new value.

The App Object

The App object defines Exchange itself: the application window on the screen, its menu items, toolbar buttons, and other aspects of the entire application, such as preference items and a list of all the open windows. You only need to create one of these objects for a given OLE automation session. App object methods (detailed in Table 8.7) allow you to:

- Quit the Exchange application.

- Hide, show, and maximize the Exchange window.

Integrating with Acrobat Exchange and Exchange LE

- Execute a menu item (a valuable ability since not all menu commands have corresponding OLE automation commands).
- Change the menu structure or toolbar contents.
- Select a tool (such as the Hand or Link tool).
- Get and set values for user preference items.

Each menu item and toolbar button has a language-independent name that is always used in OLE automation. These names are listed in Appendix A of Technical Note #5155. The GetPreference and SetPreference methods require a number to specify which preference item to operate on; these numbers are found in the SDK\IAC.H file where they are listed as C enumerated types.

Table 8.7 Exchange OLE 2 App Object Methods

Function	App Object Method
Quit the viewer program.	Exit
Close all open documents.	CloseAllDocs
Hide the viewer window.	Hide Once hidden, the user cannot control the window. In this mode, Exchange automatically exits when the last automation object is destroyed.
Show the viewer window.	Show Restores user control for the viewer window.
Maximize the viewer window.	Maximize(*Flag%*) *Flag%* is true to maximize the window, false for normal.
Return the viewer window's location and size.	GetFrame Returns a Rect object describing the window position.
Set the window to a specific location and size.	SetFrame(*Location*) *Location* is a Rect object describing the window position.
Execute a menu item by name.	MenuItemExecute(*MenuItemName$*) *MenuItemName$* is the name of the menu item. Returns true if the menu item is executed.
Test whether a menu item is enabled.	MenuItemIsEnabled(*MenuItemName$*) Returns true if the menu item is enabled.
Test whether a menu item is checked.	MenuItemIsMarked(*MenuItemName$*) Returns true if the menu item is checked.

Table 8.7 Exchange OLE 2 App Object Methods (continued)

Function	App Object Method
Remove a menu item from the menu.	MenuItemRemove(*MenuItemName*$) Returns true if the menu item was removed.
Return the name of the currently active tool.	GetActiveTool Returns the name of the tool as a string.
Set the active tool by name.	SetActiveTool(*ToolName*$, *Persistent*%) *ToolName*$ is the name of the tool. *Persistent*%, if true, specifies that the tool should remain selected after the initial operation with it is completed.
Test whether a toolbar button is enabled.	ToolButtonIsEnabled(*ToolName*$) Returns true if the tool is enabled.
Remove a button from the toolbar.	ToolButtonRemove(*ToolName*$)
Return the number of open AVDoc objects.	GetNumAVDocs Returns a long integer.
Return a handle to an AVDoc object specified by number.	GetAVDoc(*Index*&) *Index*& is the AVDoc number, ranging from one to the number returned by GetNumAVDocs. Returns an AVDoc object handle.
Return a handle to the active AVDoc.	GetActiveDoc Returns an AVDoc object representing the currently active document.
Return a code that specifies the language in use by Acrobat.	GetLanguage Returns a three-character ASCII string defining the language in use.
Set the value of a preference item.	SetPreference(*Type*%, *Value*&) *Type*% is a constant that identifies the preference item. *Value*& is the value to set for the item.
Return the value of a preference item.	GetPreference(*Type*%) *Type*% is a constant that identifies the preference item. Returns the value in a type appropriate to the request.
Lock the viewer.	Lock(*LockedBy*$) *LockedBy*$ is a string that names the application that is requesting the lock. Returns true if the lock was obtained, false if not. Call this function only before asking Exchange to draw into another application's window.
Unlock the viewer.	Unlock Used only after locking the viewer.

The AVDoc Object

The AVDoc object allows you to display an Exchange document window, complete with standard Exchange window controls for scale factor, page numbering, and splitting the window into separate panes for bookmarks and the document itself. You can control an AVDoc window in Exchange or cause Exchange to draw and operate the window within one of your own private application windows (both CVIEWER2 and VBVIEW2 in the SDK demonstrate the latter using AVDocs). In programming, you create an AVDoc for each document file you have open.

You have the choice of using an AVDoc or a PDDoc (described below) when opening a file with OLE automation. The key difference between them is that in an AVDoc window, links and bookmarks work normally (even when drawn into another application's window). In a window derived from a PDDoc object (actually the PDPage object draws the window), the PDF file is displayed but the annotations and hypertext capabilities are not functional.

The AVDoc object creates a PDDoc object that it uses as part of its implementation. If you need to display using AVDoc capabilities but also access PDDoc methods, you can retrieve the PDDoc handle from the AVDoc and use PDDoc methods with it. An AVDoc also creates an AVPageView object that you can use similarly.

The AVDoc object provides the methods listed in Table 8.8 to support the following operations:

- Open a PDF file and display it in a new window.
- Close a PDF file (and the window).
- Control the window's title, size, and location.
- Change the page view mode (PDF page only, or bookmarks and page, or thumbnails and page).
- Find a text string in this file.

- Print pages from the document.
- Select text in the document and change the view to show the selected text.

Table 8.8   The AVDoc Object Methods

Function	AVDoc Method
Return whether this AVDoc is still valid (hasn't been closed or deleted).	IsValid Returns true if this AVDoc is valid.
Open a file and display it in a window.	Open(*FullPath$*, *TempTitle$*) *FullPath$* is the path to the PDF file to open. *TempTitle$* is the title to use for the window. If blank, the file name is used as the title.
Close a file.	Close(*NoSave%*) *NoSave%*, if true, closes the file without saving.
Return a PDDoc object.	GetPDDoc Returns the PDDoc object used by this AVDoc.
Return an AVPageView object.	GetAVPageView Returns the AVPageView object used by this AVDoc.
Return the current page view mode for this document.	GetViewMode Returns a long value giving the current page mode.
Set the page view mode for this document.	SetViewMode(*Type&*) *Type&* is a constant indicating the page mode to use.
Find a text string within a document.	FindText(*Text$*, *CaseSensitive%*, *WholeWordsOnly%*, *Reset%*) *Text$* is a string giving the text to find. *CaseSensitive%* is true for a case-sensitive search. *WholeWordsOnly%* is true to match only whole words. *Reset%* is true to start the search at the top of the first page, false to continue from the current position. Returns true if the text was found, false if not.
Print pages from a document. No print dialogs are displayed.	PrintPages(*FirstPage&*, *LastPage&*, *PSLevel&*, *BinaryOk%*, *ShrinkToFit%*) *FirstPage&* is the number of the first page to print. *LastPage&* is the number of the last page to print. *PSLevel&* is 1 to generate PostScript Level 1 operators, 2 to use PostScript Level 2 operators. *BinaryOK%* is true to use binary data, false for ASCII. *ShrinkToFit%* is true to shrink the page to make it fit. Returns true if there were no exceptions generated by the printer driver.

Table 8.8 The AVDoc Object Methods (continued)

Function	AVDoc Method
Set document's selection to the specified text selection.	SetTextSelection(*AcroPDTextSelect*) *AcroPDTextSelect* is a PDTextSelection object indicating the location to select.
Clear the current selection	ClearSelection Returns true if the selection was cleared.
Change the view so the current text selection is visible.	ShowTextSelect Use this function after calling SetTextSelection to show the selection.
Display the document in a user window.	OpenInWindow(*FullPath$*, *hWnd%*) *FullPath$* is the full path to the PDF file to open. *hWnd%* is the window handle of the window to display the document in. Use the App.Lock method to lock Exchange before using this function.
Bring the document window to the front.	BringToFront Always returns true.
Return the window's title.	GetTitle Returns a string containing the title.
Set the document window's title.	SetTitle(*Title$*) *Title$* is the new name.
Maximize the document window.	Maximize(*MaxSize%*) *MaxSize%*, if true, maximizes the window, otherwise the window is set to normal size.
Set the window's size and location.	SetFrame(*Rect*) *Rect* is a Rect object defining the size and location.
Return the window's size and location.	GetFrame Returns a Rect object identifying the size and location.

The AVPageView Object

The AVPageView OLE object controls the view of a single page. Each AVDoc object contains a single AVPageView object used to display the current page in the AVDoc window. Commands in the AVPageView object (listed in Table 8.9) allow you to:

- View a particular page in the document.
- Zoom in or out.

- Scroll the window to see another part of the page.
- Move backward and forward through the navigation stack for this window.
- Convert user coordinates to device coordinates (and vice versa).

Table 8.9 The AVPageView Object Methods

Function	AVPageView Method
Return the current page number.	GetPageNum Returns a long value for the current page number (numbering starts at zero).
Change view to the specified page.	GoTo(*Page&*) *Page&* is the zero-based page number to go to. Returns true if the page was displayed.
Return the current zoom factor.	GetZoom Returns the current zoom factor as a percent (for example, 100) in a long integer.
Return the current zoom type.	GetZoomType Returns an integer indicating the current zoom type.
Change view to the specified magnification.	ZoomTo(*Type%, Scale%*) *Type%* is the zoom type to use. 0 = use the *Scale%* factor. 1 = fit page to window. 2 = fit page width to window. 3 = fit page height to window. 4 = fit visible width to window. *Scale%* is the zoom factor to use as a percent.
Scroll to the specified location on the current page.	ScrollTo(*X%, Y%*) *X%* is the X position to scroll to. *Y%* is the Y position to scroll to. Position (0,0) is at the upper-left corner of the page.
Scroll backward one full screen.	ReadPageUp Always returns true.
Scroll forward one full screen.	ReadPageDown Always returns true.
Go back one view on the navigation stack.	DoGoBack Always returns true.
Go forward one view on the navigation stack.	DoGoForward Always returns true.

Table 8.9 The AVPageView Object Methods (continued)

Function	AVPageView Method
Return an AVDoc object for the current page.	GetAVDoc Returns an AVDoc object.
Return a PDPage object for the current page.	GetPage Returns a PDPage object.
Return a PDDoc object for the current page.	GetDoc Returns a PDDoc object.
Convert point coordinates from user space to device space.	PointToDevice(*Point*) *Point* is a Point object with coordinates in user-coordinate space (where PDF objects are defined). Returns a Point object containing the equivalent device coordinates.
Convert point coordinates from device space to user space.	DevicePointToPage(*Point*) *Point* is a Point object with coordinates defined in device-coordinate space. Returns a Point object containing the points in terms of the user-coordinate space.

The PDDoc Object

The PDDoc object gives you control over the PDF file itself. You should use a PDDoc object by itself for those automation tasks that do not require you to immediately see the result of your action; it will be faster and use fewer resources than an AVDoc.

The PDDoc methods, listed in Table 8.10, allow you to:

- Create a new in-memory PDDoc you can use temporarily to copy pages to.

- Open, save, and close PDF files.

- Insert, replace, move, and delete pages in a PDF file.

- Read and change Doc Info fields.

- Create or delete thumbnails.

- Retrieve a PDPage object for any page in the file.

Some of these commands require page numbers. Page numbers start at zero, except for the following special values:

Page Number Command	Value
Before the first page	−1
The last page	−2
All pages	−3

Table 8.10   The PDDoc Object Methods

Function	PDDoc method
Create a new PDDoc.	Create Returns true if the PDDoc was created.
Open a document from a file.	Open(*FullPath$*) Returns true if the document was opened.
Save a document.	Save(*Type%, FullPath$*) *Type%* is an integer taking a value of: 0 = incremental save. 1 = write the entire file. 2 = write a copy of the file.
Close a document.	Close Returns true if the document was closed.
Delete this PDDoc from Exchange memory.	Delete
Return the file name of the PDDoc.	GetFileName Returns a string.
Return the PDF file's instance ID.	GetInstanceID Returns a string.
Return the PDF file's permanent ID.	GetPermanentID Returns a string.
Return the document's flags.	GetFlags Returns a long value containing the flags. Flag values are defined in SDK\IAC.H.
Set the document's flags.	SetFlags(*Flags&*)
Return the number of pages in a document.	GetNumPages Returns a long value.

Table 8.10 The PDDoc Object Methods (continued)

Function	PDDoc method
Insert pages from another document into this one.	InsertPages(*InsertPageAfter&, PDDocSource, StartPage&, NumPages&, Bookmarks%*) *InsertPageAfter&* specifies the page number in the destination document to insert the new pages after. *PDDocSource* is the handle of a PDDoc that is supplying the pages to insert. *StartPage&* is the page number within PDDocSource to start with. *NumPages&* is the number of pages to insert. *Bookmarks%*, if true, copies bookmarks from PDDocSource into the destination.
Replace pages in this document from another document.	ReplacePages(*StartPage&, PDDocSource, StartSourcePage&, NumPages&, MergeTextAnnotations%*) *MergeTextAnnotations%*, if true, copies text annotations from PDDocSource.
Move a page to another location within this document.	MovePage(*MoveAfterThisPage&, PageToMove&*) *MoveAfterThisPage&* specifies the destination page number.
Delete pages from this document.	DeletePages(*StartPage&, EndPage&*)
Return a handle to a PDPage object.	AcquirePage(*Page&*) *Page&* is the page number you want. Returns a PDPage object.
Return the value of a Doc Info key.	GetInfo(*InfoKey$*) *InfoKey$* is the name of the key to look for. Returns a string value.
Set a new value for a Doc Info key.	SetInfo(*InfoKey$, Buffer$*) *Buffer$* contains the new value for the key.
Create thumbnails for this document.	CreateThumbs(*FirstPage&, LastPage&*)
Delete thumbnails.	DeleteThumbs(*StartPage&, EndPage&*)
Open this document in an AVDoc window.	OpenAVDoc(*Title$*) Returns an AVDoc object.
Return the current page display mode for this document.	GetPageMode Returns a long value. See SetPageMode below.
Set the current page display mode for this document.	SetPageMode(*PageMode&*) *PageMode&* takes one of the values: 0 = do not care. 1 = use none. 2 = use thumbnails. 3 = use bookmarks. 4 = use full screen mode.
Select the text located within a particular rectangle on a page.	CreateTextSelect(*Page&, Rect*) *Page&* is the page to create the selection on. *Rect* specifies the coordinates of a rectangle containing text. Returns a PDTextSelect object.

The PDPage Object

Each page of a PDF file is represented by a PDPage object. In addition to the contents of the page itself, each PDPage is also responsible for maintaining the list of annotations on that page. You can use PDPage methods (listed in Table 8.11) to:

- Determine the size of the page.
- Draw the page into a window at a particular scaling factor. When drawn using PDPage methods, the window will display the PDF file without annotations being active.
- Add, delete, and count annotations (links and notes) attached to this page.
- Select text from this page.
- Rotate the page.

Table 8.11   The PDPage Object Methods

Command	OLE 2
Return the PDDoc for this page.	GetDoc Returns a PDDoc object.
Return the page's width and height.	GetSize Returns a Point object.
Return the page number of the current page.	GetNumber Returns a long value.
Draw the page into a specified window.	Draw(*HWND%, HDC%, XOrigin%, YOrigin%, Zoom%*) HWND is the handle of the window to draw into. HDC% is the handle of the device context to use for drawing, or zero to use the default DC for the window. XOrigin% is the starting x-coordinate on the page. YOrigin% is the starting y-coordinate. Zoom% is the zoom factor as a percent.
Return the number of annotations on this page.	GetNumAnnots Returns a long value.
Return an annotation by index.	GetAnnot(*Index&*) Index is the index number of the annotation to return (starting with zero). Returns a PDAnnot object.

Table 8.11 The PDPage Object Methods (continued)

Command	OLE 2
Return the index of the annotation object in the page's annotation array.	GetAnnotIndex(*AnnotObj*) *AnnotObj* is the handle of a PDAnnot object. Returns a long value.
Add a new annotation on the page.	AddNewAnnot(*IndexAddAfter&, SubType$, Rect*) *IndexAddAfter&* is the index of the annotation to add the new one after. *SubType$* is either "Link" or "Text". *Rect* is the handle of a Rect object that defines the location of the annotation. Returns a PDAnnot object.
Insert an annotation object into the list.	AddAnnot(*IndexAddAfter&, AnnotObj*) *IndexAddAfter&* is the index of the annotation to add the new one after. *AnnotObj* is the handle of a PDAnnot object.
Remove an annotation from the annotation list.	RemoveAnnot(*Index&*) *Index&* is the index of the annotation to remove.
Create a text selection from a list of character offsets and counts on a single page.	CreatePageHilite(*HiliteList*) *HiliteList* is a PDHiliteList object listing the characters and words to highlight. Returns a PDTextSelect object.
Create a text selection from a list of word offsets and word counts on a single page.	CreateWordHilite(*HiliteList*) Returns a PDTextSelect object.
Set the rotation value for the current page.	SetRotate(*Rotate%*) *Rotate%* takes the value 0, 90, 180, or 270.
Return the rotation value for the current page.	GetRotate Returns an integer value.

The PDAnnot Object

Each annotation on the page is represented by a PDAnnot object. The PDAnnot object has a subtype string field that identifies the type of annotation; the common types are *Link* and *Note*, but plug-ins can define other types. For portablility you should ignore types that you do not understand when you are working with these objects.

Table 8.12 lists the methods used with the PDAnnot object.

Table 8.12   The PDAnnot Object Methods

Function	PDAnnot Method
Return whether an annotation is valid.	IsValid Returns true if the annotation is valid.
Return the annotation's subtype.	GetSubtype Returns a string specifying the annotation subtype.
Return result of comparison.	IsEqual(*PDAnnot*) *PDAnnot* is the handle of another annotation to be compared with this one. Returns true if the two annotations are equal.
Return the annotation's color.	GetColor Returns a long value which is an RGB color.
Set the annotation's color.	SetColor(*RGBColor&*) *RGBColor&* is a 24-bit RGB color value.
Return the annotation's title.	GetTitle Returns a string value.
Set the annotation's title.	SetTitle(*Title$*) *Title$* is the title string to use.
Return the annotation's text contents.	GetContents Returns a string value for notes.
Set the annotation's contents.	SetContents(*Contents$*) *Contents$* is a string containing the text to appear in the annotation (notes only).
Return whether the annotation window is open.	IsOpen Returns true if the annotation is open.
Open or close an annotation.	SetOpen(*IsOpen%*) *IsOpen%* is true to open the annotation.
Return an annotation's bounding rectangle.	GetRect Returns the handle of a Rect object.
Set an annotation's bounding rectangle.	SetRect(*Rect*) *Rect* gives the coordinates on the page.
Get an annotation's date.	GetDate Returns a Time object.
Set an annotation's date.	SetDate(*Time*) *Time* is the handle of a Time object.
Perform a link annotation's action.	Perform(*AVDoc*) *AVDoc* specifies the handle of the AVDoc to display the action in.

The PDBookmark Object

The PDBookmark object defines a single bookmark within the PDF document's bookmark hierarchy. Using the PDBookmark commands listed in Table 8.13, you can

- Read or set the text of the bookmark.
- Perform the action specified in the bookmark.

NOTE: *The version of the free SDK in distribution when this book was written (summer 1995) is missing routines for the PDBookmark object in the ACROAUTO.DLL file and its source code. Look for an updated SDK to correct this problem.*

Table 8.13   The PDBookmark Object Methods

Function	PDBookmark Method
Get the bookmark by title.	GetByTitle(*PDDoc, Title$*) *PDDoc* is the handle of the PDDoc object to look in. *Title$* is the title string to search for. The string must match exactly to be found. Returns a PDBookmark object.
Delete the bookmark.	Destroy Returns true if the bookmark is destroyed.
Return whether the bookmark is still valid.	IsValid Returns true if the bookmark is valid.
Get the title of the bookmark.	GetTitle Returns a string value.
Set the title of the bookmark.	SetTitle(*NewTitle$*) *NewTitle$* is the new title string to use.
Perform the bookmark's action.	Perform(*AVDoc*) *AVDoc* is the handle of the AVDoc to perform the bookmark's action in.

Macintosh AppleEvents

Like OLE automation in Windows, AppleEvents and AppleScript allow nearly complete control of Exchange, its document windows, and PDF file components. The underlying design of the AppleEvent system for the Macintosh version of Exchange closely parallels the OLE function set described above. However, some of the AppleScript names of objects and methods are different. This is because standard AppleEvents have already been established for many common objects on the Macintosh, and Adobe has used the standard events and their names in AppleScript instead of inventing their own. The Required set of AppleEvents previously described for the Reader is one such set; the other is the core suite of AppleEvents.

The AppleEvent system, like OLE, is an object-oriented system; in fact, the objects used in AppleEvent programming are virtually the same as those defined above for OLE, but here again Adobe has stayed with the existing standards for the Macintosh in naming and organizing its objects. The result is a combination of preexisting AppleEvent names and Acrobat names, which are the same as those used in the Windows OLE implementation. The object class names you can use with AppleScript are:

- *application*—The Exchange program itself. Corresponds to the OLE App object.

- *menu*—A top-level menu. In the OLE version, menus and menu items are part of the App object.

- *menu item*—A menu item in a menu.

- *document*—A PDF document, displayed in a window. Combines AVDoc and PDDoc methods.

- *AVPageView*—A view of a page in a document window.

- *PDPage*—A page in a PDF document.

- *PDBookmark*—A bookmark in a PDF file.
- *PDAnnot*—An annotation in a PDF file.

In this section we will focus on using AppleScript to control Exchange, rather than raw AppleEvents. There are two key ways that AppleScript differs from OLE automation:

- There is a common language that is shared among the different objects. For example, you can count the pages in your document with a *count PDPage* command or a count bookmarks with a *count PDBookmark* command. In contrast, with Windows OLE each method has a unique function call.

- Objects have *properties* as well as methods; for example, the page view mode is a property of the PDPage object. You can examine the value of a property or change it using the same AppleScript commands just by substituting a different property name. Windows OLE does not have a formal notion of a property; it accomplishes the same thing through preference items (stored in the .INI file) and class methods (subroutine calls) that provide the same values.

In the sections that follow, we will detail the AppleScript commands for controlling Exchange. Usually there will be two tables, one giving the AppleScript commands controlling an object and the other the properties associated with the object. In the AppleScript tables, parameter names are shown in italics; substitute your own values as appropriate. Optional parameters to the commands are shown within square brackets. There are other minor variations on AppleScript syntax that, in the interest of brevity, we do not show; consult an AppleScript reference for more information.

In the free Macintosh SDK, there are several sample AppleScript files located in the SOURCE:Mac:Samples:SCRIPTS subdirectory and in the OPENALL-Distiller subdirectory. These files illustrate the principles of AppleScript programming.

The Apple Event Core Suite

The core suite of Apple Events generally work at the application level, but some of them can be used to manipulate all of the objects that Exchange exposes, so it is worth examining them separately from the objects themselves. We list the core suite of AppleScript commands in Table 8.14.

Table 8.14   The Apple Event Core Suite Methods

Function	AppleScript
Open a file into a window.	open *file* [invisible *flag*] *file* is the name of a file to open. *flag* equals true hides the window.
Close an open file.	close *doc* [saving *flag*] *doc* is the document to close. *flag* whether to save the file: yes—save the document. no—do not save it. ask—ask the user.
Save the document.	save *doc* to *file* *doc* is a reference to a document. *file* is a file name.
Hide the viewer window.	hide
Quit the viewer.	quit [saving *option*] *option* specifies whether to save the documents; see the close command above.
Count the number of elements of an object.	count *object* [of *container*] *object* is an object class name. *container* is the item holding the objects.
Create a new object.	make *object* [at *location*] *object* is an object class name. *location* is the place to insert the new object.
Delete an object.	delete *object* *object* is a reference to an object.
Test whether object exists.	*object* exists *object* is a reference to an object.

Table 8.14 The Apple Event Core Suite Methods (continued)

Function	AppleScript
Get the value of an object's property.	[get] *property* [as *datatype*] *property* is one of the property names for an object. *datatype* specifies a data type other than the default for this property item.
Move an object to a new location.	move *object* to *location* *object* is a reference to an object to move. *location* is the place to move it to.
Set a property value or create a reference.	set *location* to *value* *location* is the name of a property value. *value* is the new value to use.

In the sections that follow, you can use the object-oriented AppleScript commands listed in Table 8.14 with the objects described in the tables below in addition to the methods listed for the individual objects.

The Application Object

The application object is one of the core objects that Apple predefines for developers. In Apple's model, menus and menu items are separate objects that are attached to a particular application, rather than being part of the App object itself (as they are in Adobe's OLE implementation). We describe the menu objects below. The application object responds to both the required suite and the core suite of Apple events described above and adds the additional private commands listed in Table 8.15.

Table 8.15 The Application Object's Private Methods

Function	AppleScript
Close all documents.	close all docs [saving *option*] See close command above for valid options.
Remove a button from the toolbar.	remove toolbutton named *name* *name* is the language-independent name of the toolbar button.
Return whether a toolbar button is enabled or not.	is toolbutton enabled named *name* *name* is the language-independent name of the toolbar button.

The application object contains other objects as elements, which you can manipulate with AppleScript:

- *document*—Each open document. Access by document name or with an index.

- *menu*—Each of the menus on the menu bar. Access by name or index.

- *menu item*—Each menu item in a menu. Access by name.

- *AVPageView*—Each open page view. Access by document name or with an index. There is an AVPageView object for each open document.

The application object's property names are listed in Table 8.16. While many of them are equivalent to the items in the Edit | Preferences dialog boxes, some of the properties are more dynamic—like the active document and active tool.

Table 8.16   **The Application Object's Properties**

Data Value	Property Name
The application's name.	app name
Is our window frontmost?	frontmost
Exchange software version number.	version no.
The active document.	active document
The active tool.	active tool
Toolbar visiblity.	toolbar visible
Long or short menus.	long menu visibility
User interface language.	UI language
Ask for file to open at startup.	open dialog at startup
Display Exchange splash screen at startup.	show splash at startup
Default magnification level.	default zoom factor
Default zoom type.	default zoom type
Skip deletion warnings from Exchange.	skip warnings
PostScript language level used when printing.	PS level
Shrink pages to fit the printer when printing.	shrink to fit

Table 8.16 The Application Object's Properties (continued)

Data Value	Property Name
Default to case-sensitive search for finding text.	case-sensitive search
Default to whole word search.	whole word search
Default color for new notes.	note color
Default table for new notes.	text note label

The Menu and Menu Item Object

The menu object and its child, the menu item, allow you to change the menu structure of Exchange by adding and deleting menu items, or execute the menu item just as though the user selected it. These capabilities are encompassed within the App object in the OLE implementation, while on the Macintosh, menus and menu items are part of the core suite of Apple events. Table 8.17 lists the methods that operate on menus.

Each menu object contains a list of its menu items. You can generate a reference to a menu item within a menu using a numeric index or with the language-independent name.

Table 8.17 The Menu and Menu Item Methods

Function	AppleScript
Return the number of menus or menu items.	count menu items in *menu* *menu* is the name of the menu.
Execute a menu item as though the user selected it.	execute *menuitem* *menuitem* is the name of the menu item to execute.
Remove a menu or menu item from the menu.	delete *menuitem* *menuitem* is the name of the menu or menu item to delete.

When you delete a predefined Exchange menu item, the item is not permanently deleted; the menu item will be restored the next time Exchange executes, unless you delete it again. Table 8.18 lists the properties associated with menu items.

Table 8.18   **The Menu and Menu Item Properties**

Data Value	Property Name
The name of the menu or menu item.	name
The title displayed to the user.	title
Is the menu item enabled?	enabled
Is the menu item checked?	marked

The Document Object

In AppleScript, the document object is also predefined by Apple. Each document object represents a single open document in the viewer. The object includes most of the capabilities of both the OLE AVDoc and PDDoc objects. Table 8.19 lists the methods applicable to the document object. The object also contains as elements the following objects:

- PDPage objects for each page in the document. Accessed by number.

- PDBookmark objects for each bookmark in the document. Accessed by index and by title.

- An AVPageView object. There is only one per document.

Table 8.19   **The Document Object's Methods**

Function	AppleScript
Close a PDF file.	close *doc*
Print pages in a document.	print pages *doc* [first *firstpage*] [last *lastpage*] [PS Level *pslevel*] [binary output *binout*] [shrink to fit *shrink*] *firstpage* and *lastpage* are page numbers (starting with one, not zero). *pslevel* is the PostScript printing level, either 1 or 2. *binout* is true to print in binary mode. *shrink* is true to shrink the page to fit.
Return the number of elements in the document.	count *elements* in *doc* *elements* is the name of an object to count, like PDPage, PDBookmark.
Save a document to a file.	save *doc* to *file*

Table 8.19 The Document Object's Methods (continued)

Function	AppleScript
Bring document window to the foreground.	bring to front *doc*
Maximize document window.	maximize *doc* maxsize *winsize* *winsize* is true to make the window full size, false to return it to the original size.
Insert pages into a document.	insert pages *dest* after *page* from *source* starting with *firstpage* number of pages *numpages* [insert bookmarks *copy*] *dest* is a reference to the document to insert into. *page* is the page to insert after. *firstpage* is the page numbers of the source to start using. *source* is a reference to the document to get the pages from. *copy* is true to copy bookmarks with the pages.
Replace pages in a document.	replace pages *dest* over *page* from *source* starting with *firstpage* number of pages *numpages* [merge notes *merge*] *dest* is a reference to the destination document. *page* is the page number to start replacing at. *source* and *firstpage* as above. *merge* is true to merge notes on the replaced pages.
Delete pages from a document.	delete pages *doc* first *firstpage* last *lastpage*
Create thumbnails for all pages.	create thumbs *doc*
Delete thumbnails for all pages.	delete thumbs *doc*
Find text.	find text *doc* string *search* [case sensitive *case*] [whole words *words*] [wrap around *wrap*] *search* is a string to search for. *case* is true for case-sensitive search. *words* is true for whole words only matching. *wrap* is true to wrap from the end of the document to the beginning if nothing is found.
Find next note.	find next note *doc* [wrap around *flag*] *flag* is true to wrap from the end of the document to the begining if a note is not found before the end of the document is reached.
Clear text selection.	clear selection *doc*
Get Doc Info field.	get info *doc* key *name* *name* is the name of the Doc Info field to get.
Set Doc Info field.	set info *doc* key *name* value *newvalue*

Table 8.20 contains the names for properties associated with each document. You can test the *modified* property to see if the document needs to be saved. The *file alias* property is the default name to use

for the file when saving it. The document name is the name displayed in the window title for the document. All of these properties are read-only except the page view mode.

Table 8.20   The Document Object's Properties

Data Value	Property Name
Document name.	name
Has the document been modified?	modified
The boundaries of the document window.	bounds
Name document will be saved under.	file alias
Page view mode.	view mode

The AVPageView Object

The AVPageView object is named identically, and is very similar to, the OLE AVPageView object. The notable addition is the select text command, which creates a text selection; this is part of the PDPage object in OLE. Methods associated with the AVPageView object are listed in Table 8.21.

Table 8.21   The AVPageView Object's Methods

Function	AppleScript
Change view to the specified page.	goto *pageview* page *pagenum* *pageview* is the AVPageView object to use. *pagenum* is the new page number to display.
Turn to the next page.	goto next *pageview*
Turn to the previous page.	goto previous *pageview*
Scroll backwards one full screen.	read page up *pageview*
Scroll forwards one full screen.	read page down *pageview*
Change view to the specified magnification.	zoom *pageview* to *newzoom* *newzoom* is the zoom factor as a percent.
Go back one view on the navigation stack.	go backward *pageview*
Go forward on the navigation stack.	go forward *pageview*

Table 8.21   The AVPageView Object's Methods (continued)

Function	AppleScript
Scroll to a particular position on the current page.	scroll *pageview* X Amount *deltaX* Y Amount *deltaY* *deltaX* is the amount to scroll in the horizontal direction, in pixels. Positive values scroll right, negative values scroll left. *deltaY* is the amount to scroll in the vertical direction, in pixels. Positive values scroll down, negative values scroll up.
Select text for further operations.	select text *pageview* [from words *wordpairs*] [from chars *charpairs*] *wordpairs* are one or more pairs of word offsets and word lengths. A word offset is the number of words counting from the beginning of the document. A word length is the number of words to include. *charpairs* are one or more pairs of character offsets and character lengths. They are defined similarly to word offsets and lengths. Use either words or characters but not both in the same selection command.

Table 8.22 lists the properties of the AVPageView object. All except the document's name can be set as well as read.

Table 8.22   The AVPageView Object's Properties

Data Value	Property Name
The document's name in the window title	name
The current zoom factor as a percent	zoom factor
The current type of zoom as a string	zoom type Takes values: "no vary", "fit page", "fit width", "fit height", or "fit visible width".
The current page number on display	page number

The PDPage Object

This object, like its counterpart in the OLE implementation, represents a particular page in the PDF file. The list of annotations on the page is included as an element of the PDPage object; you can access the annotations by numeric index.

Table 8.23 lists the methods you can use with the PDPage object. The DrawPageToWindow Apple event, which draws a PDPage into another application's window, is not accessible from AppleScript, but only through C programming.

Table 8.23 **The PDPage Object's Methods**

Function	AppleScript
Return the number of annotations on the page.	count PDAnnot in *page* *page* is the PDPage object to look in.
Delete a page.	delete *page*
Move a page	move *page* to *location*
Draw the page into another application's window.	—

Table 8.24 lists the properties of the PDPage object. The bounds and rotation properties can be set as well as read.

Table 8.24 **The PDPage Object's Properties**

Data Value	Property Name
This page's number in the document.	number
The boundary rectangle for the page.	bounds
The rotation of the page (0, 90, 180, 270)	rotation

The PDAnnot Object

The PDAnnot object is almost identical to its OLE counterpart; however, the AppleScript version includes two additional objects that can assist you in creating annotations. The PDLinkAnnot and PDTextAnnot objects can be used with the make command to create annotation objects preconfigured to be links or notes, respectively. After you create one of these objects, you use standard PDAnnot methods to manipulate it further. Table 8.25 lists the available PDAnnot methods.

Table 8.25 **The PDAnnot Object's Methods**

Function	AppleScript
Perform an annotation's action (if any).	perform *link* *link* is a reference to a link annotation.
Delete the annotation.	delete *annot*

Table 8.26 lists the properties of a PDAnnot object. All except the index and subtype can be set as well as written.

Table 8.26 **The PDAnnot Object's Properties**

Data Value	Property Name
The annotation's label.	name
The annotation's index in the PDPage list.	index
The subtype string of the annotation.	subtype
Whether the annotation is open or not.	open state
A bounding rectangle for the annotation.	bounds
The textual contents of a note.	contents
The date the annotation was last modified.	modification date
Color of the border around the annotation.	color
The page number of a link's destination.	destination page number
The destination viewing rectangle desired.	destination rectangle
The way the destination rectangle is displayed in the window.	fit type Takes values: Left Top Zoom Fit Page/Width/Height/Rect (you choose).
The zoom factor as a percent.	zoom factor Only used if the fit type is Left Top Zoom.

The PDBookmark Object

The PDBookmark object offers the AppleScript user nearly the same functionality as its OLE counterpart. Table 8.27 lists the bookmark methods available.

Table 8.27   The PDBookmark Object's Methods

Function	AppleScript
Delete a bookmark.	delete *bookmark*. *bookmark* is a reference to a PDBookmark.
Perform a bookmark's action.	perform *bookmark*

Table 8.28 lists the properties available as part of a bookmark. All of these properties except the index are available for writing as well as reading.

Table 8.28   The PDBookmark Object's Properties

Data Value	Property Name
The bookmark's title.	name
The bookmark's index within the page.	index
The page number of the destination.	destination page number
The rectangle that will be displayed at the destination.	destination rectangle
The way the destination rectangle is displayed in the window.	fit type
See PDAnnot properties above.	
The zoom factor as a percent.	zoom factor

Integrating with the Acrobat Search Plug-in

The Search plug-in has an IAC interface independent of Exchange's interface (though of course Exchange must be running with the Search plug-in installed). However, the menu items and toolbar buttons that Search adds to the Exchange user interface are accessible via IAC with Exchange using the methods outlined above (as are those of other plug-ins you may have installed). The Search plug-in's private IAC interface is completely described in Technical Note #5155, "Acrobat Viewer Interapplication Communication Support," Appendix C.

Windows Search

The Windows version of Search provides an interface via DDE. Through this interface, the user can manipulate the list of active indexes and run a query. Both operations are performed via a DDE Poke transaction where the client application (your program) sends (or pokes) some data to the server. Because the data structure you must poke contains binary data in a specific format instead of just text, most application programs that provide DDE support through a macro language (like spreadsheets) will not be able to access Search through DDE; however, C, C++, and Visual Basic programmers will have no difficulties. Search provides commands that allow you to:

- Perform a query. All the query options available in the search dialog box are also present as options to the DDE query.
- Get a list of the search indexes available.
- Select, deselect, add, or delete search indexes.

Search responds to the service name "Acrobat Search" and the topic name "Acrobat Search". Search also requires an item name; use "Query" for the query command or "Index" for one of the index commands. There is a sample Visual Basic program that puts up its own user interface to the Search plug-in; it is located in the SAMPLES\VB\CONTRACT subdirectory of the free SDK.

Macintosh Search

The Search plug-in provides an AppleEvent interface, but like the Windows version, it requires nontext data, so there is not an AppleScript interface. The AppleEvent interface provides capabilities identical to the Windows version, but they are only accessible to C programmers. The constants required to program this interface are defined in the file SDK:searchae.h.

Integrating with Acrobat PDF Writer

PDF Writer is handicapped in the communication department vis-à-vis its fellow Acrobat programs. PDF Writer is supposed to be a printer driver, a fairly low-level piece of program code in most systems. Technical Note #5159, "Acrobat PDF Writer Control Interface Specification," describes the capabilities available.

Windows PDF Writer

One important way to control PDF Writer is through settings in the Windows WIN.INI file. These are described fully in Appendix A. There is an .INI file entry for each of the fields in the PDF Writer Printer Options dialog box and its children. Set these parameters before invoking the File | Print function in your application.

PDF Writer can tell you when it starts and finishes creating a PDF file by sending a Windows message. These messages are broadcast automatically by PDF Writer to every top-level window in your system whenever the appropriate event occurs. PDF Writer registers two messages:

- "PDFWriter Start"
- "PDFWriter Done"

To receive these messages, you must first register them with the Windows API function RegisterMessage(). See the similar example using messages from Catalog, shown at the end of this chapter.

If you're writing a program that uses PDF Writer to create Acrobat files, you can use the Windows API function Escape() to set up PDF Writer automatically. You can tell PDF Writer the name to use for the PDF file, and the Author and Creator Document Info fields. If you specify the PDF file name, PDF Writer will not display the Save As dialog box as it normally does, allowing the job to execute automatically without user intervention. The included file SDK/PDFWCTRL.H contains the information you need to use this function.

Macintosh PDF Writer

The Macintosh version of PDF Writer is even more reticent than the Windows version; it provides only a C function call programming interface. Defined in the free SDK in the files SDK:userinteraction.c and SDK:userinteraction.h, these calls let you specify the PDF file name and suppress the Page Setup and Print dialog boxes, so your print job can complete without user intervention.

Integrating with Acrobat Distiller

Acrobat Distiller provides an API that lets you distill one or more PostScript files by name, and on the Macintosh, you can also start Distiller through AppleScript without specifying files to process. Distiller does not provide for any initialization options for the job, only the name of the file to process. Distiller expects most of the initialization to occur through PostScript commands in the Distiller startup files or in the user's file. The Distiller API is documented in Technical Note #5158, "Acrobat Distiller Control Interface Specification," available in the free SDK.

Windows Distiller

The Windows version of Distiller provides the simple ability to process a list of PostScript files into PDF. There are two methods available to accomplish this: a command line interface and a more difficult message-passing interface.

The command line interface allows you to list one or more PostScript files on the program's command line. This command line is available in several ways:

- When you run the program from the Program Manager's File | Run command.

- When you click on an icon in the Program Manager's window. Command line is one of the options in the Program Item Properties dialog box used to configure a Program Manager icon.

- When you use the WinExec() function from the Windows SDK.

- Scripting languages for Windows use WinExec() and usually allow command line parameters. There is no standard scripting language but several Windows add-on products provide them.

The Distiller command line takes the following options (using square brackets to denote optional components):

```
acrodist [/q] [/o dest] source1[, source2...]
```

The */q* option tells Distiller to quit after processing all files it finds to process (including watched directories); without this option, Distiller will continue to run in the background. The */o dest* option can mean two different things depending on the value of *dest* and the remaining parameters on the command line. If the value of *dest* includes a file name (and possibly a path) and is followed by a single *source1* parameter, the *dest* name is used as the output file's name. If the value of *dest* names only a directory, all of the output files Distiller creates for one or more listed source files will be put in that directory.

Source1 names a PostScript file to convert to a PDF file. By default, the output file uses the same name but with a PDF extension; you can override this with the /o option. If there is more than one file to process, you can include the additional names after *source1*, separating them with commas.

TIP: *C and C++ programmers looking for a way to tell when Distiller has completed distilling the files they WinExec'ed should try the ExecWait() function available for download from the Microsoft Software Library on CompuServe. This function does not return until the WinExec'ed program terminates, a feature that can eliminate the need to monitor Distiller's status.*

The other means available to tell Distiller to process a file is through the Windows message-passing interface. This method is similar to that used with Catalog (described below). The data types and constants used in this method are defined in SDK\DISTCTRL.H. This interface is much more complex to implement than using the WinExec() interface described above, and it offers no additional features, so generally it should be avoided. The only reason to use it is if you want to keep Distiller running all the time as a server; in this case, you can communicate with the server using the messages defined in the header file. Messages exist to submit a list of files for processing to Distiller, and for Distiller to notify you when each file is done.

Macintosh Distiller

The Macintosh version of Distiller provides an API through the standard Apple events interface that includes the ability to work with AppleScript. The interface supports three different commands:

Command	AppleScript
Open and process a file.	open *sourcefile* [destination *destfile*] [with wait] *sourcefile* is the name of the PostScript file to process. *destfile* is the name of the output (default is *sourcefile.pdf*).

	"with wait" means that the script will wait until Distiller is finished processing the files before continuing.
Launch Distiller.	run
Quit Distiller.	quit

Integrating with Acrobat Catalog

The Windows version of Catalog supports a small API using Windows messages and DDE. This API is described in Adobe Technical Note #5157, "Acrobat Catalog Control Interface Specification," which is part of the free SDK. You can use this API to:

- Receive notification when a Catalog build stops, fails, or completes successfully.
- Query Catalog to see if it is busy or not.
- Open an index definition file (a .PDX file) and display the Edit Index Definition dialog box.
- Build an index from an index definition file you specify.
- Exit the Catalog program.

At the time this book was being written, the IAC interfaces for the Macintosh version of Catalog were not available from Adobe. Windows offers three different IAC interfaces for Catalog:

- Command line interface
- DDE interface
- Window message-passing interface

The command line interface and DDE interface have essentially the same functions—to edit an index definition file and build the index. The message-passing interface cannot accept commands, but it does respond to status queries from other programs and can notify other programs when it stops building an index.

Windows Command Line Interface

From the command line, you can start Catalog and cause it to display directly an index definition file of your choosing or begin building the index you specify. You can use the command line interface from the Program Manager or with the WinExec() system call (see the Acrobat Distiller section for more information).

To open an index definition file and display the Edit Index Definition dialog box, simply list the name and path to the index file on the command line:

```
acrocat indexfilename
```

To build the index definition file, add the option string /b in front of the index file name in the above command.

Windows DDE Interface

Catalog supports a simple DDE interface that can be used to build an index as well as display the Edit Index Definitions dialog box. There is no capability to set values in the index definition. Catalog responds to the DDE service name of "Acrocat", and the topic name "control".

DDE Command	Format
Open an index file and display the Edit Index Definition dialog box.	[FileOpen(*IndexFile*)] IndexFile is the full path to the index definition file.
Build an index.	[FileBuild(*IndexFile*)] IndexFile is the path to the index definition file.
Quit Catalog.	[AppExit()]

If you use the FileOpen command, you must have a user sitting at the keyboard to change values in the index definition and save the definition back to disk.

A Windows Messaging Interface Sample

Windows Catalog uses the Windows message-passing interface to handle queries about its status. The message-passing interface is not available from all programming languages; C and C++ are good candidates for using it. Acrobat uses Microsoft Windows's user-defined message facility, which means that the message number is defined only at runtime. Your program must register the message with Windows to obtain the correct message number to use. The following C subroutine demonstrates how to register and send a message and wait for the response using messages defined by Acrobat Catalog:

```
// IsCatalogBusy — return true if catalog is busy,
// false otherwise.

int IsCatalogBusy(void)
{
  MSG msg;
  HWND hCatalogWnd;
  UINT uQueryHelloMsg;
  UINT uQueryHelloIdleMsg;
  UINT uQueryHelloBusyMsg;

  /* get the message id of the Catalog messages */
  uQueryHelloMsg =
    RegisterWindowMessage("AcrobatCatalogQueryHello");
  uQueryHelloIdleMsg =
    RegisterWindowMessage("AcrobatCatalogResponseHello");
  uQueryHelloBusyMsg = RegisterWindowMessage(
    "AcrobatCatalogHelloImBusyResponse");

  /* find the catalog window handle by searching for the
     window title. this assumes catalog is already
running. */
```

Integrating with Acrobat Catalog

```
            hCatalogWnd = FindWindow("Acrobat Catalog", NULL);

        /* send the query message */
        SendMessage(hCatalogWnd, uQueryHelloMsg, 0, 01);

        /* wait for the response message, handling other messages
           that arrive in the mean time */
        while (1)
        {
          if (PeekMessage(&msg, NULL, 0, 0, PM_REMOVE))
          {
            if (msg.message == WM_QUIT)
            {
              PostQuitMessage(msg.wParam);
              return 0;    /* someone is trying to exit */
            }
            else if (msg.message == uQueryHelloIdleMsg)
              return 0;       /* not busy */
            else if (msg.message == uQueryHelloBusyMsg)
              return 1;       /* busy */
            else
            {
              TranslateMessage(&msg);
              DispatchMessage(&msg);
            }
          }
        }
    }
```

Notice that you must register both the message you send and the possible response messages. After sending a query message like the one above, you must wait for a response message using a Peek-Message loop (as shown). This loop is also used when you want to wait for a broadcast message from one of the Acrobat tools. The special handling of the WM_QUIT message allows the user to quit the program. This same technique can be used with the other Acrobat programs that work with the Windows message-passing interface.

Summary

The first thing to do when considering using Acrobat's IAC capabilities is to obtain the free software development kit for your platform. These kits contain working sample programs with source code that demonstrate the programming techniques. After reading this chapter, you should have a good idea of the capabilities Acrobat provides. We expect to see these capabilities carried forward into the newer Acrobat products whose IAC interfaces are not yet documented (such as the Macintosh version of Catalog and the Capture program).

In the next chapter, we look at publishing with Acrobat using different media. Acrobat on the Internet and on CD-ROM are becoming very popular ways of publishing documents. In the workgroup setting, using Acrobat with Lotus Notes is achieving similar success in corporate settings. We'll help you get started using any of these publishing media.

CHAPTER 9

Publishing with Acrobat

Overview of Publishing Technology
Preparing PDF files for Publication
CD-ROM and CD-R Publishing
Internet Publishing
Lotus Notes

Overview of Publishing Technology

In its broadest sense, publishing means presenting your work to others in the form of a document. There are now many ways to accomplish this electronically: CD-ROM, the Internet, Lotus Notes, floppy disks, electronic mail, bulletin board systems, and so forth. In this chapter we review some of these options, their advantages and limitations, and how to exploit them with Acrobat.

Overview of Publishing Technology

One important way that electronic publishing methods (as mentioned above) differ from each other is whether they deliver a single file at a time, or more than one file (a whole directory) at once. The difference relates to what you can accomplish using links between documents and files, as well as the search capabilities of Acrobat.

Files delivered one at a time (for example using e-mail, WWW, and Lotus Notes) are characterized by the need to be wholly *self-contained* (that is, no links to other documents). While a PDF document you provide may have links to other documents, there is no guarantee that those links will work because the document might not be present on the reader's system. If that is the case, you will be better off not trying to use links to other documents.

The exception to this rule is the World Wide Web: Files on the Web are delivered one at a time, but links between documents are inherently part of the Web's design. PDF files can incorporate interdocument Web links using the WebLink plug-in described in Chapter 7. However, other types of links (such as multimedia links) within PDF files you distribute as Web documents suffer from the problem mentioned above.

The alternative is to deliver your PDF files (and other required files) as a group. A group of files can use interdocument links to provide a richer flow of information without worrying about whether the link will fail. Another advantage of delivering more than one file at a time is that you can also include search indexes created with Acrobat Catalog, allowing your readers to use the full-text search capabilities of Acrobat Search.

Also, in some cases, you must be able to deliver more than one file at a time. QuickTime movies included with the Movie plug-in, for example, have to be delivered as separate files; you cannot deliver a self-contained PDF file with a movie embedded in it.

The obvious medium for delivering groups of files is a disk or CD-ROM, but another possibility is the use of a file archive (an example is the free Acrobat SDK described in Chapter 8). Archive files are created with a utility program specific to the platform your reader is using (tar on UNIX, StuffIt for Macintosh, or pkzip for Windows). Unlike disk-based document collections, these files can be delivered electronically, but they expand to provide the advantages of delivering a group of files.

Preparing PDF Files for Publication

There are some basic steps you should take with any PDF file you are distributing:

- Add values for the Document Info fields—especially if you are providing a search index using Acrobat Catalog or are using Lotus Notes or other programs that can access those fields. Remember that Distiller does not provide any values for these fields (unless you are using the pdfmark operator described in Chapter 10), so if you use Distiller you must set them by hand.

- Add bookmarks and links within your document. Bookmarks in particular are strongly recommended as they make finding your

Preparing PDF Files for Publication 323

way within a document much easier. Links that begin and end within your document, such as from the table of contents to the actual page referred to, are also helpful and easy to do.

- Use the File | Save As function in Exchange to write out your final version of the PDF file. This will clean up the edits you have made to the file and consolidate any incremental updates to the file. You can also set document security options at this time if you require them.

If you have a collection of documents to distribute there is a lot more you can and should do with them:

- Organize the document collection into smaller subgroupings of related files.
- Provide an introductory document for your collection.
- Provide a search index (generated with Catalog).
- Use links between documents to tie your collection together.
- Test everything.

Planning Your Document Collection

Before you begin linking your documents together with delicate strands of hypertext, you should have a good solid plan for what you are going to do. Your plan should list all of the documents and the links you plan to create between them. You will need this list when you enter the debugging phase of your publishing project. You do not have to compile this entire list before you begin, but you must keep it up to date as you add more links.

Organizing Document Collections for Publication

The first step in preparing a collection of PDF documents is to organize the files into subgroups if you need to. Place subgroups of files in different directories or folders whenever you have strong distinctions in subject matter between the files. A good way to distinguish subgroups is by end user: If different people will be using the files, split them into subgroups along those lines.

For example, the internal technical documentation of a product may be grouped separately from promotional and marketing information about the product; but both subgroups may be on the same CD-ROM. One of the chief advantages of subgrouping like this is that you can index the subgroups independently with Catalog. Then, the person interested only in technical matters can include the technical document index in his list of search indexes, skipping the unwanted references to similar topics in the marketing subgroup.

To begin building your document collection, create a top-level directory on your hard disk. This will become the root directory of your CD-ROM, disk, or file archive. Each subgroup of PDF files is placed in its own subdirectory within this directory. If you have enough files, do not hesitate to create sub-subgroupings of your collection, each with its own nested subdirectory.

When you have arranged the files, you can begin indexing and creating links between them. Both links and Catalog indexes need to know where the files are stored. You should use relative path names to files when you create links, so that the files can be moved to a different disk drive and root directory or folder without damaging the links. If you change the locations of some of your files, you may have to change links and recompute Catalog file indexes to account for the new locations.

Introducing Your PDF Document

Typically, your PDF document will have some kind of separate introduction to orient the reader. At the very least, you may want to alert them to the fact that you are using Acrobat PDF, in case they do not have a viewer installed. The type of introduction depends on the medium used:

- *E-mail.* Usually your basic text message provides the introduction. Often the mail system will allow the recipient to launch the Acrobat viewer by clicking on the PDF file attachment.

- *Lotus Notes.* Acrobat works with Notes Field Exchange to provide access to the Document Info fields in your PDF file from within Notes. The Notes database you are working with can display pertinent values selected from these fields. Files embedded in Notes with OLE can display an Acrobat icon; clicking on the icon will open the Acrobat viewer. We discuss this in more detail later in the chapter.

- *WWW document collections.* You should create an introductory document using HTML (not PDF—see the Resources section for information on HTML). This will be the home page of your document collection. Write it using HTML so that Web users without the Acrobat Reader installed can learn something about your documents. It should of course contain links to the PDF files that form your document collection, along with descriptive information about the files. Mention that the files are being distributed in Acrobat PDF format so the reader will not download the files only to discover that she cannot view them. Users who have to pay for their Internet connection by the minute will also appreciate knowing the file size if it is larger than a few kilobytes.

- *Disk, CD-ROM, and file archive collections.* You should create an introductory document in Acrobat PDF. This file should have a brief abstract or synopsis of each referenced document, with a link to the document itself. Name the file so that it stands out as a starting point for browsing the collection.

Indexing Document Collections

Whenever you distribute a document collection using a CD-ROM or file archive, provide an index of the collection created with Acrobat Catalog. Catalog has special options for distributing static indexes (that is, indexes that will not change because the document collection will not change). This option is called Optimize for CD-ROM and it is available in the Index Options dialog box (see Chapter 5 for more information on this option and indexing in general). You can use this option for other media besides CD-ROM; the key point is that you cannot add to an index that has been optimized. Since CD-ROM is a read-only medium, this option always applies to them.

To take full advantage of the subgroups you have created, index each subgroup separately. The PDX file created by Catalog should be in the same directory as the document collection, with the search index subdirectory beneath it. Remember that if you change a PDF file in your collection you will usually need to regenerate your Catalog indexes.

Creating Links between Documents

Ideally you do not begin this process until you have final copy on all of your documents. This is to avoid the tedium of reentering annotations and links into your PDF files. The key thing to remember when creating links between documents and other files is that all of your files must be on the same disk drive and in their final positions relative to each other before you begin. While Exchange will allow you to create links to documents or files on other drives, when you deliver your document to someone else, those files will not be present (unless you have prearranged for this).

Testing Your Documents

Providing links, bookmarks, and text search indexes for a document collection endows that collection of files with some of the characteristics of computer programs, including, unfortunately, bugs. Bugs in a document collection show up when a link does not take you to the right place in the file, an annotation like a movie does not play, a font is displayed incorrectly, or a search returns the wrong pages from your file. We have two approaches to dealing with this problem.

The Right Way to Create Documents

The first approach, easily stated but much harder to perform, is to do things right the first time. Often, the errors in our documents show up because of changes made in the later stages of development that result in work being redone. Time pressures at this stage cause work to be rushed and details forgotten. In an ideal world, you would develop your documents in the following order:

1. Write, edit, and correct the document contents.
2. Produce PDF files.
3. Position the files in the directory structure for final delivery.
4. Create interdocument links and search indexes.

Seldom are we so lucky as to get it all done correctly the first time. Usually at least a part of one of the documents requires a change. If the change results in a different flow of text across a page, or causes text to move onto new pages, this may affect links coming from other documents and Catalog indexes. Acrobat cannot tell you which documents have links to the pages you are changing; in order to ensure correctness, you must have a list of the interdocument links so you know when one is affected by a change. This situation also affects links within a PDF document as well, but here we have some hope that automated tools will relieve us from the burden of creating intradocument links from scratch. Such tools are becoming available for PDF; in the next chapter we talk about using the pdfmark operator for this purpose.

TIP: *When you need to correct pages in a PDF document that already contains links and bookmarks, you may save yourself some work by using Exchange to insert and replace pages in the file rather than starting over with a new PDF file.*

Verifying Correctness

The second approach is to test the files; since the first approach usually fails us, testing the files is essential. There are certain requirements that must be met for an adequate test. The first requirement is that the person or persons who created the product should not be involved in performing the final test. Developers are notoriously poor testers, with a tendency to be less than thorough. They already know that things work right, so they don't test them the way a more naive person would. If top quality is your goal, send your developers home when it's time to test, and bring in people unfamiliar with the work who will use it the way your end users will.

The second requirement is that the files should be tested on a machine separate from the usual development environment, with a different installation of Acrobat. This is to verify that there are no dependencies that you have forgotten about in your usual installation. In particular, if you are relying on Acrobat to handle an unusual font correctly, make sure you test on a machine where that font is not installed. If your files are going to be viewed with the Reader, you should test with it even though you probably don't use it yourself (or *because* you don't).

The third requirement is to have a test plan for larger projects, so you know what to test. This is the really hard part; you have to be very dedicated to your product's quality to sit down and prepare a test plan for it. The test plan should identify the key features that need testing and the expected result. The test plan acts as both a guide to testing and a checklist for verifying correctness, and it is essential if you are using outsiders to test your product.

Surveys of people who have already completed electronic publishing projects reveal that invariably testing was the one area where they wish they had spent more time and effort. Mistakes caught late in the process become progressively more expensive to correct as more people get involved. For example, Internet service bureaus may charge you a service fee to change your Web installation, while changes to a CD-ROM can mean doubling its cost. Do yourself a favor and allocate enough time to make sure you find the bugs rather than someone else finding them.

CD-ROM and CD-R Publishing

CD-ROM has become the publishing medium of choice for a permanent collection of documents. CD-ROM offers a storage capacity of up to 650 megabytes of data at a very low cost per megabyte. In large quantities they are very cheap to produce but can be reasonably priced even for quantities of one or two using the new recordable compact disc format (called CD-R). CD-R discs are fully compatible with standard CD-ROM players, and in the past six months, CD-R recorders have dropped in price to under $2,000, making do-it-yourself CDs a reality. In this section we provide a brief introduction to using CD technology in general and with Acrobat.

Introduction to CD-ROM Technology

CD-ROM is based on the same technology as the audio compact disc (this is the primary reason for CD-ROM's low cost). Each CD-ROM contains 99 tracks that can hold digital audio or computer data (or a combination). The newer CD-R format simply allows you to record some of the 99 tracks now, with the option to record more later. However, you can never erase anything from a compact disc, so you cannot record over what you have already written, even with a CD-R disc.

CD Disc and File Formats

Compact disc technology has evolved a series of progressively more complex recording formats over the past ten years. Each new format brought new capabilities to the medium. This is an incomplete list of the recording formats currently in use:

- *Digital CD audio (the Red Book standard).* The original audio compact disc.

- *CD-ROM (the Yellow Book standard).* A compact disc containing computer data.

- *CD-ROM/XA (extended architecture).* An enhanced version of the Yellow Book standard that allows interleaving of data, audio, and video. It's primarily used for games and full multimedia presentations.

- *Multisession CD-R (the Orange Book standard).* Unlike any of the methods listed above, CD-R allows more than one data recording session.

Typically you will be creating compact discs in either the CD-ROM (if you have a larger batch of discs manufactured) or CD-R (for small numbers of discs) formats. The difference is usually immaterial because most current computer CD readers can handle any of the formats.

The next question to answer is what file system you will use on your CD-ROM. The file system determines how files are stored on the CD-ROM, what format file names are permitted, and what directory structure is allowed. Typically, there is a "native" file system for your computer that you can use on a CD-ROM; these native formats can be read only by the target computer. Examples are the Macintosh HFS file system and various UNIX file systems, all of which can be implemented on a CD-ROM. The advantage of using a native file system is that all the features of that file system are available (like long file names).

The ISO 9660 file system was developed to provide a CD-ROM format that works across many platforms. This format works because it represents the lowest common denominator among competing standards for Macintosh, UNIX, and MS-DOS CD-ROMs. A file name on an ISO 9660 disk must consist of eight or fewer uppercase alphanumeric characters (A–Z and 0–9) and the underscore (_) character, followed by a three-character file extension. Directory names can have up to eight characters, and subdirectory names are separated by a forward slash character (/). No more than eight levels of subdirectories are allowed.

An alternative to using the ISO file system is to use a hybrid CD-ROM format. In this format, an ISO 9660 file system exists for files available on all platforms, but an additional native file system is also present, which contains files with their long file names intact. Adobe uses this method for distributing the Acrobat SDKs on CD-ROM; the Windows user will see the ISO files with their eight-character names, but a Mac user will find additional files with long file and folder names. These files cannot be seen by the Windows or UNIX user.

The simplest solution for general purpose publication currently is to use the ISO 9660 file system with its short file names. Contact your CD-ROM service bureau well in advance if you are attracted to the hybrid format, and remember that it will take some extra testing to make sure it all works right. Of course, the whole issue of file system support is about to be shaken up again as Windows 95 will provide for long file names in a new file system not compatible with the Macintosh file system.

Steps in Creating a CD-ROM

The process of creating a CD-ROM is straightforward:

1. Create an image of the CD-ROM file system you are constructing on a hard disk. The final versions of all of the files required by your application are put into their respective directories inside this image.

2. Test the files in this image to make sure you have the correct files in the right places. Beyond this point, it will usually cost you extra money to correct any errors.

3. If you are using an outside duplicating service, copy this image to the file delivery medium the service requires. Usually the service requires files to be delivered on a magnetic tape (8mm or DAT tape cartridges are typical), a removeable hard disk like a SyQuest disk, or even a regular hard disk that you remove from your computer and ship to the service bureau.

4. Your data is prepared for the CD in a process called premastering. Premastering creates an image of the data in the format required for the CD-ROM file system. Premastering software is used for this purpose; if you do your own CD-R recording, you will have to purchase premastering software with your CD-R recorder. If you use a production house, they will charge you for premastering.

5. At this point, the data is ready for recording. If you are making a single disc, you are done after writing the disc. If you are having a batch of compact discs manufactured, at this point the manufacturer will create and send you a test disc (make sure this is in-

cluded in your contract). This is your last opportunity to make any changes to the disc before manufacturing; of course, any changes you make will usually incur another charge for premastering the changes.

6. After approval of the test disc, your order is manufactured. There is a setup charge for the equipment (called a mastering charge) and a charge per disc replicated.

7. You can also have a label printed onto the surface of the CD-ROM from artwork that you supply. The charge for this service depends on how many colors your print requires; a basic single-color label may be included in the replication price.

8. You can have your CD-ROMs shipped to you for packaging, or you can arrange for the manufacturer to package them for you (for an extra charge). Larger manufacturers will also handle printing covers or inserts to include with your CD-ROM from artwork you supply, or you can have the printing done elsewhere and shipped to the CD manufacturer for insertion.

Using Acrobat with CD-ROM

PDF files are easy to use with CD-ROM; they require no special tweaking to work properly. Follow the guidelines above for preparing your files. When preparing your search index with Catalog, be sure to use the Optimize for CD-ROM feature in the Options dialog box. This will minimize space requirements for the index.

PDF files have no real-time requirements, so their layout on the disk is not critical. However, if you include links to Apple QuickTime Movie files or other multimedia files, make sure you verify that they play properly from your CD-ROM without glitches. Glitches can occur when the CD-ROM reader has to perform a long seek across the disk to find another piece of a long multimedia file. Each such file should be recorded in a solid block rather than spread out in pieces on the disk. Files are assigned space on your CD-ROM during the premastering process; you should provide instructions for premastering that indicate which files require special handling.

Internet Publishing

The explosion of interest in the Internet has created new opportunities for electronic publishing. People are turning to online services to find sources for the most up-to-date information, as well as obscure information that did not have any real market previously. Home pages on the World Wide Web even provide opportunities for politically correct self-promotion, such as putting one's resume or business catalog online.

These publications are ideal candidates for PDF files because, unlike other formats in use on the Internet, PDF files preserve document formatting. Most Internet services do not provide for formatted text and graphics; they use simple ASCII text, or in the case of HTML, a combination of text and graphics without any specific format control. Prior to the introduction of Acrobat, the standard file format for text and graphics distribution on the Internet was Adobe's PostScript. The advantages of PDF over PostScript, including file size and text search capability, combined with the ready availability of free Reader software, make it likely that PDF will overtake raw PostScript as a distribution file format for published material.

Internet Publishing Possibilities

There are several tools you can use to serve documents to others on the Internet:

- E-mail-based services allow you to send documents to a subscriber list via Internet e-mail. You create a mailbox and assign a mailing list program to service it, and the program will manage the list automatically. For example, a new subscriber can add herself to your mailing list by sending your mailing list manager an e-mail message; the program reads the message and adds her to your list without your intervention.

- You can create a file archive accessible via FTP (file transfer protocol). When users want a file from your archive, they use anonymous FTP to attach to your FTP server and copy the file to their machine. The drawback of FTP is that it is somewhat arcane and not particularly user-friendly.

- Gopher is a menu-based system for navigating the Internet. Your gopher server provides a menu listing the files you have to offer; when the user selects one, the gopher server transfers the file to her system. Prior to the advent of the World Wide Web, Gopher was the tool used to provide global access to data for those unwilling to learn FTP and go get it themselves. The World Wide Web has largely superceded gopher for this task today.

- WAIS (Wide Area Information Server) is a full-text index and search engine (similar to Acrobat Search) that you can use to provide documents in response to a search request. You index a document collection using *waisindex* (similar to using Acrobat Catalog), then users connect to your index and perform searches. WAIS servers return a list of documents that match the search criteria. There are both free and commercial versions of WAIS software available; currently, however, the free version will not knowingly index PDF files.

- The World Wide Web is the newest information service on the Internet. The Web allows you to provide pages for others to view with their Web browsers. Pages can include both text and pictures and can incorporate hypertext links to other pages on the Web. A Web page can also have links to FTP archives, Gopher servers,

WAIS servers, and Internet news groups, so that the Web has become the most popular (and user-friendly) way to access all services on the Internet.

All Internet publishing services are based on having a computer attached directly to the Internet to provide the service. You can provide your own computer if you have a direct Internet connection (for example, as part of your corporate network), or you can hire an Internet service provider to handle operating the Internet service for you. Of course, the services described above can be used internally on a corporate network without providing Internet access.

Internet Access Providers

To get access to the Internet, you usually must go through an Internet access provider (someone who has purchased or leased a high-volume connection to the Internet and is reselling that connection). To provide any of the above services, you have two options: lease your own full-time connection to the Internet, or use an access provider's computers to furnish the service.

You do not need an expensive computer to provide an Internet information service; unless your connection is very busy, dedicated PCs or Macintosh computers (with the right software) can handle the job. Free server software is available from several sources, if you do not need a secure server. A secure server provides encryption so that users can send their credit card numbers to you over the network without fear of their being stolen. Secure servers are commercially available for larger computers like Sun workstations, and they will set you back several thousand dollars at the moment.

Probably more important is the size of your Internet connection; the range here is anywhere from a 14.4K baud modem connection up to a T1 leased line (or larger). Your computer needs to be able to respond quickly to each request, as people are notoriously impatient with online services. An overloaded connection to the network can result in people giving up on your site. Your requirements depend on how busy your site is, as well as how much other information travels over your connection, but a 56K baud leased line is the minimum acceptable for any serious frequent use, with a full ISDN connection preferred.

Most access providers can also act as a service bureau to provide you with any of the publishing services listed above, running on their computers or on a computer you furnish for the purpose on their premises. Usually they will charge you a setup fee and a monthly charge for providing the service, sometimes with extra charges for storage consumed by your data. They may also charge you any time you make a change to your document installation. Make sure your access provider has sufficient capacity to handle your requirements, including the size of their Internet connection.

When you begin to publish on the Internet, one of the most important investments you make is in your Internet address. It does not matter too much what your address is; what counts is that you keep it. This is an issue for smaller publishers who do not establish their own service connection, instead relying on an access provider. If you change access providers, your Internet address will change too. There is no capability for forwarding messages from your old Internet address to your new one, so address changes can result in missing connections and lost business.

Charging Fees for Electronic Document Delivery

This is an area that is still maturing. Currently, most information provided over the Internet is free. The World Wide Web is the primary focus for commercial services, but software to provide for secure business transactions over the Web is just starting to be available.

Another possibility that is viable today is to use an online service like CompuServe or America Online to publish your files. You can make arrangements with the service provider to handle billing for you when someone requests a file. Users can select a file for downloading and they are automatically billed by the service provider when the download occurs. The online service takes a percentage of the purchase price for providing the service. As an example, you can find some relatively expensive financial newsletters distributed in PDF format in this way from CompuServe (see GO PUBONL).

A third alternative to consider is shareware publishing. In this mode of retailing, people download your documents and then pay you for them if they find the documents useful. Usually you provide extra services as an incentive to pay the bill, such as additional information or free updates. Of course, this is a less reliable source of income than one where the customer pays you up front, but it may be surprisingly practical depending on your clientele.

Web Publishing with Acrobat

Adobe has gone out of their way to make sure that PDF files are easy to use as part of a World Wide Web document. Adobe is providing a new version of the Reader that can accept the WebLink plug-in described in Chapter 7, enabling the PDF file to contain links back to other documents on the Web. This version of the Reader is being incorporated into Web browser packages, ensuring that many people will be able to view PDF files.

Some simple guidelines to follow when preparing your documents for use on the Web:

- Use a standard HTML page as your home page, not a PDF document. Use hyperlinks to link the PDF files to that page. Your links should indicate that the file is an Acrobat PDF file, so the reader doesn't accidentally download something she is not prepared to view.

- Keep files as short as possible. Do not ask users to download your entire catalog of color pictures in order to see one item; create intermediate pages with links that allow them to download only the information they need.

Lotus Notes

Publishing works at the workgroup level too, with Lotus Notes. Acrobat PDF files can be attached to or embedded in a Notes database, allowing presentation-quality documents to be shared in the group. Notes distributes documents by replicating copies of them throughout the Notes distributed database. Notes is another publishing medium that requires self-contained PDF files; Notes cannot deliver more than one document at a time. For this reason Notes is better suited to ad hoc publishing efforts and sharing works in progress rather than permanent publication. Notes is capable of combining PDF files with other resources and generating full-text searches across its entire database, something no other product currently offers.

There are two techniques you can use to incorporate PDF files into Notes databases: embed them with OLE or attach them as independent files. We'll discuss the implications of using one method or the other.

Using File Attachments

Attaching a PDF file to a Notes database form gives you an Acrobat icon on your form which displays the name of the file (use the File | Attach command from Notes menu to select the file to attach). The PDF file will be replicated along with the rest of the database this form is attached to. This is a good way to distribute a file to a group, but it turns out to be a poor way to receive updates on the file from other users.

When someone wants to see the attached file, they just double-click on the icon. Notes asks if they want to detach the file (that is, remove it from the database and copy it to a separate disk file) or launch it (using Windows standard file extension matching to launch the Reader or Exchange). However, neither case is very helpful for updates. Detaching the file requires that it be manually reattached again after being modified, while launching the file first creates a temporary copy of the PDF file on disk, and this file is passed to Exchange. Changes to the temporary file never make it back into Notes.

Using OLE

There is another choice, which is to embed the file into Notes using OLE. Using OLE, the PDF file can be edited and updated by just double-clicking on the file within Notes. You can embed a PDF file into any Rich Text field on a database form.

There are two alternative menu commands you can use in Notes to embed a file: Edit | Insert | Object or Edit | Paste Special. The difference is that Insert Object will start Exchange to complete the embedding operation, while with Paste Special there is no direct interaction between Notes and Exchange. The advantage of starting Exchange is that Notes/FX fields are updated when Exchange closes the file (see below). Paste Special does not update the Notes/FX fields you may be using, but it works faster than Insert Object.

To use Paste Special, you must first copy the PDF file to the clipboard so that it is available for pasting. Use the Exchange Edit | Copy File to Clipboard command to put the file on the clipboard. If you select and copy only a portion of the file, it will not be pasted as a PDF OLE object, but as a text or graphics object (depending on what you copied to the clipboard).

When you embed a PDF file into another program using either the Insert Object or Paste Special menu commands, Exchange gives you two choices of representation for the PDF file. You can select a Picture representation, which draws an icon for the PDF file, or select Rich Text Format (RTF) to include the full text of the PDF file within the Notes database. This selection is different from the type of the Notes field, which should be a Rich Text field in any case. You may be offered other choices for representing the OLE file, but Picture and RTF are the only options recognized by Exchange. Other possible selections, like Bitmap and Text, will be rendered in Picture format by Exchange.

If you choose the Rich Text Format representation, the Rich Text field in your form will expand to hold the entire PDF file. All of the text of the RTF field can be indexed and included in a full-text search of the Notes database. By embedding PDF files into RTF fields in Notes and then indexing their database you can achieve the same functionality provided by Acrobat Catalog, and use Notes to perform your searches rather than Acrobat Search.

If you choose the Picture representation, you will see an Acrobat icon in the Rich Text field in your form. You can double-click the icon to edit the PDF file with Exchange, but the text of the PDF file is not searchable from Notes.

For either the Picture or RTF representations, when you double-click on the field in the Notes database, Exchange will be started in its OLE server mode. In this mode Exchange's File menu is altered so that instead of a Save command there is an Update command which updates the embedded version of the file in Notes. Instead of the normal File | Exit command, there is an Exit and Return to Notes command, which you should use after updating the file to return to Notes.

Using Notes/FX with PDF Files

When you use OLE to embed a PDF file into Notes, Acrobat defines a set of fields that Notes databases can reference directly using the built-in features of Notes Field Exchange (or Notes/FX). These fields include the Document Info fields from the PDF file as well as other information about the PDF file. There are two sets of fields maintained in every PDF file: A set of fields provided by Acrobat to Notes as read-only fields, and a set of fields that can be changed by either Acrobat Exchange or Notes (called two-way fields). The names of these fields are listed in Tables 9.1 and 9.2, respectively.

Table 9.1   Read-only Notes/FX Fields Supplied by Acrobat

Notes/FX Field Name	Field Type	Meaning
DocumentClass	Text	"Adobe Acrobat Document"
PDFAddingOrChangingNotes	Text	"Allowed" if adding or changing notes is allowed, otherwise "Not Allowed"
PDFChangingTheDocument	Text	"Allowed" if changing the document is allowed, otherwise "Not Allowed"
PDFCreationDate	Text	The creation date of the PDF file
PDFCreator	Text	The creator of the PDF file
PDFModDate	Text	The modification date of the PDF file (shown in the Document Info | General Info dialog box)
PDFOpenPassword	Text	"Yes" if the file requires an open password; otherwise "No"
PDFPrinting	Text	"Allowed" if printing is allowed, otherwise "Not Allowed"
PDFProducer	Text	The program that produced the PDF file
PDFSecurityMethod	Text	The security method shown in the Acrobat document's Security Info dialog box
PDFSecurityPassword	Text	"Yes" if the file requires a security password, otherwise "No"
PDFSelectingTextAndGraphics	Text	"Allowed" if copying text or graphics to the clipboard is allowed, otherwise "Not Allowed"
SizeInK	Number	The size of the PDF file on disk in kilobytes
SizeInPages	Number	The number of pages in the PDF file

Table 9.2 Two-way Notes/FX Fields Supplied by Acrobat

Notes/FX Field Name	Field Type	Meaning
Categories	Text	The Doc Info Keywords field
PDFAuthor	Text	The Doc Info Author field
PDFTitle	Text	The Doc Info Title field
Subject	Text	The Doc Info Subject field

You access this data from Notes by creating fields in a database form that have exactly the same names and types as shown above. You must also create a Rich Text field in the database form that will hold the PDF document itself; you may give this field any name you want. Embed a PDF file into the Rich Text field using either of the two methods described above (Insert Object or Paste Special). The first time Exchange is launched with the embedded file and the file is saved or just closed, Exchange will update Notes with the values of the Notes/FX fields. The advantage of using Insert Object to add the file is that the fields are updated when the file is first added, rather than later on when someone selects it.

In addition to the fields predefined by Acrobat, you can create custom Doc Info fields in your PDF file and access them from Notes too. You must name your Notes database fields with exactly the same name and data type as the Doc Info fields you created.

Summary

There are a number of new technologies for electronic publishing, including the Internet and online services, the CD-ROM, and the Lotus Notes groupware product. Each of these places different restrictions on the capabilities Acrobat provides for linking documents together into larger published works. The important design consideration for a publisher is whether or not you can reliably access more than one file; if so, you can break your files down into smaller pieces and incorporate interdocument links and Catalog-generated search indexes to tie them together. Both CD-ROM and file archives offer this capability, while Lotus Notes does not. PDF documents on the World Wide Web are somewhere in-between; they can incorporate links to other documents on the Web (PDF, HTML, or others), but they cannot rely on Catalog indexes, standard PDF links to other files, or multimedia links.

This completes our discussion of the Acrobat tools themselves and how to use them. In the next chapter we take up a discussion of generating PDF files, either through special PostScript operators or by writing PDF yourself directly.

CHAPTER 10

Writing PDF Source Code

Enhancing PostScript Files with Distiller Commands

Writing PDF From Scratch

Adobe has taken great pains to isolate most Acrobat users from ever having to concern themselves with the internal structure of a PDF file. Thankfully, they have done a good job, and for most users the structure of a PDF file can remain an arcane mystery. On the other hand, high on the wish list of any Acrobat power user is the automatic creation of PDF file objects like bookmarks directly from the source application. Some tools are already available that feature this level of integration (Frame Technology's FrameMaker, Corel's Ventura 4.2, and plug-ins for Adobe's PageMaker).

If your tools do not already support PDF features directly, there are two ways you could add that support: Through OLE automation with Exchange (described in Chapter 8) or through writing your own PostScript or PDF files. We take up the latter solution in this chapter. First we describe the **pdfmark** PostScript operator, which allows you to create PDF objects through PostScript code that is read by Distiller and incorporated into a PDF file. Secondly, we take a look at the structure of a PDF file itself; if you are a developer who generates PostScript directly, this section will give you an idea of how you might support PDF directly.

Enhancing PostScript Files with Distiller Commands

Distiller recognizes several special PostScript operators that make it easy to add PDF features to a PostScript file:

- **setdistillerparams.** Sets parameters for converting PostScript to PDF.

- **currentdistillerparams.** Returns the value of Distiller parameters for PDF conversion.

- **pdfmark**. Creates PDF objects like bookmarks in the Distiller output file.

Distiller parameters are covered in detail in Chapter 4, but also see the section below for a definition you should include in your PostScript file if you are using **setdistillerparams**. In the rest of this section, our focus will be on the **pdfmark** operator. Before describing the operator in detail, we'll try to answer the question, "How can I use this if I do not write my own PostScript directly?"

Using PostScript Operators Independently

Most of us do not generate our own PostScript; we sensibly rely on our standard device drivers to handle this for us. Even so, you can generate PostScript files with **pdfmark** or **setdistillerparams** operators and apply them to PostScript files generated by your application. The mechanics of doing so are simple: After you have created your PostScript file containing the operators, use the RunFileEx procedure described in Chapter 4 to combine the PostScript file generated by your application with your file and feed the result to Distiller (see "Combining Several PostScript Files into a Single PDF Document").

The slightly more difficult question is how to create the PostScript operators in the first place. First, you could manually create a static list of the these commands you need in a disk file (entering them with a standard text editor). For Distiller parameters this is standard practice anyway, and for some PDF objects, like bookmarks, generating a **pdfmark** manually is not as hard as you might think.

However, we would really like a method that automatically finds key features in our source document and writes a corresponding **setdistillerparams** or **pdfmark**. Fundamentally this task requires a program that scans through your source document to find these key features (you will also have to decide on what features in your

Enhancing PostScript Files with Distiller Commands 349

source file to translate into PDF). You will have to tailor a solution to your own situation, but here are a few possible answers:

- Use your application's macro language. For example, in Microsoft Word you could write a macro that looks for particular styles used in your document and generates **pdfmark** commands from them into a separate text file (or use a document buffer and save the text to a standard text file).

- With plain text source files, use a text processing tool like Awk or Perl (both UNIX utilities now widely available on other machines). For example, you could program either of these tools to recognize HTML tags in a text file and use them to create an appropriate **pdfmark**.

- You could also process the PostScript file produced by the application itself using one of these tools. For example, if you want to control image compression directly for each image, then you must enter **setdistillerparams** operators before each image in the PostScript file. This cannot be done through a separate file using the RunFileEx procedure. However, you can scan the PostScript file produced by your application and insert the appropriate **setdistillerparams** commands. You will want to search for the PostScript commands your application uses to define the images and insert the **setdistillerparams** commands just before the image starts.

The setdistillerparams Operator

The **setdistillerparams** operator (and its companion operator, **currentdistillerparams**) was described in Chapter 4 in the Startup section. You can place PostScript files in the Distiller STARTUP directory or folder and they will be executed by Distiller as it initializes.

The **setdistillerparams** operator is often used in these files to supply default values for the various Distiller parameters.

You can also include the **setdistillerparams** and **currentdistillerparams** operators in your PostScript files (ones not used solely for initialization). You must include the following PostScript code in the front of your file, before any instances of the operators are used, to enable PostScript interpretors that do not understand these operators to skip them:

```
/currentdistillerparams where { pop }
{ userdict /currentdistillerparams { 1 dict } put } ifelse
/setdistillerparams where { pop }
{ userdict /setdistillerparams { pop } put } ifelse
```

The pdfmark Operator

The **pdfmark** operator allows you to specify PDF features in your PostScript file. When processed by Distiller, the PDF features you specify will be created automatically. An application developer can incorporate the use of **pdfmark** to create PDF features directly from the source material, rather than adding those features manually later. Pdfmark is documented in the file PDFMARK.PDF, located in the Distiller HELP subdirectory.

Like the **setdistillerparams** operator, **pdfmark** is only understood by Distiller; but you can add the following PostScript code to the front of your file that makes **pdfmark** transparent to other PostScript interpretors:

```
systemdict /pdfmark known not
{ userdict /pdfmark systemdict /cleartomark get put } if
```

Generic pdfmark Syntax

The **pdfmark** operator manages all of Acrobat's PDF capabilities from a single syntactic structure:

```
[ key-value-pairs name pdfmark
```

The *name* field gives us the type of **pdfmark** to create; the proper names are listed in Table 10.1. Names in a PostScript file always start with a forward slash character (/), including the **pdfmark** names shown in the table (see the **pdfmark** code samples that follow). Each name has an associated set of key-value pairs that define the component values of the **pdfmark**. For example, an ANN **pdfmark** has a key called Contents; the value of this key defines the text contents of the note. We list all of the valid key-value pairs for each **pdfmark** in the sections that follow.

Table 10.1 pdfmark Names and Types

pdfmark Name	Type
ANN	Annotation—a note
ARTICLE	Article
DEST	Named destination
DOCINFO	Document Information fields
DOCVIEW	Document view when opened
LNK	Link
OUT	Bookmark
PAGES	Page cropping
PS	PostScript pass-through

A key is also a PostScript name, and like the **pdfmark** name it should always be written with a forward slash (/) within the **pdfmark** text you generate. The value portion of the key-value pair may contain different types of data. A value may be another name, a number, a string, or an array containing any of these types. In the sections that follow we provide some examples.

Page Coordinates

Sometimes the **pdfmark** operators require you to specify coordinates for objects on the page. These coordinates will always be specified in terms of the PostScript *user space* you are using (the user space is the coordinate system used by the other PostScript operators within the file the pdfmarks are a part of). If your **pdfmark** commands are embedded within the standard PostScript output of your application, the coordinate system in effect will be the one established by your PostScript device driver.

By default, both the PostScript and PDF user spaces are defined with the origin at the lower-left corner of the page, with the positive x-axis extending horizontally along the bottom edge of the page, and the positive y-axis extending vertically up the page. The unit of measurement on each axis is $\frac{1}{72}$ of an inch (approximately one point), so the point one inch from the lower-left corner of the page is (72, 72). These values can be modified using standard PostScript commands, so your PostScript driver may use something other than the default user space coordinates. If you are modifying your application to write **pdfmark** operators into your standard PostScript output, you can simply use the coordinate transformations other elements of your file are using.

If you are entering **pdfmark** commands in a separate file to be included with your PostScript, you can assume that the default user space coordinate system will be in effect. This is true as long as your other PostScript files are well-behaved; that is, they save the graphics state when they start and restore it when done.

Destinations

Several of the **pdfmark** commands (DOCVIEW, LNK, and OUT) change the current view of the document, switching to a new page in the current file or perhaps to an entirely different document. There are several ways to specify these destinations, which we will review here. Each of these pdfmarks contains an optional key called Action. The Action key can take any of the values described below (plus there may be others defined by plug-ins). The value of the Action key determines what other keys must be present, as follows:

- *Article*—Starts reading an article. You can generate an action of this type with a **pdfmark**, and Exchange will display it, but Exchange does not support editing this action type in a link.

- *GoTo*—Moves to a new view of the current file. This is the default action if the Action key is not present. Requires a Dest, Page, or View key to describe where to go.

- *GoToR*—Same as a GoTo except a File key is allowed; if present, the view is found in the file named in the File key (or its relatives, described below).

- *Launch*—Launches another application program. Requires a key to specify a file to launch; this includes the File key and others as described in the section below.

Custom dictionaries have been added as an Action value for Acrobat version 2.1. These dictionaries allow plug-ins to implement their own actions. An example is the WebLink plug-in.

Named Destinations   A named destination lets you give a name to a particular page view of your PDF file. The named destination specifies a page number and viewing mode in your file; the names and destinations are kept in a dictionary that is part of the PDF file. Named destinations have two advantages: They are easily changed and they can be used for links between documents, giving interdocument links a measure of independence. When a named destination is used along with a File key in a GoToR action, the viewer looks for the name of the destination in the Dest dictionary of the new file, not the file the link is in. For example:

```
[ /File BOOK.PDF
  /Dest /Chapter1
  /LNK
pdfmark
```

This **pdfmark** specifies a link to a new file, BOOK.PDF. When the link action is performed, this file is opened and the name *Chapter1* is looked up in the named destination dictionary located in the new file. The BOOK.PDF file itself can define where its first chapter starts; other programs can refer to that location by name. Note that there are no default named destinations; if you want to use them you must create them yourself.

You create a named destination with a **pdfmark** named DEST. A named destination can be used in any of the **pdfmark** commands listed above in place of a Page and View combination. This is a simple example of a DEST **pdfmark** named Chapter1 that opens page 3 in a view of the full page.

```
[ /Dest /Chapter1
  /Page 3
  /View [ /Fit ]
  /DEST
pdfmark
```

Exchange has a limit of 4,000 named destinations per file. Distiller does not enforce this limitation, so you must be careful not to create more than 4,000 DEST **pdfmark** operators in your file, or the file will not work properly with Exchange.

Destinations within the File   The GoTo and GoToR actions require you to specify a new location for the view. You can specify this location with a named destination (which specifies the location), or you use the following two key-value pairs independently to describe a position within a document:

- *Page* gives the page number (page numbers start at 1). Destinations that do not change the current page should omit the Page key and value. A value of 0 is considered a null destination, which does not change the view.

- *View* describes the viewing mode to use. The value of the View key is a PostScript array. The first element in the array is the name of a viewing mode, followed by various parameters; the viewing mode names and their parameters are listed in Table 10.2. If omitted, the viewing mode does not change.

Table 10.2 Viewing Mode Array Values

Viewing mode	View Name	Example
Fits the page to the window	Fit	/View [/Fit]
Fits the visible contents of the page to the window	FitB	/View [/FitB]
Fits the width of the page to the window	FitH	/View [/FitH *top*] *top* is the distance from the page origin to the top of the window.
Fits the width of the visible contents of the page to the window	FitBH	/View [/FitBH *top*]
Tries to fit the specified rectangle to the window. More of the document may be shown depending on the window size.	FitR	/View [/FitR *x1 y1 x2 y2*] *(x1,y1)* and *(x2,y2)* are coordinates that specify a rectangle on the page.
Fits the height of the page to the window	FitV	/View [/FitV *left*] *left* is the distance from the page origin to the left side of the window.
Fits the height of the visible contents of the page to the window	FitBV	/View [/FitBV *left*]
Displays the page from a particular point at a specified zoom	XYZ	/View [/XYZ *left top zoom*] The point *(left,top)* is at the upper-left corner of the display window, and at the magnification level is specified by *zoom*.

Specifying a New File for Viewing   Pdfmarks provide a rich set of file-naming keys to describe a file location from within a link or bookmark (required for GoToR and Launch actions). A system-independent version of a file name, or platform-specific names, may be specified with the File key. If both types are present, the platform-specific key takes precedence when viewed on that platform. For example, a Macintosh viewer will check for a file specified with MacFile first; if one is not found it will check for a file specified with File. Table 10.3 lists the valid path parameters.

Table 10.3   **File Name Specifications Used in a pdfmark Destination**

File Parameter Name	Type	Example File Spec
File	string	/c/acroexch/help/help_e.pdf
MacFile	string	:Macintosh HD:Acrobat 2.1:HELP:help_e.pdf
DosFile	string	c:\acroexch\help\help_e.pdf
UnixFile	string	/acroexch/help/help_e.pdf

The path stored for a platform-specific key should be in the native format for files on that system. The path stored for the File key should be in Acrobat's system-independent format, which replaces all disk drive and directory punctuation in the path with a UNIX-style slash (/). For example, an MS-DOS file name of c:\filename.ext is converted to /c/filename.ext for the File parameter value; a Macintosh file :Macintosh HD:Filename.ext is converted to /Macintosh_HD/Filename.ext.

As you can see from that last example, the system-independent format does not necessarily provide a path that will work on other systems. Few people other than Macintosh users are likely to have a disk volume or directory named Macintosh_HD. The good news is that there is a way to specify a file name that is more portable: use a relative path for the file.

A relative path starts at the location of the current PDF file and contains only directory names (including ".." as the parent of the current directory) and the desired file name itself—no disk volume names. Because of this the relative path can only refer to other files on the same disk volume as the current PDF file.

To specify a relative path in Adobe's system-independent format, do not start your string with a file separator (/). Specify the path in terms of named subdirectories, the current ("./") and parent ("../") directories and combinations of these, all separated by slash characters, and ending in a file name. For a file in the current directory, just the file name alone will do. A file in the parent directory is specified as *../filename.ext*, while a file in a subdirectory is specified as *subdir/filename.ext*.

Specifying a File for Launch   The Launch action requires a file specification for the file to launch. If supported by the operating system (for example, Macintosh or Windows), this file may be a data file associated by its file type with an application program (such as TEXT on Mac or .TXT on Windows; both are associated with simple text editors). In this case the application program registered for the file is launched. Alternatively, the file named in the **pdfmark** may be a program itself.

The Launch action can use all of the file specification options provided by the GoToR action described above: the File system-independent file specification key and the three system-dependent keys. An additional file specification option is provided for Windows programs: the WinFile key and its associated keys shown in Table 10.4. Like the other platform-specific options, the WinFile key is ignored on non-Windows computers, but receives priority over a File specification on a Windows computer. The Acrobat viewers implement this feature by calling the Windows ShellExecute() function (a part of the Windows 3.1 API) with the values specified by these keys.

Table 10.4   **Windows Launch Action Keys**

Key	Type	Value
WinFile	string	The MS-DOS path of an application to launch.
Dir	string	The MS-DOS path of a directory to launch the application in
Op	string	Either the string *open* to display the file or *print* to print it
Params	string	A string containing any parameters required by the Windows application

Setting the Default Document View

You can control the document view when the Acrobat viewer first displays a PDF file by using the DOCVIEW **pdfmark** (Table 10.5 lists the commonly used keys). This **pdfmark** can optionally accept any Action type, but usually only the GoTo action is used, along with a Page and View key to set the page view, and the PageMode key to select display of bookmarks, thumbnails, or a full-screen view. This is very useful for opening your document to a particular page, such as the Table of Contents page, which may not be on the first page of the file. Here is an example of a DOCVIEW **pdfmark** that opens the file on the third page using the Fit Visible Width viewing mode and displaying bookmarks:

```
[ /Page 3
  /View [ /FitBH 0 ]
  /PageMode /UseOutlines
  /DOCVIEW
pdfmark
```

Table 10.5 Subset of the Keys Used with the DOCVIEW pdfmark

Key Name	Type	Value
Action	name	Usually GoTo or Article
Dest	integer or name	An integer specifying an article to display or the name of the article for an Article action, or an optional named destination for a GoTo action
Page	integer or name	An integer page number to specify the destination page for a GoTo action
View	array	An array that specifies the destination viewing mode for GoTo action. (See Table 10.2.)
PageMode	name	One of the valid PageMode names: FullScreen—displays in Full Screen mode UseNone—displays the PDF page only UseOutlines—displays PDF page with Bookmarks alongside UseThumbs—displays PDF page with Thumbnails alongside

Setting Doc Info and Related Fields

Using the DOCINFO **pdfmark** you can make entries directly into the PDF Document Info dictionary. The key-value pairs for this **pdfmark** are arbitrary, meaning you can define your own custom Doc Info fields by simply creating them. All the strings you specify will appear in the dictionary. The values that Acrobat viewers expect to be present are listed in Table 10.6 (however, missing values do not cause errors). This sample **pdfmark** sets the Title key value and a private key called ISBN:

```
[ /Title (Acrobat: Your Personal Consultant)
  /ISBN (1-56276-336-1)
  /DOCINFO
pdfmark
```

Notice the use of parentheses to enclose an ASCII string; this is standard PostScript practice, but you can use the other string encodings allowed by PostScript as well. Note also that you do not have to set all of the Doc Info fields in the same **pdfmark**; you can have more than one DOCINFO **pdfmark** command in the file.

Table 10.6   **Keys Used with the DOCINFO pdfmark**

Name	Type	Value
Author	string	Author's name
CreationDate	string	Date file was created, in PDF date format
Creator	string	The application that manages the source file
Keywords	string	Keywords associated with the document
ModDate	string	Date document was last changed
Producer	string	The program that created the PDF file
Subject	string	Document's subject
Title	string	Document's title

Creating Notes

The ANN **pdfmark** lets you add a note to your file. The keys accepted by this **pdfmark** are shown in Table 10.7. Only the Rect and Contents keys are required. Each note is attached to a particular page; you can specify the page for this note using the SrcPg key or if you omit this key, the note is attached to the current page in the PostScript file. Using SrcPg, the **pdfmark** can appear anywhere in the PostScript input file (such as your own separate file). Here is an sample note:

```
[ /Rect [ 25 25 100 300 ]
  /Contents (This is a note, \n on two lines.)
  /Open true
  /Title (Roy Christmann)
  /Subtype /Text
  /ANN
pdfmark
```

Table 10.7   **Keys Accepted by the ANN pdfmark**

Name	Type	Value
Color	array	An array containing an RGB color
Contents	string	The text of the note (required)
ModDate	date	The date the note was last changed
Open	Boolean	Whether the note is open or not
Rect	array	An array in the format [llx lly urx ury] that specifies the location of the note (required) llx is the lower-left x-coordinate. lly is the lower-left y-coordinate. urx is the upper-right x-coordinate. ury is the upper-right y-coordinate.
SrcPg	integer	Page number where note appears
Subtype	name	The annotation subtype. New for Acrobat 2.1, it should be set to /Text or omitted.
Title	string	The note's title

Creating Bookmarks and Links

The bookmark **pdfmark** uses the name *OUT* (referring to an outline). A link **pdfmark** uses the name *LNK*. These two marks share a large block of keys—the ones that define a destination. Table 10.8 lists all the keys associated with a destination.

The Action key itself is optional; if it is not present, it defaults to GoTo. If the Action requires a file name (it is a GoToR, Launch, or optionally an Article action), then File or one of its brethren must be present. Platform-specific keys are ignored by viewers on different platforms, so you should specify a system-independent path if possible.

The ID key is optional; it provides the ability to verify the destination file's PDF ID fields against values you store here. To do so, you must know the other document's ID when you write the **pdfmark**. The ID is calculated by most Acrobat software (including Exchange and Distiller) and written to the end of the PDF file when it is created and modified. In this sense they act like version numbers for the PDF file. You can use Exchange to get the IDs for a particular document using OLE automation (the PDDoc.GetID method, see Chapter 8). If you specify an ID key and value here, Exchange tries to match the ID fields when it executes the link, and if there is a mismatch, an error message dialog box is displayed warning the user that the file may not be the correct version.

Table 10.8   Keys Used with the Action Key

Key	Type	Value
Action	name	GoTo, GoToR, Launch, or Article
Dest	integer or name	An integer specifying an article to display or the name of the article for an Article action; a named destination for a GoTo or GoToR action
Page	integer or name	An integer page number or one of the names *Next* or *Prev* to specify the destination page for a GoTo and GoToR actions
View	array	An array that specifies the destination viewing mode for GoTo and GoToR actions (see Table 10.3)
File	string	System-independent path for GoToR, Article, and Launch actions

Table 10.8   Keys Used with the Action Key (continued)

Key	Type	Value
MacFile	string	Macintosh path for GoToR, Article, and Launch actions
DOSFile	string	MS-DOS path for GoToR, Article, and Launch actions
UnixFile	string	UNIX path for GoToR, Article, and Launch actions
ID	array	An array of two strings that specify a PDF file ID. If this key is present and the destination of a GoToR or Article action does not match the ID named, the user is warned.
WinFile	string	MS-DOS name of application to Launch using Windows ShellExecute for a Launch action
Dir	string	Windows default directory for Launched application
Op	string	"open" or "print", used if WinFile specifies a document to open
Params	string	Windows-specific Launch parameters
Unix	string	Unix-specific Launch parameters

Bookmarks   Bookmark pdfmarks must be written to the PostScript file in the same order that the bookmarks will appear in the document (otherwise they may appear anywhere in the input). In addition to the Action keys listed above, bookmarks also contain the two keys shown in Table 10.9, which define aspects of their appearance. The Title key is optional; if not present the bookmark title will be blank.

Table 10.9   Keys Used Only with the OUT pdfmark

Name	Value Type	Value
Title	string	The text that appears in the bookmark (required)
Count	integer	Specifies subordinate bookmarks if any (see text)

The absolute value of the Count key gives the count of the number of bookmarks subordinate to this one in the bookmark list. The next bookmarks that follow in the file become the subordinate bookmarks. The Count key should not be specified in the **pdfmark** if there are no subordinate bookmarks. The sign of the Count key value tells whether the current bookmark is open (that is, its subordinates are displayed) or closed; a positive value means the bookmark is open.

The example that follows creates three bookmarks with three separate pdfmarks; the first uses the Count key so it is followed by a subordinate bookmark. Notice that nothing in the second bookmark reveals that it is subordinate. The last example launches a file SOUND.WAV, which is a sound file in Windows (but may mean nothing on another system).

```
[ /Count 1
  /Page 2
  /View [ /FitW ]
  /Title (Main Bookmark)
  /OUT
pdfmark
[ /Page 3
  /View [ /FitW ]
  /Title (Subordinate Bookmark)
  /OUT
pdfmark
[ /Action /Launch
  /File (sound.wav)
  /Title (Listen to sound file)
  /OUT
pdfmark
```

Links Links combine the keys listed in Table 10.8 with the keys in Table 10.10. The Rect key (required) specifies the location of the link on the page in user coordinates. The other keys are optional; if the SrcPg key is not specified, the link will be attached to the current PostScript page. The optional Border array specifies what the border will look like; it can be used to specify a dashed line instead of a solid one, or to set the line weight the border rectangle is drawn in.

Table 10.10 **Keys Used with the LNK pdfmark**

Name	Type	Value
Rect	array	An array in the format [*llx lly urx ury*] that specifies the boundaries of the link on the page *llx* is the lower-left x-coordinate. *lly* is the lower-left y-coordinate. *urx* is the upper-right x-coordinate. *ury* is the upper-right y-coordinate.
SrcPg	integer	Page number where link appears
Border	array	Specifies the border appearance
Color	array	An array containing an RGB color
ModDate	date	The date the link was last changed
Subtype	name	/Link

Creating Articles

Articles are composed of beads, which are just rectangles containing text. To create an article, you simply define the set of beads that compose the article by writing a **pdfmark** for each one. The pdfmarks should be listed in your PostScript file in the order you want the article beads viewed when the user selects an article. In each bead, you must include the Title key and the string you want to use for the name of the article, and this string must match every other **pdfmark** for this article, because it is through identical Title strings that the article beads are recognized.

In addition to the fields listed in Table 10.11, you can optionally specify the DOCINFO keywords Author, Subject, and/or Keywords and their values; doing so will associate the values with this particular article. Here is an example of a two-bead article:

```
[ /Title (Creating Articles with pdfmark)
  /Author (Roy Christmann)
  /Keywords (Article, pdfmark)
  /Rect [ 200 300 300 500 ]
  /Page 2
  /ARTICLE
pdfmark
```

```
[ /Title (Creating Articles with pdfmark)
  /Rect [ 200 170 300 430 ]
  /Page 4
  /ARTICLE
pdfmark
```

Table 10.11   Keys Used with the ARTICLE pdfmark

Name	Type	Value
Rect	array	An array in the format [*llx lly urx ury*] that specifies the boundaries of the article bead on the page (required) *llx* is the lower-left x-coordinate. *lly* is the lower-left y-coordinate. *urx* is the upper-right x-coordinate. *ury* is the upper-right y-coordinate.
Page	integer	Page number where article bead is located
Title	string	The name of the article (required—must be the same for each bead in the article)

Writing PDF From Scratch

The PDF file format is built on top of PostScript, so for developers who write their own PostScript, it is reasonable to look into the possibility of writing PDF as well. This saves the user the extra time and expense of processing a PostScript file with Distiller. In the remainder of this chapter we will examine what is involved in writing a PDF file from scratch. To understand this discussion, you should be familiar with programming in PostScript Level 2.

The bibles of PDF are the various specifications published by Adobe, and you must possess these to write PDF yourself. They are listed in the "For Further Reading" section of the book. First is the *Portable Document Format Reference Manual,* which contains the complete specification for PDF 1.0, the format supported by Acrobat version 1.0 software. This is supplemented by Technical Note #5156, "Updates to the Portable Document Format Reference Manual" (found in the free SDK described in Chapter 8) which describes changes to the format for Acrobat version 2.0. With the release of a set of new capabilities in Acrobat 2.1, look for a new update to the PDF specification as well.

If you are considering writing PDF, you will find it useful to look at PDF files produced by Distiller and PDF Writer. By disabling Text and Graphics Compression in the Options dialog box for Distiller or PDF Writer, you can clearly see what PDF these programs are producing.

Describing a Page in PDF Format

PDF is based on PostScript, but the PostScript capabilities of Acrobat are carefully constrained. Probably the hardest part about writing your own PDF is that you have to give up the full power of PostScript and use only the subset that PDF allows.

PDF uses a special set of 56 operators to render text and graphics on a page. These operators are fully described in the PDF Reference Manual. Conceptually they are constructed out of PostScript operators stored in ProcSet resources within the viewer, but Adobe says that the actual drawing of PDF operators by the viewer is not done through a PostScript interpreter but directly. If you want to write PDF, you have to draw your page in terms of these operators in the PDF file (they are listed in Table 10.12).

It is possible to use the PDF drawing operators as PostScript operators by defining them appropriately in your PostScript file. Adobe does not provide this information as part of an SDK, but by printing a PDF file from Exchange using a PostScript printer driver and redirecting the output to disk, you can see what PostScript is generated for the operators in the PDF file. In fact, in this output you will find a series of header files that define the PDF operators in terms of PostScript. These header files contain Adobe Systems copyright notices. Adobe has been flexible about the use of copyrighted code, as long as you preserve the copyright notices if you reuse the PostScript; contact the Adobe Developers Association for details.

Table 10.12 PDF Drawing Operator Summary

Graphics State Operators	**Function**
q, Q	Save and restore (respectively) current graphics state
cm	PostScript concat
d	PostScript setdash
i	PostScript setflat
j	PostScript setlinejoin
J	PostScript setlinecap
M	PostScript setmiterlimit
w	PostScript setlinewidth

Color Operators |
--- | ---
g, G | PostScript setgray for filling and stroking, respectively
k, K | PostScript setcmykcolor for filling and stroking, respectively
rg, RG | PostScript setrgbcolor for filling and stroking, respectively

Path Operators |
--- | ---
m | PostScript moveto
l | PostScript lineto
c, v, y | Variations on the PostScript curveto
re | Draws a rectangle
h | PostScript closepath
n | Terminates path without filling or stroking it
S | PostScript stroke
s | PostScript closepath and stroke
f, f* | PostScript fill and eofill, respectively
B, B* | PostScript fill/eofill and stroke
b, b* | PostScript closepath, fill/eofill, and stroke
W, W* | PostScript clip/eoclip (the star character means use eoclip)

Text Operators |
--- | ---
BT, ET | Start and end, respectively, a group of text operators
Tc | Set character spacing
Tf | Set font size
TL | Set text leading
Tr | Set text rendering mode
Ts | Set text rise

Table 10.12 **PDF Drawing Operator Summary (continued)**

Text Operators	Function (Continued)
Tw	Set text word spacing
Tz	Set horizontal scaling
Td, TD, T*	Variations on a move to the start of the next line
Tm	Set the text transformation matrix
Tj, ', ", TJ	Show a text string with line and character positioning options

Image Operators

BI, EI	Start and end an image, respectively
ID	Marks the start of image data (comes between BI and EI)

Miscellaneous Operators

Do	Executes an Xobject
d0	PostScript setcharwidth for a Type 3 font
d1	PostScript setcachedevice for a Type 3 font

One of the key differences between PDF and PostScript concerns text handling. In a PDF file, Acrobat tries to maintain all the text drawn in the document as strings in the file, drawn with the PDF text operators. This includes spaces between words in a paragraph (but each line of text is maintained separately). PostScript developers often have not worked within such constraints; within a PostScript file, they may position and draw each word or even each character individually. This has implications for the ability to do a full-text search of a PDF file. Acrobat can recognize and search on words that are drawn with individual commands, but if characters are drawn individually, Acrobat cannot turn them back into words, which means searching the text is impossible. Generally speaking, you need to use the text operators to draw whole words (or preferably whole lines of text) in a PDF file rather than positioning and drawing individual characters.

PDF File Structure

A PDF file contains four sections that define the different elements of the file:

- A header that marks the file as a PDF file. The header is simply the first line of the file, which must be the PostScript comment "%%PDF-1.0" (or substitute for the 1.0 the version number of the PDF spec you are using in the file).

- A body which contains all of the objects in the file: the page descriptions, font descriptions, info dictionary, and so forth.

- A cross-reference table which allows random access to the body section of the file. This table contains object numbers and byte offsets to the object's position within the file.

- A trailer which contains special key words that identify the start of the cross-reference table and other key elements of the file.

A PDF file is meant to be read from the end, as that is where the pointers to other data in the file are stored. The list above is modified for a PDF file that has had an incremental update; in this situation, there will be more than one body, cross-reference table, and trailer in the file. If you scan from the front of the file looking for these objects, you will find the wrong ones if there has been an incremental update because the most recent objects are written last. The trailer defines where to begin reading such a file. Since the file is meant to be read backwards, we will describe it that way.

Direct and Indirect Objects

Just about everything in the PDF file is considered an object of some type. PDF objects include all the usual PostScript data types (Booleans, numbers, strings, names, arrays, dictionaries, and streams). A direct object is one of these objects that is defined in place, without being named. An indirect object is a regular object wrapped up and packaged with an object number and a version number. The object numbers are used by other components of the file to refer to this object, and the version number allows for incremental update of the object. This is a definition of an indirect object, in this case the number 10:

```
8 0 obj
10
endobj
```

In this example, the number 10 is assigned object number 8 and version number 0. The actual object you are naming is placed between the **obj** and **endobj** keywords. Now, another PDF operator could refer to this indirect object using the syntax in the following example, which defines a dictionary containing the name Length whose value is the indirect object numbered 8 with version number 0:

```
<< /Length 8 0 R >>
```

Indirect objects can be used in forward definitions, meaning that you can refer to the indirect object in the file before it has been written to the file. The PDF file format uses indirect objects for virtually every entity in the file, from a page description to an annotation. The indirect objects are named in the cross-reference tables and in other tables in the file. Interpreting a PDF file amounts to finding the indirect objects in the file in the right order. The trailer section of the file is where you start.

The PDF Trailer

The trailer section of a PDF file is shown in the code sample below. Working backwards from the end of the file, the very last line of a PDF file contains the PostScript comment "%%EOF." The two lines before it define the byte offset of the most recent cross-reference table from the start of the file (the numeric argument of the **startxref** statement).

```
trailer
<<
/Size 12
/Root 2 0 R
/Info 1 0 R
>>
startxref
12543
%%EOF
```

Just before the **startxref** statement is the trailer dictionary. This dictionary contains key-value pairs that define the following:

- *Info*. The indirect object identifier for the Info dictionary object.

- *Prev*. The offset from the beginning of the file to the previous cross-reference table (present only if the file has been incrementally updated).

- *Root*. The indirect object identifier for the Catalog object, which defines access to all other objects in the file (required value).

- *Size*. How many total entries are defined in the PDF file's cross-reference tables (required value).

To start reading a PDF file, you would obtain the byte offset of the cross-reference table and the object number of the PDF file Catalog object. The next step is to look up the Catalog object in the cross-reference table to find out where it is.

The Cross-Reference Table

The cross-reference table is the table that defines the location of all of the indirect objects in the PDF file (and since everything is an indirect object, this table is very important). The table contains records of a fixed length so that it is easy to find the next record. It starts at the byte offset specified in the trailer with the keyword **xref**. Following the **xref** keyword are one or more subsections of the table (see example below). When a file is first created it has only a single subsection, but incremental updates that define new objects create new subsections in the table.

```
xref
0 3
0000000010 00000 n
0000000112 00000 n
0000000769 00000 n
```

Each subsection starts with a line specifying the object number of the first object in the subsection, followed by a count of the number of objects (in the example above, the first object is zero, and there are three objects defined). Object numbers are assigned contiguously within the section. The first object record in the subsection follows on the next line. Each record is 20 bytes long including the line terminator, and contains two numbers and a keyword. The first number is always 10 digits long (padded with zeroes if necessary); it specifies a byte offset within the PDF file. This is where the indirect object definition begins. The second number is the generation number, which specifies which generation of the object is defined at this location. It is always five digits, zero padded. A single space character separates the two numbers and the keyword. The keyword identifies whether the object is defined (keyword **n**) or free (keyword **f**).

Acrobat maintains a sophisticated procedure for updating this table and tracking free objects, but the first generation of a PDF file does not have to worry about that. This table is really nothing more than the byte offset where each indirect object starts in the output file. Creating this table requires some minor bookkeeping to keep track of these offsets as they are written (remember this table is written after the objects themselves).

The Body of the PDF File

The body of the PDF file is nothing more than a list of indirect objects. There are certain objects (like the Catalog object) that have to be present; other objects are present if they are required to define some element of the page. Almost all of these objects are in fact PostScript dictionaries that contain key-value pairs to define the attributes of the object. The objects that can be incorporated into the body of a PDF file are:

- *Catalog.* The starting point for reading the PDF file, the Catalog contains the indirect object numbers for the Pages object, the Outlines object, and a value for the opening view of the PDF file.

- *Pages.* The root of the Pages tree. The Pages tree is a set of dictionaries, each describing the location of a Page object in the file. The dictionaries are arranged in a tree structure so that the viewer can quickly find a reference to any page in the file.

- *Page.* Each page in the file is defined by a Page object, which is a dictionary containing definitions of values defining the page contents.

- *Thumbnails.* A dictionary followed by a stream containing the image data for the thumbnail. Each page will have its own thumbnail object.

- *Annotations.* A dictionary describing an annotation. Annotations have subtypes which identify their contents: Link and Text (meaning note) are the two original subtypes.

- *Outlines.* Essentially, the list of bookmarks in the document. The Outlines object contains indirect references to the first and last Outline objects in the list.

- *Outline.* An individual bookmark. An Outline object is a dictionary with keys defining the bookmark text, the action taken by the bookmark and the position of this Outline object in the bookmark hierarchy.

- *Resources.* A dictionary naming indirect objects that are resources of the page. Resource types are: Encoding, Font, FontDescriptor, ColorSpace, and Xobject.

We will not go into further details on these objects here, but interested parties are invited to investigate further in the PDF references cited earlier in the chapter.

Summary

In this chapter we've learned how to create PDF objects from within our own applications using the **pdfmark** operator. You should be able to define a link, annotation, bookmark, or other PDF object using **pdfmark** and add those definitions to a document created with Distiller. We also poked around under Acrobat's hood to get a feel for what is involved with writing raw PDF directly. It is clear from our investigation that writing a first-generation PDF file is not at all difficult. It is our hope to see more applications that can automatically generate PDF features like links and annotations directly from the source application's data structures.

APPENDIX

Windows INI File Settings

Reader and Exchange
PDF Writer

Reader and Exchange

Reader settings are in the file ACROREAD.INI, while Exchange uses ACROEXCH.INI. Many of the entries in this file either represent preference items you can access from the Edit | Preferences menu, or they are purely internal values of no interest. The exceptions are listed below:

Name	Example	Definition
MaxDoc	MaxDoc=1	Sets default Exchange subwindow size to full screen (=1) or cascaded (=0)
MaxApp	MaxApp=0	Sets default Exchange window size to maximized (=1) or not (=0)
ShortMenu	ShortMenu=0	Use short menus (=1) or not (=0)
ShowToolBar	ShowToolBar=1	Display the toolbar (=1) or not (=0)
MaxPageCacheZoom	MaxPageCacheZoom=131072	The maximum page magnification that will be cached
MinPageCacheTicks	MinPageCacheTicks=12	Drawing time threshold for page caching (in 12ths of a second). Pages that draw faster than this amount of time are not cached.
MaxPageCacheBytes	MaxPageCacheBytes=4194304	Size of the page cache in bytes
FullScrolling	FullScrolling=0	Increases the page size (=1) so that the page will not scroll until the bottom of the page is visible, or use normal page size (=0)
DefaultSplitterPos	DefaultSplitterPos=140	Sets the position of the bar between the page view pane and the bookmark/thumbnail view pane. Minimum value is 100.

Name	Example	Definition
DrawMissingThumbs	DrawMissingThumbs=1	Draws the page contents into the thumbnails regardless of whether the file has thumbnails in it (=1) or leaves missing thumbnails blank (=0).
ThumbViewScale	ThumbViewScale=8192	Sets the display size of thumbnails, between 65535 (= 100%), and 2000 (= 3%)
DefaultOverviewType	DefaultOverviewType=1	Sets default page mode if none specified in the document to one of the following: no change (=0), page only (=1), page and thumbnails (=2), page and bookmarks (=3), full screen mode (=4)
CaseSensitive	CaseSensitive=0	Enables case-sensitive text search (=1) or not (=0) by default
WholeWords	WholeWords=0	Enables matching whole words only (=1) or not (=0) by default

PDF Writer

These settings are found in the [Acrobat PDFWriter] section of WIN.INI.

Name	Example	Definition
PDFFileName	PDFFileName =c:\tmp\file.pdf	Full path file name for the PDF output file
cpunits	cpunits=0	Units for custom page sizes: inches (=0), millimeters (=1), points (=2)
cpwidewhole	cpwidewhole=612	The whole number portion of the page width, in points
cpwidepart	cpwidepart=0	The fractional portion of the page width, in 1/1000 of a point

Name	Example	Definition
cpheightwhole	cpheightwhole=792	The whole number portion of the page height, in points
cpheightpart	cpheightpart=0	The fractional portion of the page height, in 1/1000 of a point
cpmarginwhole	cpmarginwhole=17	The whole number portion of the margins, in points
cpmarginpart	cpmarginpart=760	The fractional portion of the margins, in 1/1000 of a point
orient	orient=1	Page orientation: portrait (=1), landscape (=2)
custom	custom=1	Custom paper size (=1) or not (=0)
compASCII	compASCII=0	Use ASCII-85 filter on the PDF file (=1)
comptg	comptg=1	Compress text and graphics (=1) or not (=0)
compcolor	compcolor=1	Compress color and grayscale images (=1) or not (=0).
compmono	compmono=1	Compress monochrome images (=1) or not (=0).
monotype	monotype=2	Compression type for monochrome images: CCITT Group 3 (=0), CCITT Group 4 (=1), LZW (=2), RLE (=3)
colorqual	colorqual=2	Compression type for color images: JPEG High (=0), JPEG Medium-High (=1), JPEG Medium (=2), JPEG Medium-Low (=3), JPEG Low (=4), LZW (=5)
res	res = 2	Resolution used for images: Screen (=0), 150 dpi (=1), 300 dpi (=2), 600 dpi (=3)
bDocInfo	bDocInfo=1	Display document info dialog box (=1) or not (=0)
bExecViewer	bExecViewer=1	Launch the viewer after creating PDF file (=1) or not (=0)

Name	Example	Definition
bAlwaysEmbed	bAlwaysEmbed=1	Enable always embed list (=1) or not (=0)
bNeverEmbed	bNeverEmbed=1	Enable never emded list (=1) or not (=0)
bEmbedAllFonts	bEmbedAllFonts=1	Embed all fonts (=1) or not (=0).
EmbedNever_Num	EmbedNever_Num=0	Number of fonts in the never embed list
EmbedAlways_Num	EmbedAlways_Num=1	Number of fonts in the always embed list
EmbedNever{0...}	EmbedNever0 =Helvetica	A font name in the embed never list. List each font separately.
EmbedAlways{0...}	EmbedAlways0 =Symbol	A font name in the always embed list

The Embed Always and Embed Never lists are specified similarly to the custom Doc Info fields described in Chapter 5. Each font in the list is specified on its own line, with a number ranging from 0 to EmbedNever_Num –1 (or EmbedAlways_Num in the case of the Embed Always list). Here is a more complete example:

```
[Acrobat PDFWriter]
EmbedAlways_Num =2
EmbedAlways0 = Zapf Chancery
EmbedAlways1 = AvantGarde
```

References for Further Reading

Acrobat Technical Documentation
Creating Hypertext Documents
Interapplication Communication
Publishing on the Internet
CD-ROM Publishing

Acrobat Technical Documentation

Tim Bienz and Richard Cohn, *Portable Document Format Reference Manual,* Addison Wesley, 1993, ISBN 0-201-62628-4. The starting point for understanding the internals of PDF format. Make sure you get the update listed below as well.

PostScript Language Reference Manual, 2nd Edition, Addison Wesley, 1990, ISBN 0-201-18127-4.

The following are the technical documents available in the free SDK described in Chapter 8. The files take the number of the technical note as their name. They are also available separately from Adobe's FTP site (ftp.adobe.com) in the directory /pub/adobe/DeveloperSupport/TechNotes/PDFfiles.

Technical Note #5116, "Supporting the DCT Filters in PostScript Level 2." Describes how to use the JPEG compression algorithm when writing PostScript or PDF.

Technical Note #5150, "pdfmark Reference Manual." How to use the PostScript pdfmark operator with Distiller.

Technical Note #5151, "Acrobat Distiller Parameters." How to use the PostScript setdistillerparams operator with Distiller.

Technical Note #5152, "Adobe Acrobat Product Overview and Compatiblity." Brief introduction to the product line and a few notes for PostScript compatibility with PDF.

Technical Note #5155, "Acrobat Viewer Interapplication Communication Support." Essential companion to any effort to use OLE, DDE, or AppleScript with Acrobat viewers.

Technical Note #5156, "Updates to the Portable Document Format Reference Manual." Explains the changes in PDF since version 1.0.

Technical Note #5157, "Acrobat Catalog Control Interface Specification." Describes the IAC interfaces to Catalog.

Technical Note #5158, "Acrobat Distiller Control Interface Specification." Describes the IAC interfaces to Distiller.

Technical Note #5159, "Acrobat PDF Writer Control Interface Specification." Describes how to interface to PDF Writer.

Creating Hypertext Documents

William Horton, *Designing and Writing Online Documentation*, John Wiley and Sons, 1994, ISBN 0-471-30635-5. An excellent guide to designing hypertext documents. The primary focus of the book is product documentation but Horton's ideas apply to any hypertext document that tries to inform rather than merely entertain.

Interapplication Communication

OLE 2 Programmer's Reference, Microsoft Press, 1994, ISBN 1-55615-629-4. Volume 2 discusses using OLE automation from a C/C++ perspective. Not exactly an easy read, but an essential reference.

Bob Cristello, "Build Smart Documents with Acrobat and OLE," *Visual Basic Programmer's Journal*, July 1995 (Vol. 5, No. 7). This article presents a sample program using Visual Basic to build an OLE container app for a PDF file and Exchange to draw the file into the VB window.

Derrick Schneider, *The Tao of AppleScript*, Hayden Books, 1994, ISBN 1-56830-115-4. A good introduction to AppleScript programming for the non-programmer.

Danny Goodman, *Danny Goodman's AppleScript Handbook*, Random House, 1994, ISBN 0-679-75806-2. A meatier AppleScript book for the more experienced programmer.

Publishing on the Internet

Larry Aronson, *HTML Manual of Style*, Ziff-Davis Press, 1994, ISBN 1-56276-300-8. A concise reference to the capabilities of HTML and its variants, with examples.

Cricket Liu, et. al., *Managing Internet Information Services,* O'Reilly & Associates, 1994, ISBN 1-56592-062-7. The definitive guide to setting up your own Internet information service. Covers servers for the World Wide Web, Gopher, WAIS, FTP, and mailing list processing.

CD-ROM Publishing

Les Cowan, *CD-ROM: Publishing Medium—Publishing Tool*, Micro Publishing Press, 1995, ISBN 0-941845-12-5. This book discusses CD-ROM publishing in general, including selecting software to access the information you publish. Acrobat is mentioned as one of the alternatives. Good discussion of how to produce a CD-ROM.

INDEX

A

ACROAUTO.DLL, 269
Acrobat
    components of, 1–3
    integrating other applications with, 8–9, 258–318
    packages, 3
    support for, 9–11
    technical documentation, 383–384
    uses for, 3–4
    using with CD-ROM, 333–334
    Web publishing with, 338–339
Acrobat Capture. *See* Capture
Acrobat Catalog. *See* Catalog
Acrobat Distiller. *See* Distiller
Acrobat Exchange. *See* Exchange
Acrobat Reader. *See* Reader
Acrobat Search. *See* Search
ACROEXCH.INI file settings, 377–378
ACROREAD.INI file settings, 377–378
AcThread plug-in, 245–246
AddBook plug-in, 246–247
Add Font Name dialog box (Distiller), 118
AddInfo plug-in, 247–248
AddPS plug-in, 248
Add Query dialog box, 253
ADFs (automatic document feeders), 197–198
Adobe PageMaker, 97
AEVIEW, 273
ANN pdfmark, 360
AppleEvents, 262–263
    application object properties, 300–301
    application objects, 299–300
    AVPageView object, 304–305
    core suite methods, 298–299
    document objects, 302–304
    for Exchange, 296–308
    Macintosh Reader support for, 274
    menu and menu item objects, 301–302
    PDAnnot object, 306–307
    PDBookmark object, 307–308
    PDPage object, 305–306
AppleScripts, 263–265. *See also* AppleEvents
    core suite commands, 298–299
    object classes, 296–297
    object properties, 297
application integration. *See* IAC
archive files, 322
Article box, 69
ARTICLE pdfmark, 364–365
articles, 68–70
    creating, 68–70, 364–365
    read aloud, 256–257
    selecting and changing, 70
    using, 27–29
Articles dialog box, 29
AutoZoom mode in Reviewer, 207–208

B

balloon help message, 249
Balloon plug-in, 249
base URL, setting for a document, 235–236
Bookmark plug-in, 249. *See also* bookmarks
Bookmark Properties dialog box, 73–75
bookmarks, 7, 15–19
    changing the destination for, 78
    creating, 71–75, 78–79, 361–363
    creating a hierarchy of, 77–78
    in Exchange, 71–79
    magnification options, 75–76
    selecting and editing, 76–77
Boolean expressions, using in searches, 144–145
browsing a document in Reader, 18–20
buttons (toolbar), deleting or renaming, 250

Index

C

Capture, 174–228. *See also* Reviewer
    accessing the scanner, 178–179
    choosing scanning resolution, 194–195
    dictionaries, 189–190
    image files in, 184–187
    input folders, 184–187
    log files, 200
    main window, 176
    output file formats, 179–180
    output folders, 187–189
    overview of, 175–181
    PDF Writer, 177, 182–183
    Processing dialog box, 191
    processing scans, 198–200
    removing input folders, 186
    removing output folders, 188
    requirements for, 177–178
    scanner drivers, 178–179, 184
    scanner setup, 183–184
    scanning double-sided pages, 198
    scanning landscape images, 197
    scanning multiple pages, 193–194
    scanning options, 196
    scanning a page, 191–192
    scanning tips, 196–197
    scheduling processing, 199
    setting preferences, 182–183
    setting up, 181–190
    setting up input folders, 186–187
    setting up output folders, 188–189
    Setup Processing Options dialog box, 181
    suspect words in, 180, 205–208
    text conversion, 180–181
    using, 190–200
    using automatic document feeders, 197–198
    using continuous monitoring, 200

Catalog, 133, 150–173
    automatic index builds, 158–160
    building and rebuilding indexes, 156–157
    choosing index options, 155–156
    creating an index, 151–153
    custom Doc Info fields, 162–164
    disk and file options, 169
    distributing indexes, 326
    documents to index, 153–155
    drop folders, 172–173
    index build errors, 160–161
    indexing groups of documents, 167–168
    Index Preferences, 165–169
    integrating with, 314–317
    large document indexing, 166–167
    logging, 170–172
    preferences, 164–173
    Preferences dialog box, 165–166, 170–172
    preparing documents for indexing, 161–162
    purging an index, 157–158
    Schedule Builds dialog box, 159
    setting index defaults, 170
    setting purge time, 165
    stopwords in, 142
    Windows command line interface, 315
    Windows DDE interface, 315–316
    Windows messaging interface example, 316–317

CD-ROM
    disc and file formats, 330–332
    publishing, 329–334, 385
    steps in creating, 332–333
    technology, 330–333
    using Acrobat with, 333–334

CD-ROM:Publishing Medium—Publishing Tool, 385

Clipboard, copying to, 29–30

color/grayscale image compression, 45–49

color image compression, 45–49, 104–107

compound documents, 31

compression (image)
    color, 45–49, 104–107
    grayscale, 45–49, 107–110
    monochrome, 110–111
Compression Options dialog box (PDF Writer), 45
compression options (PDF Writer), 44–49
CONTRACT, 270
conversation, IAC, 261
conversion, text. *See* text conversion
Create Link dialog box, 80, 234
Crop Pages dialog box, 67
cropping pages in Exchange, 66–67
cross-reference table, PDF file, 371–372
Cstmize plug-in, 250
Customize dialog box, 251
CVIEWER and CVIEWER2, 270

D

DDE (Dynamic Data Exchange), 261
    of Catalog, 315–316
    of Reader, 273–274
DDE services, Windows, 275–295
DDE support, Windows, 277–278
Delete Pages dialog box, 65
deleting pages in a document, 63, 65
Designing and Writing Online Documentation, 384
dictionaries
    in Capture, 189–190
    in Reviewer, 211–212
Distiller, 90–131
    color image compression, 104–107
    configuration, 97–127
    downsampling, 103–104
    error logging, 128–129
    font embedding, 112–113, 116–120
    font location, 111–112
    font options, 102

general options, 101–102
grayscale image compression, 107–110
integrating with, 311–314
Job Options dialog box, 100
main window, 94
monochrome image compression, 110–111
vs. PDF Writer, 38–39, 53, 92–93
PostScript files with, 347–365
preferences, 98–99
Preferences dialog box, 98
in single-user mode, 93–94
Startup directory, 122–124
using as a PDF server, 128
watched directories, 120–122
Distiller Assistant (Windows), 95–96
Doc Info fields
    searching, 146–147
    setting, 359
    using, 322
    using custom, 162–164
DOCINFO pdfmark, 359
Document Information dialog box, 41
document links. *See* links
document notes. *See* notes (PDF document)
documents. *See* PDF documents
Document Statistics dialog box, 255
document views. *See* Reader
DOCVIEW pdfmark, 357–358
double-sided pages, scanning, 198
downsampling in Distiller, 103–104
drawing operators (PDF), table of, 367–368
drawings, annotating documents with, 251–252
drop folders (Catalog), 172–173

E

Edit Custom Dictionary dialog box (Capture), 189
EPS (Encapsulated PostScript) images, 38
error logging in Distiller, 128–129

Index

Exchange, 36–89
    AppleEvents for, 296–308
    articles in, 68–70
    bookmarks in, 71–79
    full vs. short menus, 54–55
    INI file settings, 377–378
    Insert dialog box, 62
    inserting files in, 61
    integrating with, 275–308
    links in, 79–84
    notes in, 84–88
    pages in, 59–67
    saving files, 56
    Search menu in, 135
    Security dialog box, 57
    security options, 56–58
    setting properties, 55
    thumbnails in, 58–59, 62
    using, 53–89
    versions of, 54
    Windows DDE services, 275–295
    Windows DDE support, 277–278
Exchange Doc Info Fonts dialog box (Distiller), 119
Exchange LE, 54, 275
Exchange OLE object programming, 280–281
Exchange OLE object structure, 280
Exchange OLE 2 objects, 279–280
    App object, 282–284
    AVDoc object, 285–287
    AVPageView object, 287–289
    PDAnnot object, 293–294
    PDBookmark object, 295
    PDDoc object, 289–291
    PDPage object, 292–293
Exchange Windows OLE 2 automation, 279–295
Export Notes dialog box, 88
Extract File dialog box, 256
extracting pages to a file, 65–66
Extract Pages dialog box, 66

F

file aliases, 303
file formats, Capture, 179–180
file formats, PDF, 366–368
files. *See* PDF documents; PDF files; PostScript files
Find function, in Reader, 24–25
font embedding, 6, 112–113, 116–120
Font Embedding dialog box
    Distiller, 117
    PDF Writer, 50–53
fonts, PDF document, 5–6
fonts in Distiller
    location, 111–113, 116–120
    options, 102
FullPath plug-in, 250–251
Full Screen display mode (Reader), 23
Full Screen Preferences dialog box (Reader), 34
full-text searching, 134–135
further reading list, 382–385

G

General compression options (PDF Writer), 46
General Preferences dialog box (Reader), 32
Go Back, 19–20
Go Forward, 19–20
Go To Article, 245
grayscale image compression, 45–49, 107–110

H

Hand tool, using, 23
help balloon, 249
HTML (Hypertext Markup Language), 3
Hypertext documents, creating, 384
Hypertext links. *See* links

I

IAC (interapplication communications), 8, 259–265
    Exchange capabilities, 275–308
    Macintosh, 262–265
    Reader capabilities, 273–274
    reference books, 384–385
    SDK on the Internet, 266
    Search interface, 308–309
    Windows, 260–262
image compression
    color, 45–49, 104–107
    grayscale, 45–49, 107–110
    monochrome, 110–111
indexes, selecting for a search, 141–142
indexing PDF documents. *See* Catalog
index parameter file (.PDX), 151
Index Selection dialog box, 142
INI file settings, 376–380
Input Folder Setup dialog box (Capture), 185
Insert dialog box (Exchange), 62
inserting files in Exchange, 61–62
inserting pages in Exchange, 60–63
installing plug-ins, 231–232
Internet
    access providers, 336–337
    getting the SDK from, 266–273
Internet publishing, 334–339
    charging for, 337–338
    reference books, 385
ISIS scanner drivers, 178, 184
ISO 9660 file system, 331

J

Job Options dialog box (Distiller), 100
JPEG compression, 45, 47, 49, 105, 107–108

K

KillLink plug-in, 251

L

landscape images, scanning in Capture, 197
links, 6–7, 19, 79–84
    creating, 80–81, 326–327, 361–364
    editing, 83
    magnification options, 75–76
    using, 83–84
link styles, 81–83
LNK pdfmark, 361, 364
log files in Capture, 200
Lotus Notes, 9
    publishing with, 339–343
    using file attachments, 339–340
    using Notes/FX with PDF files, 342–343
    using OLE, 340–341
LZW compression, 45, 47, 49, 106–108

M

Macintosh AppleEvents. *See* AppleEvents
Macintosh Distiller, integrating with, 313–314
Macintosh IAC, 262–265
Macintosh PDFWriter, integrating with, 311
Macintosh print drivers, 97, 113
Macintosh Reader, 274. *See also* Reader
Macintosh SDK
    directory structure, 272
    free, 271–273
    header files and libraries, 271
    sample applications, 272
Macintosh Search, integrating with, 309
Markup plug-in, 251–252

Index

menu items
    adding, 251, 247–248
    deleting and renaming, 250
MergeNote plug-in, 252
message passing, Windows, 260
modeless dialog box, 137
monochrome image compression, 49, 110–111
Movie Player Properties dialog box, 239
Movie plug-in, 237–242
    Border Appearance, 242
    choosing movie files, 238
    choosing movie properties, 239
    movie authoring, 238–242
    Movie Poster, 241
    Player options, 239–241
    playing a movie, 242
    window, 240
Movie Poster, 241

N

Named Queries dialog box, 253
Named Queries plug-in, 252–253
navigation stack, 20
New Index Definition dialog box, 152
Note Preferences dialog box, 86
Note Properties dialog box, 86
Notes (Lotus). *See* Lotus Notes
notes (PDF document), 8, 25–27, 84–88
    creating, 84–85, 360
    editing, 85
    hiding and showing, 252
    importing and exporting, 86–88
    preferences, 85–86
    properties, 85–86
    summarizing, 88

O

object classes, AppleScript. *See* AppleEvents; AppleScript
objects, OLE 2. *See* OLE 2 objects (Exchange)
objects (PDF file), direct and indirect, 369–370
OK stamp, 254
OLE (object linking and embedding), 31
    in Lotus Notes, 340–341
    under Windows, 261–262
OLE object programming, 280–281
OLE object structure, 280
OLE 2 automation, 279–295
OLE 2 objects (Exchange), 279–280
    App object, 282–284
    AVDoc object, 285–287
    AVPageView object, 287–289
    PDAnnot object, 293–294
    PDBookmark object, 295
    PDDoc object, 289–291
    PDPage object, 292–293
OpenAll plug-in, 253
Open URL dialog box, 237
OUT pdfmark, 361–362
Output Folder Setup dialog box (Capture), 187

P

page layout, captured, 212–227
page layout objects, 213–216
PageMaker, 97
page numbering, 60
page numbers used with DDE commands, 276
Page Only view (Reader), 15–17
pages
    cropping, 66–67
    deleting, 63, 65
    describing in PDF format, 366–368
    in Exchange, 59–67

Index

extracting to a file, 65
inserting, 60–63
replacing in a document, 63–64
rotating, 67
page scaling, 21–23
Page Setup dialog box (PDF Writer), 43
page setup options in PDF Writer, 42–53
page size, selecting in PDF Writer, 44
passwords in Exchange, 56–58
path (PDF file), displaying, 250–251
PDF document indexing. *See* Catalog
PDF documents. *See also* PDF files
    basics of, 5–8
    creating, 37–42, 327–328, 384
    creating with PDF Writer, 39–42
    with drawings and pictures, 6, 251–252
    setting a base URL, 235–236
    text and fonts, 5–6
    using WebLink in, 234–237
    verifying correctness of, 328
    word count, 255
PDF document viewing. *See* Reader
PDF drawing operators, table of, 367–368
PDF file format, describing a page in, 366–368
PDF files. *See also* PDF documents
    body, 372–374
    converting other files to, 253
    cross-reference table, 371–372
    direct and indirect objects in, 369–370
    displaying the full path of, 250–251
    preparing for publication, 322–329
    trailer section, 370–371
    using Lotus Notes/FX with, 342–343
    writing from scratch, 365–374
PDF file structure, 369–374
pdfmark operator, 350–365
    ANN, 360
    default document view, 357–358
    destinations, 352–357
    DOCINFO, 359

    DOCVIEW, 357–358
    generic syntax, 350–351
    names and types, 351
    page coordinates, 351–352
    setting Doc Info, 359
    specifying a file for launch, 357
    specifying a file to view, 355–357
    viewing mode array values, 355
PDF (Portable Document Format), 1, 4
PDF server, using Distiller as, 128
PDF source code, writing, 346–374
PDF trailer, 370–371
PDF Writer, 36–89. *See also* Exchange; PDF documents
    Capture version, 177, 182–183
    compression options, 44–49
    Compression Options dialog box, 45
    creating documents with, 39–42
    vs. Distiller, 38–39, 53, 92–93
    Document Information dialog box, 41
    Font Embedding dialog box, 50
    font embedding options, 50–53
    INI file settings, 378–380
    integrating with, 310–311
    Options dialog box, 42
    Page Setup dialog box, 43
    page setup options, 42–53
    Save As dialog box, 41
    selecting page size, 44
PDF Writer dialog box, 40
PIE (PDF Info Editor), 163
plug-in interface, 9
plug-ins, 230–257
    installing, 231–232
    removing, 232
    from the SDK, 243–257
    table of SDK Windows, 244–245
Plug-in SDK, 9, 265
Plus tab, 69

Index

Portable Document Format Reference Manual, 365
PostScript files. *See also* PDF files
    combining, 129–130
    with Distiller commands, 347–365
    generating, 94–97
    inserting, 248
PostScript operators, using, 348–349
PostScript printer drivers
    font handling, 113–116
    using, 96
PostScript user space, 351
publishing, 320–344
    CD-ROM and CD-R, 329–334, 385
    creating an introduction, 325
    creating links, 326–327
    distributing indexes, 326
    on the Internet, 334–339, 385
    with Lotus Notes, 339–343
    organizing document collection, 324
    planning document collection, 323
    preparing PDF files, 322–329
    technology, 321–322
    testing documents first, 327–329
purging an index, 157, 165

Q

Quark XPress, 97
queries (Search), saving, 252–253
QuickTime controller, 240
QuickTime movie keystrokes, 242

R

Reader, 12–35
    Articles feature, 27–29
    browsing a document, 18–20
    copying to the Clipboard, 29–30
    document view scaling, 20–23
    Full Screen display mode, 23
    INI file settings, 377–378
    integrating with, 273–274
    Notes feature, 25–27
    screen layout options, 14–17
    setting preferences, 31–35
    text searches, 24–25
    versions of, 13–14
    Windows DDE interface, 273–274
    and Windows OLE, 31
replacing pages using thumbnails, 64
Reviewer, 175–177, 200–227. *See also* Capture
    adding words to the dictionary, 211–212
    commands for viewing, 204–205
    correcting conversion errors, 205–212
    correcting text format errors, 210–211
    document views, 203–205
    main window, 201–202
    preferences, 202–203
    suspect-word options in, 206–208
    text blocks in, 216–220
    text conversion repair examples, 220–227
    text editing in, 209–210
    text lines in, 216–220
    using AutoZoom mode, 207–208
    working with page layout, 212–227
Reviewer files, saving, 212
Rotate Pages dialog box (Exchange), 67
rotating pages in Exchange, 67

S

scaling a document view (Reader), 20
scaling a page (Reader), 21–23
Scan Images to Input Folder dialog box (Capture), 192
scanner, accessing with Capture, 178–179

scanner drivers, Capture, 178–179, 184
scanner setup with Capture, 183–184
scanning with Capture. *See also* Reviewer
    double-sided pages, 198
    landscape images, 197
    multiple pages, 193–194
    options for, 196
    a page, 191–192
    resolutions in, 194–195
    tips for, 196–197
Scan and Process Images dialog box (Capture), 192
scan processing in Capture, 198–200
Schedule Builds dialog box (Catalog), 159
screen layout options (Reader), 14–17
SCRIPTS, 272
SDKs (software development kits), 265
    Acrobat, 265–273
    getting from the Internet, 266–273
    Macintosh, 271–273
    plug-in, 9, 243–257
    Windows free, 266–271
    Windows plug-in, 244–245
Search, 133
    commands, 139–141
    dialog box, 140
    forming search expressions, 143–147
    full-text search, 134–135
    integrating with, 308–309
    preferences, 136–138
    saving named searches, 252–253
    selecting indexes, 141–142
    specifying search expressions, 147
    using, 135–150
    using Sounds Like, 150
    using Thesaurus, 150
    using Word Assistant with, 148–150
    using Word Stemming, 149–150
Search dialog box, 140

Search expressions
    Boolean, 144–145
    with Doc Info fields, 146–147
    forming, 143–147
    specifying, 147
    using wildcards, 145–146
Search Preferences dialog box, 136
Search Results dialog box, 141
Search menu in Exchange, 135
Search operators, table of, 147
Search Results dialog box, 141
Security dialog box (Exchange), 57
security options in Exchange, 56–58
Select File Containing Notes dialog box, 87
Select Object Type dialog box (Reviewer), 214
setdistillerparams operator, 122–127, 349–350
Setup Processing Options dialog box (Capture), 181
Setup Scanning Device dialog box (Capture), 183
Setup Suspect-Word Options dialog box (Reviewer), 206
SnapZoom plug-in, 254
Sounds Like, using in a search, 150
source code (PDF), writing, 346–374
Spread plug-in, 254
Stamper plug-in, 254
standard PDF fonts, 5
Stats plug-in, 254–255
stopwords, 142
Store File dialog box, 256
Store plug-in, 255–256
StoryTell plug-in, 256–257
superscripts and subscripts, captured, 211
support from Adobe, 9–11
suspect-word options in Reviewer, 206–208
suspect words in Capture, 180, 205–208
SYLK format, copying data in, 254
synthetic fonts, 5

T

Table of Contents, tool for, 246–247
Table of Figures, tool for, 246–247
technical documentation, Acrobat, 383–384
text, PDF document, 5–6
text blocks in Reviewer, 216–220
text conversion
    in Capture, 180–181
        correcting errors in, 205–212
        correcting format errors in, 210–211
        repair examples, 220–227
text editing in Reviewer, 209–210
text lines in Reviewer, 216–220
text searches in Reader, 24–25. *See also* Search
Thesaurus, using in a search, 150
thumbnails, 7, 15–17, 19
    deleting pages using, 65
    in Exchange, 58–59, 62
    replacing pages using, 63–64
Thumbnail view (Reader), using, 24
toolbar buttons, deleting and renaming, 250
TWAIN scanner drivers, 179, 184

U

URLs (Uniform Resource Locators), 232, 235–236
user space (PostScript), 351

V

VBTEST, 270
VBVIEW and VBVIEW2, 271
viewing mode array values, 355
viewing PDF documents. *See* Reader
View Options dialog box (Reviewer), 203

W

WAIS (Wide Area Information Server), 335
watched directories
    in Capture, 184–185, 193–194
    in Distiller, 120–122
Watched Directories Options dialog box, 121
Watched Directory Alert dialog box, 99
WebLink plug-in, 232–237
    compatibility, 233–234
    configuring, 232
    selecting a base URL, 235–236
    using, 237
    using in documents, 234–237
Web page, opening from Viewer, 236
Web publishing with Acrobat, 338–339
wildcards, using in searches, 145–146
Windows DDE interface, 261
    of Catalog, 315–316
    of Reader, 273–274
Windows DDE services, 275–295
Windows DDE support, 277–278
Windows Distiller Assistant, using, 95
Windows IAC, 260–262
Windows INI file settings, 376–380
Windows Launch action keys, 357
Windows message passing, 260
Windows messaging interface example, 316–317
Windows OLE, 31, 261–262
Windows OLE 2 automation, 279–295
Windows PostScript printer drivers, 96, 114–116
Windows SDK
    directory structure, 267
    free, 266–271
    header files and libraries, 268
    sample applications, 269–271
    table of plug-ins, 244–245
WIN.INI file settings, 378–380
Word Assistant, 148–150
Word Assistant dialog box, 148

word confidence threshold in Capture, 180
word count (document), displaying, 255
WordFind plug-in, 257
word stemming, using, 149–150
World Wide Web page, opening from Viewer, 236
World Wide Web publishing, 338–339. *See also* WebLink plug-in
writing a PDF file from scratch, 365–374
writing PDF source code, 346–374
WWW Link Preferences dialog box, 233

Z

zooming with SnapZoom, 254
Zoom tools, using, 21–22

Ziff-Davis Press Survey of Readers

Please help us in our effort to produce the best books on personal computing.
For your assistance, we would be pleased to send you a FREE catalog
featuring the complete line of Ziff-Davis Press books.

1. How did you first learn about this book?

Recommended by a friend . . . . ☐ -1 (5)
Recommended by store personnel . . . . ☐ -2
Saw in Ziff-Davis Press catalog . . . . ☐ -3
Received advertisement in the mail . . . . ☐ -4
Saw the book on bookshelf at store . . . . ☐ -5
Read book review in: _____ ☐ -6
Saw an advertisement in: _____ ☐ -7
Other (Please specify): _____ ☐ -8

2. Which THREE of the following factors most influenced your decision to purchase this book? (Please check up to THREE.)

Front or back cover information on book . . . ☐ -1 (6)
Logo of magazine affiliated with book . . . . . ☐ -2
Special approach to the content . . . . ☐ -3
Completeness of content . . . . ☐ -4
Author's reputation. . . . . ☐ -5
Publisher's reputation . . . . ☐ -6
Book cover design or layout . . . . ☐ -7
Index or table of contents of book . . . . ☐ -8
Price of book . . . . ☐ -9
Special effects, graphics, illustrations . . . . . . ☐ -0
Other (Please specify): _____ ☐ -x

3. How many computer books have you purchased in the last six months? _____ .   (7-10)

4. On a scale of 1 to 5, where 5 is excellent, 4 is above average, 3 is average, 2 is below average, and 1 is poor, please rate each of the following aspects of this book below. (Please circle your answer.)

Depth/completeness of coverage   5 4 3 2 1   (11)
Organization of material   5 4 3 2 1   (12)
Ease of finding topic   5 4 3 2 1   (13)
Special features/time saving tips   5 4 3 2 1   (14)
Appropriate level of writing   5 4 3 2 1   (15)
Usefulness of table of contents   5 4 3 2 1   (16)
Usefulness of index   5 4 3 2 1   (17)
Usefulness of accompanying disk   5 4 3 2 1   (18)
Usefulness of illustrations/graphics 5 4 3 2 1   (19)
Cover design and attractiveness   5 4 3 2 1   (20)
Overall design and layout of book   5 4 3 2 1   (21)
Overall satisfaction with book   5 4 3 2 1   (22)

5. Which of the following computer publications do you read regularly; that is, 3 out of 4 issues?

Byte . . . . ☐ -1 (23)
Computer Shopper . . . . ☐ -2
Home Office Computing . . . . ☐ -3
Dr. Dobb's Journal . . . . ☐ -4
LAN Magazine . . . . ☐ -5
MacWEEK. . . . . ☐ -6
MacUser . . . . ☐ -7
PC Computing . . . . ☐ -8
PC Magazine . . . . ☐ -9
PC WEEK. . . . . ☐ -0
Windows Sources . . . . ☐ -x
Other (Please specify): _____ ☐ -y

Please turn page.

6. What is your level of experience with personal computers? With the subject of this book?

	With PCs	With subject of book
Beginner............	☐ -1 (24)	☐ -1 (25)
Intermediate.........	☐ -2	☐ -2
Advanced............	☐ -3	☐ -3

7. Which of the following best describes your job title?

Officer (CEO/President/VP/owner)........	☐ -1 (26)
Director/head........................	☐ -2
Manager/supervisor....................	☐ -3
Administration/staff...................	☐ -4
Teacher/educator/trainer................	☐ -5
Lawyer/doctor/medical professional.......	☐ -6
Engineer/technician...................	☐ -7
Consultant..........................	☐ -8
Not employed/student/retired............	☐ -9
Other (Please specify): _____	☐ -0

8. What is your age?

Under 20........................	☐ -1 (27)
21-29............................	☐ -2
30-39............................	☐ -3
40-49............................	☐ -4
50-59............................	☐ -5
60 or over.......................	☐ -6

9. Are you:

| Male............................ | ☐ -1 (28) |
| Female.......................... | ☐ -2 |

Thank you for your assistance with this important information! Please write your address below to receive our free catalog.

Name: _____
Address: _____
City/State/Zip: _____

Fold here to mail.

3369-18-21

BUSINESS REPLY MAIL
FIRST CLASS MAIL   PERMIT NO. 1612   OAKLAND, CA

POSTAGE WILL BE PAID BY ADDRESSEE

Ziff-Davis Press
5903 Christie Avenue
Emeryville, CA 94608-1925
Attn: Marketing

NO POSTAGE NECESSARY IF MAILED IN THE UNITED STATES